THE LAST ELEVEN?

By the same author

URGENT FURY

THE
LAST ELEVEN

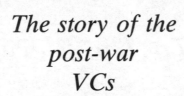

*The story of the
post-war
VCs*

by
MARK ADKIN

LEO COOPER · LONDON

To The Eleven

First published in Great Britain in 1991
by Leo Cooper, 190 Shaftesbury Avenue, London WC2H 8JL
an imprint of Pen & Sword Books Ltd., 47 Church Street,
Barnsley, S. Yorks S70 2AS.

Copyright © Mark Adkin 1991

A CIP catalogue record for his book is available
from the British Library.

ISBN: 0-85052-214 5

Typeset by Yorkshire Web, 47 Church Street, Barnsley, S. Yorkshire
Printed in Great Britain by Mackays of Chatham PLC,
Chatham, Kent

CONTENTS

Maps.vii
Acknowledgments.ix
Introduction.1
Prologue.11
Military Symbols used on maps.18

PART ONE - KOREA
1 Major Kenneth Muir VC   page 23
2 Lieutenant Philip Kenneth Edward Curtis VC   page 38
3 Lieutenant-Colonel James Power Carne VC DSO DL   page 54
4 Private William Speakman VC   page 73

PART TWO - BORNEO   page 89
5 Lance Corporal Rambahadur Limbu VC (later MVO)   page 93

PART THREE - VIETNAM   page 113
6 Warrant Officer Class 2 Kevin Arthur Wheatley VC   page 116
7 Major Peter John Badcoe VC   page 130
8 Warrant Officer Class 2 Rayene Stewart Simpson VC DCM   page 143
9 Warrant Officer Class 2 Keith Payne VC   page 156

PART FOUR - THE FALKLAND ISLANDS   page 171
10 Lieutenant-Colonel 'H' Jones VC DSO   page 175
11 Sergeant Ian John McKay VC   page 192

Postscript . 205
Notes . 207
Bibliography . 210
Index . 211

MAPS

1 Korea   21
2 27 Brigade's Planned Advance to Songju   28
3 The Argylls Attack Hill 282   29
4 Muir's Battle on 282   31
5 A Company on Castle Hill, 22nd April, 1951   42
6 Curtis Assaults the Bunker   49
7 29 Brigade's Deployment on the Imjin River   58
8 The Final Phases of the Imjin Battle   60
9 Operation Commando, 3rd-5th October, 1951   76
10 The Struggle for 'United'   79
11 South East Asia and Borneo   90
12 Deployment of 2/10 GR in the Bau District   99
13 C Company 2/10 GR Approach Gunong Tepoi   100
14 The Battle on Gunong Tepoi   104
15 Vietnam   111
16 Wheatley's Patrol Route from Trabong   119
17 Wheatley Ambushed   120
18 Wheatley's Struggle to Save Swanton   122
19 Area of Badcoe's Three Actions   134
20 Badcoe's Three Actions   135/6/141
21 Simpson's Two Actions   147/9
22 Payne's Area of Operations   160
23 Payne's Actions 24th-25th May, 1969   162/5
24 The Falkland Islands   172
25 2 Para's Initial Advance on Darwin   183
26 Jones Attacks Enemy Trench   185
27 3 Para's Planned Attack on Mount Longdon   197
28 McKay's Final Charge   199

ACKNOWLEDGMENTS

The gracious permission of Her Majesty the Queen was obtained to republish the two quotations from Queen Victoria's Journal which are quoted in the Introduction.

Although I was able to obtain a great deal of information from reference to the published works listed in the bibliography, this book could not have been written without the help of individuals. To check my facts, to ask questions, to obtain photographs or copies of letters, maps, papers, regimental journals, and newspaper articles, I had to meet and correspond with a host of people.

I sought to locate those who knew the VC winners personally, and preferably those who had fought with them. Many were willing to be interviewed, and many more wrote at length in response to my questionnaires. Unfortunately I could not visit Australia, but I was given enormous assistance by people and organizations who not only wrote, but sometimes telephoned with information.

To them all I extend my grateful thanks. I hope those who read the book will feel I have done justice to these eleven extraordinary soldiers, bearing in mind I was limited to a chapter on each. In particular, I wish to acknowledge the value of the assistance rendered by the following individuals, who went out of their way to give of their time and expertise.

KOREA:

General Sir Anthony Farrar-Hockley, Adjutant of the Glosters at the Imjin battle; His Excellency Lieutenant General Sir Alexander Boswell, now Governor of Guernsey, but formerly the Intelligence Officer of the Argylls; Brigadier A.D.R.G. Wilson, formerly A Company Commander of the Argylls; Colonel The Viscount Slim, one-time Adjutant of the Argylls; Lieutenant-Colonel H.L.T. Radice, the archivist at the Regimental Headquarters of the Glosters; Lieutenant-Colonel A.W. Scott-Elliot, Regimental Secretary of the Argylls; Lieutenant-Colonel D.C.R. Ward, Regimental Secretary of the King's Own Scottish Borderers; Major A.R. Brooks, a former platoon commander in B Company, the KOSB; Major P.M.K. Mackellar, a former platoon commander in B Company, the Argylls; Major V.T. Smedley, Royal Signals, on the staff at the UN Command, Korea; Major P.W. Weller, once Officer Commanding Support Company of the Glosters; Major W.H. White, curator of the Duke of Cornwall's Light Infantry museum; Major A. Wilson, second-in-command of A Company, the Glosters at the Imjin; the Reverend S.J. Davies, the Glosters' Padre at the Imjin; Mr T.A. Cunningham-Boothe, of the British Korean Veterans Association, who fought at the Imjin with the Royal Northumberland Fusiliers; Mr P. Haley, a former member of B Company the, KOSB; Mr R.A. Hudson, a former member of the KOSB 'battle patrol'; Mr S. Mercer, an ex-member of the platoon of Lieutenant Curtis VC; Mr J. Murdoch, formerly the Company Sergeant Major of B Company, the KOSB; Mr C.J. Papworth, then the RAMC corporal with A Com-

pany, the Glosters; Mr D. Pillinger, Military Historical Society of the U.K.; and Mr N.H. Tuggey, who was Lieutenant Curtis' platoon sergeant at the Imjin.
BORNEO:
Lieutenant-Colonel H.C.S. Gregory, the Secretary of the 10th Gurkha Association; Major C.E. Maunsell, who was Rambahadur Limbu's company commander during the battle; and Captain Rambahadur Limbu VC MVO, who was kind enough to respond to my letters from Brunei.
VIETNAM:
Captain S.L. Stanton, former USSF officer and author of *Green Berets at War;* Captain J.D. Thurgar; Mr W.H. Connell; Ms R.M. Merritt, curator of the J.F. Kennedy Special Warfare Center museum at Fort Bragg, U.S.A.; Mrs H. O'Hagan, niece of Warrant Officer Simpson; Mrs S. Simpson, the wife of Warrant Officer Simpson; Mr A. Staunton; Mr A. Thompson, from the Department of Defence in Canberra; and Mr W.A. Tomlinson, the Queensland President of the Australian Army Training Team Vietnam Association.
THE FALKLANDS:
Brigadier C.D. Farrar-Hockley, then Officer Commanding A Company 2 Para at Goose Green; Lieutenant-Colonel M.H. Argue, formerly the Officer Commanding B Company 3 Para at Mount Longdon; Lieutenant-Colonel C.P.B. Keeble, who took over command of 2 Para at Goose Green after Lieutenant-Colonel Jones was killed; the Reverend D. Cooper, formerly the Padre of 2 Para; Captain J.G. Carruthers, Regimental Headquarters of the Parachute Regiment; Lieutenant L.S. Tuson RE, formerly with the Falkland Islands Field Squadron RE; Warrant Officer 2 P. A. Hennegan, the Cheshire Regiment; Warrant Officer 2 B. Norman, formerly Lieutenant-Colonel Jones' bodyguard; Mr P. Harper; Mrs S. Jones, wife of Lieutenant-Colonel Jones VC OBE; Mrs F. McKay, mother of Sergeant McKay VC; and Mrs M. McKay, wife of Sergeant McKay VC.

Other organizations whose staff have been unstinting with their assistance include The Army Medal Office, at Droitwich; the Australian War Memorial; the Buckingham Palace Press Office; the Central Chancery at Buckingham Palace; the Gurkha Welfare Trust, who made available the booklet 'My Life' by Rambahadur Limbu VC; the Imperial War Museum; the Ministry of Defence Library; the National Army Museum; and the Victoria Cross and George Cross Association, particularly Mrs D. Grahame, its Secretary. I would also like to thank Mr W.R. Dalzell, a former art master of mine from many years ago, for his expertise on architecture, and Buckingham Palace in particular.

My final debt of gratitude is to my wife, Sandhira, without whose skill on the word processor, and infinite patience, this book could never have been finished.

Introduction

'It is ordained that the Cross shall only be awarded for most conspicuous bravery, or some daring or pre-eminent act of valour or self-sacrifice or extreme devotion to duty in the presence of the enemy.'
  The conditions for the award of the Victoria Cross in the Royal Warrant of 30 September, 1961.

At 9.55 a.m. precisely, on 26 June, 1857, the officer commanding the artillery saluting troop shouted 'Fire'. The crack of the cannon startled both people and pigeons on a hot summer morning in Hyde Park. The start of the Royal Salute signalled the imminent arrival of the 39-year-old Queen Victoria, to hold the first Investiture of a new award for great gallantry — the Victoria Cross.

The Park had been packed for several hours. Since before 7 o'clock crowds had been gathering around the open northern space, bounded to the east by Park Lane. On either side of the Grosvenor Gate, official enclosures had been erected for invited guests, although seats were only provided for diplomats and parliamentarians in the front. Her Majesty's position was marked by a standard, hanging limply in the heat. There was a blazing sun, with no breeze. *The Times* correspondent thought the swelter intense, and described how, 'the ladies seemed to suffer much from it, and even strong hearty gentlemen were not too fastidious to extemporize rude fans from coat-tails, handkerchiefs, and morning journals . . .' Costermongers did a brisk business under the trees behind the throng.[1]*

Drawn up facing the Grosvenor Gate were some 9,000 troops, sweltering in their ceremonial uniforms. Parading that morning were a troop of Horse Artillery, two batteries of Field Artillery, battalions of the Grenadier and Coldstream Guards, Fusiliers, Cameron Highlanders, the Rifle Brigade, and Marines. Grouped together, as a solid mass of glittering horsemen, were the 1st and 2nd Life Guards, the 6th Dragoons and the 11th Hussars. The last contingents to march on were 100 naval ratings from HMS *Excellent* and HMS *Osborne*, followed by the band of Chelsea Pensioners, and boys from the Duke of York's School.

A few minutes before 10.00 a.m. a single file of 61 officers and men marched to the front of the parade, to halt and face the Queen's standard. These were the Crimean War veterans, whose outstanding bravery was being publicly recognised. Twelve belonged to the Royal Navy, two were Marines, the remainder were soldiers. Four or five wore civilian clothes, having left the Services, and one was in police uniform. This was ex-Sergeant George Walters, formerly of the 49th (Berkshire) Regiment, who had saved the life of General Adams at the battle of Inkerman. His appearance prompted *The Times* to comment, 'Surely for such a man a better post may be found than that of a constable at 18s a week.' At ten precisely, as Her Majesty appeared, the parade presented arms, Colours were lowered gracefully to the grass, while the bands struck up the National Anthem.

The Queen had breakfasted early, and was clearly happy and excited at the prospect of events in the Park. She later wrote '. . . ½ p.9 we went down and mounted our horses, I, in my full uniform, riding "Sunset"'.[2] It was the first time she had ridden on horseback at a public review in London. She had on a scarlet jacket, with a general's sash over her left shoulder, and plume of red and white feathers in her hat. She rode forward between her beloved Prince Albert, in a field-marshal's uniform, and Prince Frederick William of Prussia in a Prussian colonel's. After the parade had ordered arms the Queen, flanked by the Duke of Cambridge, who had commanded the 1st Division in the Crimea, and trailed by the royal retinue, rode along the front rank of the troops.

There was slight consternation when Her Majesty returned to her place by the standard, as she showed no inclination to dismount. A table with the VCs had been set up, together with a dais, it clearly being the intention that the Queen would stand on the dais to present the medals. She, however, remained firmly seated on Sunset, so recipients had to approach close

* See page 207 for notes.

to her horse, to permit her to lean forward to fasten the Crosses on their chests. Seated side-saddle as she was, this could have caused problems. Thankfully Sunset remained motionless for the full twelve minutes of the actual presentation — much to the relief of those nearby.

The first man to march forward was Commander Henry James Raby RN. As a lieutenant in the Naval Brigade at the siege of Sebastopol he, assisted by two other seamen, had rescued a wounded soldier under intense enemy fire. The first Army recipient was the imposing figure of Sergeant-Major John Grieve of the 2nd Dragoons (Royal Scots Greys), who had ridden in the charge of the Heavy Brigade at Balaclava. Seeing one of his officers surrounded by Russians he had spurred forward, decapitated one with his sword, and scattered the others, thereby saving the officer.

The march past followed. First in slow, then in quick time, the long lines of scarlet-clad troops paraded past their Sovereign, officers saluting with their swords, Colours dipping, while the VC holders stood stiffly at attention on the left of the passing column. Last came the horse artillery and cavalry, all at a fast, jingling, clattering canter. It took a long time before all the units were back in their original positions. Victoria later remarked, 'I never saw finer troops, nor better marching, excepting the Life Guards who did not come by well in quick time.'[3] The naval contingent impressed the spectators, receiving a spontaneous cheer as it came past bare-headed, saluting Her Majesty with an 'eyes right'.

Ninety-nine years later in 1956, a century after the Victoria Cross had been instituted, 299 holders assembled once again before their Sovereign. This time it was to be Queen Elizabeth who inspected them, but the venue was the same — Hyde Park. The march past of these gallant veterans was a deeply moving occasion. Some were old, most were middle-aged, a mere handful wore uniform. But clinking and glittering proudly on their chests were hundreds of medals, awarded for campaigns and battles on the sea, in the air, and on the land, around the globe. With remarkable fearlessness these men had fought in the filth of Flanders, the jungles of Burma, the deserts of North Africa, the mountains of Korea, the skies above Europe, and on, or under, the grey waters of the Atlantic. Now they were collectively saluting their Queen for the last time.

This gathering was instrumental in the founding of The Victoria Cross Association, (soon to become The Victoria Cross and George Cross Association). Under the patronage of Her Majesty The Queen, and with Her Majesty Queen Elizabeth The Queen Mother as President, this Association holds reunions in London every two years. Inevitably, as only seven awards of the VC have been made since then, the ranks of living holders have thinned. In 1989 only 49 recipients remained alive, the last surviving VC holder of the carnage of 1914-1918 died that year, and none was still serving.[4]

It was the Crimean War that brought home the fact that Britain had no suitable way of rewarding exceptional bravery on the battlefield. The Germans had had the Iron Cross since 1813, while the French had instituted the Legion of Honour as long ago as 1803. Queen Victoria, ever one to acknowledge the value of her soldiers and sailors, took a personal interest in remedying this omission. The award which bears her name has come to be recognised as probably the most prestigious decoration for courage in the face of an enemy in the world.

Victoria chose the design herself, after suggesting improvements, and rejecting the proposal that it be made of copper. She wrote, 'The cross looks very well in form, but the metal is ugly; it is copper and not bronze'.[5] The medal she finally agreed has remained unchanged to this day, except that since 1918 the blue ribbon for Navy awards has been replaced by crimson. Each Cross is still made by the same London jewellers, Messrs Hancocks, from the bronze of Russian cannons captured at the siege of Sebastopol, large ingots of which are stored at the Army's Central Ordnance Depot at Donnington.

It can only be bestowed for actions 'in the presence of the enemy' and, until 1977, was the only British decoration, apart from a Mention in Despatches, that could be awarded posthumously. Since that year all military bravery decorations, except for the DSO (which, because it is an appointment to an Order, can only be conferred on a living person) may be given to a serviceman killed in action. The VC carries a small annuity of £100 a year. Its award requires the approval, indeed the close scrutiny, of the Sovereign. Recommendations are carefully examined up the military chain of command, particularly at Ministry of Defence level. There is a requirement for at least three witnesses, who must make sworn written statements as to the exact circumstances of the action involved. Lack of surviving witnesses has often been the reason outstanding deeds have gone unrewarded. Sometimes these witnesses do not speak English, and are illiterate, as in the case of Sergeant Nigel Leakey's award while serving with the King's African Rifles in Abyssinia in 1941. The witnesses' statements are translated from Swahili, and signed with thumbprints. Similarly with the Australian, Major Peter Badcoe, whose exploits are described in chapter seven, two witnesses were completely illiterate.

It is not just a British award, but also a Commonwealth one. There is no barrier of colour, creed, sex (women are eligible) or rank. Unlike many military decorations that have various grades, some of which are reserved for officers, a person of any rank can win the VC. It is the highest decoration that the Sovereign can confer. The VC recipient holds an honour that

4

takes precedence over all others within Britain or the Commonwealth. This, coupled with the rarity of its bestowal, gives the Cross its unrivalled prestige.

In the 128 years between 21 June, 1854, when the Mate of HMS *Hecla*, Charles Lucas, saved his ship in the Baltic by picking up a live shell and throwing it overboard, and 11 June, 1982, when Sergeant Ian McKay of 3 Para charged an Argentinian machine gun on the rocky summit of Mount Longdon in the Falklands, the VC has been bestowed 1354 times.[6]

The records of the VC reveal, not only accounts of supreme self-sacrifice and devotion to duty, but some fascinating human stories. The youngest winners were only just over 15 years old. Andrew Fitzgibbon was a hospital apprentice attached to the 67th (Hampshire) Regiment when it assaulted the north Taku Fort in China in 1860. His attention to wounded under fire, until he was himself hit, won him the Cross. The other boy was a drummer of the 64th (North Staffordshire) Regiment at Cawnpore, India, in 1857, who, although wounded, fought hand to hand with two enemy artillerymen. The oldest was nearly 62. Lieutenant William Raynor was in the Bengal Veteran Establishment and found himself defending the Magazine at Delhi in May, 1857. He was one of only nine men who fought for five hours against incredible odds before they deliberately exploded the Magazine to prevent it falling into rebel hands. Miraculously Raynor survived.

No less than four families have two brothers who have gained the VC, while on two occasions it has been won by father and son. Fourteen men who were not born British or Commonwealth citizens have received this honour; five Americans, one Belgian, three Danes, two Germans, one Swede, a Swiss and a Russian. This last was Corporal Filip Konowal who was born in the Ukraine, but fought with the Canadian Army in World War 1, where in 1917 he single-handedly attacked and destroyed enemy gun emplacements until severely wounded. Additionally, it has been presented to the American Unknown Soldier, buried at the Arlington National Cemetery. This is the only ungazetted award. The U.S. government conferred their equivalent decoration, the Congressional Medal of Honor, on the British Unknown Warrior in Westminster Abbey.

A little known fact is that the Warrant establishing the VC permits it to be bestowed by ballot, when the act of gallantry has been performed by a body of men. This is still possible today, as Clause 13 of the original 1856 Warrant remains unchanged. Forty-six Crosses have been awarded by ballot, the last being the four given to crew members of HMS *Iris II* and HMS *Daffodil* in action at Zeebrugge in April, 1918.

Civilians have won it; three members of the Bengal Civil Service during the Indian Mutiny, and a Chaplain in the Bengal Ecclesiastical Department in Afghanistan in 1879. One person was recommended twice but never received it. General Sir Ian Hamilton was a subaltern at the battle of Majuba Hill in the first Boer War when his actions merited a VC recommendation. It was turned down on the grounds that he was too young, and would have plenty of other chances. Nineteen years later, when he was a brigadier during the second Boer War, another recommendation was rejected as it was felt he held too high a rank.

Three men have won the VC twice. Surgeon-Captain Arthur Martin-Leake received his first one in 1902 in South Africa for tending wounded under close range fire until hit himself. His bar was also for rescuing wounded, again while exposed to constant danger, in Belgium in 1914. He commanded an ARP unit during World War 2 and died, aged 79, in 1953. The second double VC, also in the RAMC, was Captain Noel Chavasse who in 1916, and again in 1917, rescued and treated wounded under fire. He died two days afterwards from the wounds he received. The third was 2nd Lieutenant Charles Upham. Upham is a New Zealander, who in Crete in 1941 displayed incredible leadership and courage. Although wounded twice, and suffering from dysentery, he rescued a wounded soldier, participated in close-quarter fighting, and later personally killed or wounded some 22 Germans. Just over a year later in the Western Desert he destroyed an enemy tank, together with several guns and vehicles, although his arm was shattered. He still lives in New Zealand.

The Royal Artillery (RA) boasts 51 winners, which is more that any other unit in the British Army. Next comes the Royal Engineers (RE) with 41, and then the RAMC with 27. Among the infantry regiments pride of place is held by the Rifle Brigade with 27. Apart from the more obvious military memorials, many individuals live on in the names of streets, buildings, pubs, restaurants, schools, or even railway engines.

Countless servicemen have shown the sort of remarkable courage in battle required for a VC but never received it. They are the men whose actions went unnoticed, or the witnesses to their deeds were killed, or whose self-sacrifice resulted in a lonely death and unmarked grave. This is true no matter what the nationality of the person, no matter whether the award is the Victoria Cross, the Legion of Honour or the Congressional Medal of Honor. It is why the tomb of a nation's unknown warrior usually has the highest gallantry decoration bestowed upon it.

Courage is a coin with two sides — the moral and the physical. People of character who possess the former can be expected, when tested, to display the latter. The reverse is not quite so often true. This book is concerned with examples of the physical side of courage. The willingness to risk prolonged agony, mutilation and death, to achieve an objective in combat, be it the destruction of an enemy or the saving of a comrade, or a combination of both. Everybody has some courage but most of us are seldom required to display it. It is there within us, in varying degrees, whether we are civilians or soldiers. The policeman who tackles an armed robber, the fireman who rescues somebody, the woman who jumps into an icy river to save a drowning child, or even the person with a terror of flying who nevertheless refuses to give in, and flies frequently, all exhibit physical courage.

It is, I think, true to say that without fear there can be no courage. Courage conquers fear, smothers for a time the instinct of self-preservation. For the soldier, who may be required to face fear on a daily basis for prolonged periods, courage must be nurtured and preserved. Every man has his limit. Eventually, if required to overcome intense danger without respite, a man's courage runs out. No matter how rich a person may be, heavy, unremitting expenditure will ultimately bankrupt him unless he is given time to recoup losses. Soldiers on the battlefield spend their courage, at times in short, intense bursts, at others it dribbles away, almost unnoticed, in overcoming the continual hazards of survival.

The military seeks to reinforce a soldier's stock of daring, to conserve it, to augment it, so that when the time comes there will be sufficient to carry him forward when all his instincts urge the opposite. A combination of factors enhance the courage of the warrior. His training, if thorough and rigorous enough, gives him self-confidence. He knows that he is good, that he is fit, physically and mentally, he becomes confident of his professional ability, and convinced of his superiority over others less well trained. Training is a key factor in building high morale and self-assurance.

Discipline plays its part. Ill-disciplined units seldom excel in combat. It does not have to be the discipline of the martinet, although this has in the past produced amazing acts of gallantry, in the trenches of World War I for example, but a high standard of self-discipline is indispensable on the modern battlefield, where close control by senior officers is often impossible.

Fear is contagious, but so is courage. During a crisis the example of one man, for good or ill, can produce momentous results — the attack surges forward, or the troops flee in panic. The leader is the crucial figure. In action all eyes turn to the officer or NCO on the spot. If his courage fails it is unlikely the unit will succeed unless another, stronger, personality takes over immediately. But the leaders are human, they have the same instincts, the same fears, as those they lead. So how can they sustain themselves and carry their burden of responsibility in moments of great stress? Some do not, but most do. The military leader has constantly to be thinking of others rather than himself. This is the core of his training and his great advantage. In the heat of battle all is chaos and confusion, so the leader's time is taken up trying to bring about some sort of order, trying to achieve an objective, so there is less opportunity for him to dwell on his own safety. He knows an example is expected of him and so his fear of failure is often greater than his fear of death. Most soldiers facing combat are more scared of show-ing their distress, than of the actual enemy. Once given a task, any task, no matter how trivial, most people can forget their fears. Activity, both mental and physical, is an effective antidote to fright.

This leads me to perhaps the most important factor in sustaining battle field courage — the desire not to let down one's friends. Men who have lived together, trained together, suffered together, over a period of many months, sometimes years, are linked by powerful bonds of comradeship. Within the company, platoon or section, particularly the latter as it is a small intimate sub-unit, each individual knows, and is known by, all the others. Every member understands that he cannot survive alone, that he is totally dependent in battle on the actions of others. Their skills, stamina, and courage are critical to his personal survival. All are companions in a close-knit team, whose strongest wish is not to let their buddies down. The stories in this book contain several outstanding examples of this devotion to comrades, which ultimately can lead to the laying down of a life to save another.

Before turning to the record of the eleven men whose heroism was in every case except one displayed in the midst of conflict with fellow soldiers nearby, a word or two on the courage of those who face their perils alone is appropriate. To be brave on your own, perhaps for long periods, without friends to sustain or encourage, is an unsurpassed form of bravery, for which there can never be a VC. I will give two examples of this, taken from the Glosters, whose epic stand at the Imjin River during the Korean War resulted in the award of two VCs. The first concerns a young 2nd Lieuten-ant called Terry Waters who was captured, grievously wounded, by the Chinese after the battle. He, along with a number of his soldiers, were incarcerated in The Caves, a notorious dark cavern, half-filled with water. There they were deprived of all amenities or treatment for the injured and sick, existing entirely on meagre meals of boiled maize. When offered decent conditions in return for joining a movement condemning U.S. aggression all vehemently refused. Waters, however, realized that with men dying under these conditions daily, he must appear to agree in order to save his men. He gave them a direct order to pretend to co-operate, although he himself refused all attempts to get him to reject his principles and live. Promises of medical treatment and nutritious food failed to make this gallant young man give way. Waters died in The Caves some five weeks after capture. He was subsequently awarded a posthumous George Cross.

The other instance involved the adjutant of the Glosters, Captain Anthony Farrar-Hockley.[7] He too was captured and, for repeated attempts to escape, was subjected to horrific bouts of torture. He was almost drowned with a wet cloth over his face, beaten, burned with cigarette ends, kept tied up in the dark for days on end with no relief, even to visit the latrine. Enteritis and countless lice completed his misery. Just as he was nearing the end of his endurance his torture ceased, and a threat of execution, which would have been a relief for him, was inexplicably not carried out.

In the 45 years since the Second World War, eleven VCs have been won. Although at the time of writing, October 1990, they are the last eleven, it would be rash to predict they will remain so — hence the question mark after the title of this book. Only a few weeks ago the likelihood of Britain being involved in another conflict on the scale of the Falklands campaign was extremely remote. Now, however, British and Commonwealth forces are among the hundreds of thousands in the sand of Saudi Arabia involved in a far greater clash. While it is conceivable that Sergeant McKay will go down in history as the last winner of this coveted award, the odds must be against it.

Of the eleven, four were conferred during the war in Korea, one to a Gurkha in Borneo, four to Australians in Vietnam, and two in the Falklands.

It has been said that the VC is more difficult to win in modern times, while to survive the action is miraculous. This concept has some truth. When Queen Victoria instituted the award it was the only way of rewarding acts of battlefield bravery. This century has seen the introduction of a wide range of lesser awards for meritorious service or gallantry. Officers can now receive the Distinguished Service Order (DSO) or the Military Cross (MC), while other ranks can qualify for their equivalents, the Distinguished Conduct Medal (DCM) and Military Medal (MM). These have been bestowed for deeds that might earlier have merited the VC. With posthumous awards it is significant to record that of the last eleven VCs six recipients died winning them. A high proportion. The last one to live was an Australian, Warrant Officer Payne, who won his on 24 May, 1969 — over 20 years ago. The last British award that was not posthumous (discounting the Gurkha in 1965) was to Private Speakman in 1951, almost 40 years ago.

The common thread of exceptional courage runs through each of these stories; but there is variety. Two Crosses were given to senior officers, lieutenant-colonels commanding battalions — one for his leadership in defence, the other in attack. At the opposite end of the rank structure are a private and a lance corporal, the former defending, the latter attacking. Several were gained for acts of self-sacrifice to save others, while one was the culmination of three separate actions.

It is most uncommon in this century for officers of the rank of lieutenant-colonel to receive the VC as their duties normally prevent them from becoming involved in actual combat. Capable active service command of a battalion, involving a degree of personal risk, normally earns a DSO for the commanding officer, provided he survives.

In each case I have made purely personal observations on the individual's actions in the context of the larger battle. Did it have any effect on the outcome, or was it purely a brilliant flash of courage without any wider significance? These are entirely my own comments and have no official acceptance.

I make no apologies for the number of maps in the text. I believe them to be an essential aid to understanding military events. In some instances, particularly in Vietnam, topographical details are approximate, but they do, nevertheless, help to illustrate the action.

For the sake of simplicity all timings are local.

Prologue

'The Queen has been graciously pleased to approve
the award of the *VICTORIA CROSS* to:'

The opening words of the Supplement to *The London Gazette* confirming
the granting of a Victoria Cross.

Outside Buckingham Palace it was a chilly winter morning. Inside an
exceptionally tall young soldier was sweating, nervously wiping the damp-
ness from the palms of his hands on his dark tartan trews. Private William
'Big Bill' Speakman dwarfed both palace officials, and all the other
assembled award winners clustered in the Annexe to the Ball Room. He
was 6 feet 6 inches tall — slightly more in his heavy army boots, the toe
caps of which now gleamed like black glass.

It was 27 February, 1952, almost four months since Speakman's actions
on an unknown hill in Korea had earned him his country's highest decoration for gallantry. His unit, the 1st Battalion the King's Own Scottish Borderers (KOSB), was still in Korea, but Speakman had been flown home,
almost straight from his hospital bed, to receive his Cross from the hands
of Her Majesty Queen Elizabeth II. The Investiture that was about to begin
should have been held by her father King George VI — he had personally
approved the honours being bestowed that day — but his death early that

11

month had brought Princess Elizabeth hurrying home from a holiday in Kenya to assume the throne.

The Palace was still in mourning. The Queen would be wearing black when she presented the honours that the King had granted. Although she was now the reigning monarch, the medals lying on the velvet cushions bore her father's head, not hers. It was only twelve days since she had ridden with The Queen Mother and her sister, Princess Margaret, in the black-draped carriage immediately behind the gun-carriage bearing the King's body from Westminster Abbey to Paddington station. She was very young, only 25, to shoulder the responsibilities of the Crown. The soldier, fidgeting apprehensively as he gazed at his opulent surroundings, was a year younger. At a few moments past eleven o'clock a lowly private soldier would be the first person to receive a decoration from the new Queen. Surely she must have felt some satisfaction in the fact that it was to be the VC that was the first insignia she pinned on anybody. That the recipient was of humble origins, youthful, but a man of great courage and stature, was perhaps an appropriate omen for her reign. Not only was it the Queen's first Investiture, but it was also her first semi-public ceremony to be held since her accession exactly three weeks before.

Speakman had spent hours preparing for this moment. Because of his height he was never an easy man for the quartermaster to kit out, so the Investiture warranted the making of a completely new, tailor-made, uniform. Although he had enlisted into The Black Watch, he was attached to the KOSB in Korea, so it was their uniform he wore that morning. Inside the Palace everyone was bareheaded, morning dress was worn by civilians, while the uniforms of Service recipients were devoid of swords or medals, although ribbons could be worn. Speakman's battle dress jacket already had the crimson ribbon, with its miniature bronze cross in the centre, sewn on the right of five others, indicating service in the Second World War and Palestine, as well as with the United Nations forces in Korea.[1] He wore the old style, 1938 pattern, web belt, perfectly blancoed light green, the burnished brass buckle flashing golden light with every slight movement. But the Borderers were a lowland Regiment, so Speakman did not wear the distinctive kilt and sporran of a highlander, but trews, or trousers, bearing the Leslie tartan.

Speakman was then a single man, so the three guests he was permitted to bring were his mother and the Mayor and Mayoress from his home town, Altrincham, Councillor and Mrs Warren. They were at that moment seated expectantly in the Ball Room, along with some 300 other privileged guests, waiting to watch the proceedings with a mixture of pride and awe.

There were 109 recipients of honours assembled that day. Fifty-five would kneel before Her Majesty while she bestowed the accolade of knighthood. Fifty-four were members of the Services or civilians receiving awards for gallantry or meritorious service.

Speakman and his party had arrived early, and they entered the Palace through the Grand Entrance in the West Wing, which contains the State Apartments. These Apartments are on the secluded side of the building, invisible to the crowds that assemble daily at the top of the Mall to watch the changing of the guard. The visitors were then in the Grand Hall. Like many of the other rooms in this part of the Palace the Grand Hall is decorated in white and gold, set off with a rich red carpet. It is surrounded by coupled columns of single blocks of pale grey marble, specially imported from Italy over 150 years ago. Each pillar is topped with gilded bronze Corinthian capitals, and a gilt frieze borders the ceiling. A few Regency chairs stand at the sides of the hall, as do a number of delicate china vases, several of which contained huge bouquets of fresh flowers.

The eyes of everybody stepping for the first time into the hushed, rarified atmosphere of royalty, which is so apparent in the Palace, are drawn to the stairs which lead from the Grand Hall. There are three flights of steps, each covered with matching crimson carpets. Those on the right, or northern side, lead to a small landing on which is set a magnificent marble chimney piece, with a gold-faced clock above the hearth. The short stairs facing the visitor take him through into the Marble Hall, which opens into the Semi-State Apartments on the ground floor. To his left is the Grand Staircase.

Speakman and the others were guided up the Grand Staircase, under the all-seeing eyes of the imposing portraits which gaze down from the white and gold walls. This staircase was built by King George IV's favourite architect, John Nash. In 1825 the King had summoned him to carry out major alterations and improvements to the Palace. It too is built of marble, with an elaborate gilded bronze balustrading which cost £3900 at 1830 prices. At the first landing the stairs divide into two flights, curving left and right to meet again at the double doors of the Guard Chamber. This is the ceremonial entrance to the Green Drawing Room.

At this point of the Investiture the sheep are separated from the goats. While Speakman and the other recipients went through to the Green Drawing Room, the guests were led, via the East Gallery, into the Ball Room itself where they were shown the seats from which they would observe the ceremony.

The Green Drawing Room is lit by beautiful chandeliers, the countless prisms of crystal glass doubling, and redoubling, the light of the candles. Green and gold again predominate. The walls are covered by green stamped brocade, and the ceiling ornamented with gilded frieze work. A deep crimson and gold Axminster carpet enhances the muted atmosphere. From here one can go either into the Throne Room or to the Picture Gallery, which, with a length of 155 feet, divides the Palace like a spine running north-south along the first floor. Another Regency room, the Picture Gallery, boasts a priceless collection of old masters acquired by successive monarchs. Despite its comparative narrowness, the pale yellow and orange carpets, and orange brocade walls, well lit by the curved glazed ceiling, give an impression of spaciousness.

Here in the Green Drawing Room and Picture Gallery recipients of honours are assembled and briefed. Here officials of the Lord Chamberlain's Office take over. The responsibility of this Office is the smooth running of the Royal Household. On this occasion the Lord Chamberlain was the Earl of Clarendon, so it was members of his staff who organized, supervised and carried out the Investiture up to the moment the Queen actually bestowed an honour. Quietly, quickly and efficiently, the recipients were divided into groups according to the type and precedence of the awards they were receiving. The VC has absolute precedence, so Speakman was positioned at the head of the first group, coming before peers, top-ranking Service chiefs and those being appointed to high Orders of Chivalry. No wonder he was worried.

First, it was necessary to check attendance; get everybody into the right order in smaller groups of 10-15 persons, and ensure names were going to be correctly pronounced. At this stage Speakman was 'hooked up', that is a small hook was fastened just above his ribbons to facilitate the hanging on of the Cross. There would be no pushing or poking with pins. A member of the Household explained to the groups the exact procedure each individual was to follow. It was now approaching eleven o'clock.

The small party to be invested first, with Speakman walking immediately behind the official, was led to the East Gallery, then through the rear of the Ball Room to the Annexe, whose double doors opened directly to within a few feet of where Her Majesty would be standing. Here the group stopped for a final check to ensure they were still in the correct order. Speakman was now by the side doors alongside a Gentleman Usher, who smiled reassuringly up at the smart soldier. There was nobody ahead of him that he could watch; if any mistakes were to be made he would learn nothing from them. He was to lead the way, out in front of the distinguished gathering to meet his Queen face to face. He was more nervous than he had ever been on that bleak Korean hill four months earlier. At least there he had not felt so alone.

The Ball Room is one of the most impressive rooms in the Palace. Constructed in 1854 by Sir James Pennethorne, pupil of Nash, it is 123 feet long and 60 feet wide. It is used for the more regal occasions when large numbers of guests will be present, such as state balls, banquets and Investitures. The focal point is at its western end, where attention is drawn to the Throne Dais. Here the splendid crimson velvet of the Throne Canopy towers up above the two gilded State Chairs. It was designed by Sir Edwin Lutyens and made from the Imperial Shamiana used at the coronation Durbar at Delhi in 1911. It is decorated with elegant and intricate gold thread embroidery, the centrepiece of which is the huge Royal Coat-of-Arms on the backcloth. Surmounting the arch, which encompasses the Canopy, are profiles of Queen Victoria and the Prince Consort, supported by figures representing Fame and History. From the edge of the Dais, directly in front of the State Chairs, the Queen stands to bestow awards. At the opposite end, beyond the rows of crimson-covered chairs for the guests, is the organ and musicians' gallery, occupied that morning by a Guards' band in full ceremonial uniform, playing light background music. White, gold and red are again the colours of the Ball Room. The ceiling is deeply coffered, while the Canopy, carpeting on the Dais, chairs, and the three tiers of benches down each side of the room, are upholstered in crimson. The floor is of polished wood.

It was just a few minutes after eleven when the band struck up the National Anthem. Speakman gave his clammy hands their last wipe, as all in the Ball Room rose to stand motionless as Her Majesty entered. She looked incredibly young, very lovely, in a simple black dress set off with a pearl necklace, and diamond brooch at her left shoulder. She wore neither hat nor gloves. The Queen was accompanied by the Lord Chamberlain, closely followed by the Duke of Edinburgh in naval uniform, and members of the Palace Household. It was a unique scene in a sumptuous setting. The young monarch was about to perform an ancient royal prerogative, that of rewarding brave and loyal subjects with personal honours.

Her Majesty walked to the edge of the Dais and spoke in a clear voice, 'Ladies and gentleman, please be seated'. To her right, and slightly to the rear, stood her military equerry, ready if necessary to whisper a discreet prompt. To his right again, the Earl of Clarendon, in a morning suit, positioned himself to make the formal announcement of each recipient. On the Queen's left, slightly behind, stood the Master of the Household. It was his task to present each Badge (insignia or medal) on the crimson velvet cushion to Her Majesty, from the gleaming array set out on trays on the table in front of him. Behind the Queen, the sergeant major of the Yeomen of the Guard kept a watchful eye on the other Yeomen who acted as the Queen's escort, one being positioned on either side of the archway, just forward of the Dais. On this occasion there were no Gurkha Orderly Officers present. The custom of the Sovereign having six Indian Army Orderly Officers had lapsed in 1947. It was not until seven years later, in 1954, that the Queen reintroduced the practice, but with just two Gurkha officers.

The Lord Chamberlain spoke. 'To be decorated with the Victoria Cross. Private William Speakman, the King's Own Scottish Borderers.' As the Earl of Clarendon finished speaking the Gentleman Usher at the door gave Speakman a nod, and with heart racing he strode forward into the Ball Room, grateful for the fact that a strip of carpeting deadened the clumping of his boots, and removed the risk of a humiliating slip on the floor. He could concentrate his mind on what he had to do. He halted opposite Her Majesty, turned left to face her, and remembered to bow not salute. The Lord Chamberlain then read a resume of his citation, before Speakman took a pace forward to position himself within the Queen's reach. Even standing on the Dais as she was, Speakman towered over his Queen. It was an historic moment, unfortunately lost to posterity as no photography is ever permitted inside the Palace. She fastened on the Cross before chatting to Speakman for a moment or two, congratulating him, and asking how long he had served in the Black Watch and the KOSB. A handshake concluded his Investiture. Speakman took a step back, bowed, turned right, and marched out through the opposite doors.

Once outside Speakman was 'unhooked', and his Cross taken from him, to be put in its box before being handed back. He was then directed to a seat at the rear of the Ball Room to enable him to observe the remainder of the ceremony. Within an hour it was all over. The National Anthem signalled Her Majesty's departure, and recipients and guests were reunited before filing out of the Palace to face the Press.

Speakman put it simply: 'It was a great experience, and a great honour.'

Military symbols used on maps

UNIT SIZES

A section, 6–10 men

Two sections, 12–20 men

A platoon, 20–35 men

A company, 100–150 men

A battalion, 450–800 men

A regiment, 800–1,500 men

A brigade, over 1,500 men

A division, over 8,000 men

(+)   A reinforced unit

(−)   An understrength unit

A unit in a defensive position

TYPES OF UNIT

Infantry

Artillery

Tanks

Infantry in armoured personnel carriers (APCs)

An headquarters

An observation post (OP)

AN EXAMPLE

B ⊠ KOSB   B Company 1st Battalion Kings Own Scottish Borderers

WEAPONS AND INDIVIDUALS

51 mm light mortar   105 mm howitzer

81 mm medium mortar   155 mm howitzer

120 mm heavy mortar   Minefield

Light machine gun (LMG)

Medium machine gun (MMG)   Wounded man

Heavy machine gun (HMG)   Dead man

1. Major Muir receives a welcoming bouquet from a Korean schoolgirl on arrival at Pusan docks, as the Argylls disembark from HMS *Ceylon*. *(Hulton Picture Library)*.

2. Hill 282 as it looks today. B Company secured the right-hand summit and C Company the left-hand one. It was on this hill that the Argylls were attacked with napalm by U.S. aircraft, and upon which Major Muir died winning his VC. *(Major V.T. Smedley, Royal Signals)*.

3. Lieutenant P.K.E. Curtis. He is wearing the cap-badge of The Duke of Cornwall's Light Infantry, not that of the Glosters to whom he was attached when he won his VC. *(Imperial War Museum)*.

4. The forward (northern) slopes of Castle Hill as it is today. It shows part of the view from 3 Platoon (Lieutenant Waters) area, with the Imjin River in the distance. *(Major V.T. Smedley)*

PART ONE

Korea

On a small-scale map Korea appears as an ugly, 530-mile-long and 150-mile-wide appendage, spoiling the otherwise graceful curves of China's Pacific coast. It reaches out across the sea almost to touch the southern-most Japanese island of Kyushu. China and Japan have shaped the Korean people's history. Over the centuries the razor-backed ridges, steep hills and narrow valleys have often been witness to warfare. Genghis Khan's Golden Horde conquered the country; the sixteenth century saw 300,000 Japanese with matchlock muskets rampaging up the peninsula; next it was the Manchus, sweeping south. Finally, in 1904, the Japanese Emperor's imperial armies arrived to wage the Russo-Japanese war. As the victors, they remained, placing Korea under military occupation for 40 years. When, in 1945, the Russians and Americans split the country along the bureaucratic boundary of the 38th Parallel, over 70,000 Japanese civil servants and 600,000 soldiers had to be shipped home. The vicious use of murder and torture by the Japanese rulers had turned antipathy between the two peoples into hatred.

In rural areas old customs still prevail; age receives respect. Men of over 50 wear birdcage-shaped hats, a married woman's hair is tightly tied in a bun, and white is the colour of mourning, worn for the death of a father, mother, or son; never a wife — she can easily be replaced.

The Korean of today is descended from the Mongols. For 2000 years the people survived on primitive agriculture; life plodded forward at the pace of the bullock cart. The peasant population lived a hard, timeless, dreary existence, their daily routine dictated by the seasonal demands of the rice paddy, or the overriding urgency for warmth in the winter. The average Korean is a resilient, hardworking, uncomplaining individual. He has all the natural attributes of a good infantry soldier.

The tranquillity of The Land of the Morning Calm was shattered at 4.00 a.m. on Sunday, 25 June, 1950, by the crack and crump of shells and mortar bombs landing on the forward positions of President Syngman Rhee's South Korean army. It was the start of a three-year war that would kill some 34,000 Americans, 700 British, 415,000 South Koreans, and 800,000 North Koreans and Chinese. Countless thousands of civilians died, over 400,000 houses were destroyed, making more than 3.5 million people homeless.

By 1952 no less than sixteen nations had troops in the field under the UN flag. Within six months the fighting would sweep down to the sea in the south, then back north to the Yalu River, before finally stabilizing across the centre of the peninsula. Here the front came to resemble that of World War 1, both sides burrowing into the hillsides, with mile after mile of trenches, bunkers and barbed wire. The period from July to December, 1950, however, was one of the most shameful for the US Army. It was the period of the 'bugouts' when battalion after battalion failed to fight, turning tail after a few shots and fleeing south. Major-General William Dean, the commander of the first US division to arrive (the 24th Infantry) straight from the soft, almost civilian, life style of Japan, frantically fired senior commanders in the field as he desperately sought to stop the rot. Later, after General MacArthur's masterly landing behind the enemy's lines at Inchon, when the UN forces were approaching the Yalu, China poured her 'volunteers' over the frontier. This event saw the start of the second, bigger, 'bugout', which witnessed the entire American 8th Army and its South Korean allies in retreat, abandoning equipment, weapons, dead, and sometimes wounded, in the stampede to join the refugees on the roads south. Only in the east did the US Marines hold together, during their bitter withdrawal from the Chosin reservoir to the port of Hamhung for naval evacuation.

Kim Il Sung had sent seven infantry divisions, spearheaded by Soviet T-34 tanks, across the Parallel that summer morning 40 years ago. His invasion prompted an instant reaction from the UN Security Council. In a never-to-be-repeated resolution, the Council agreed unanimously to a UN military response to rescue South Korea. There was no Soviet veto, as their delegate was boycotting meetings as a protest at the UN's refusal to expel Nationalist, and admit Communist, China. The USSR was never to be caught out again. As the US searched desperately for troops to be flown in, within hours rather than days, their embassy in the South Korean capi-

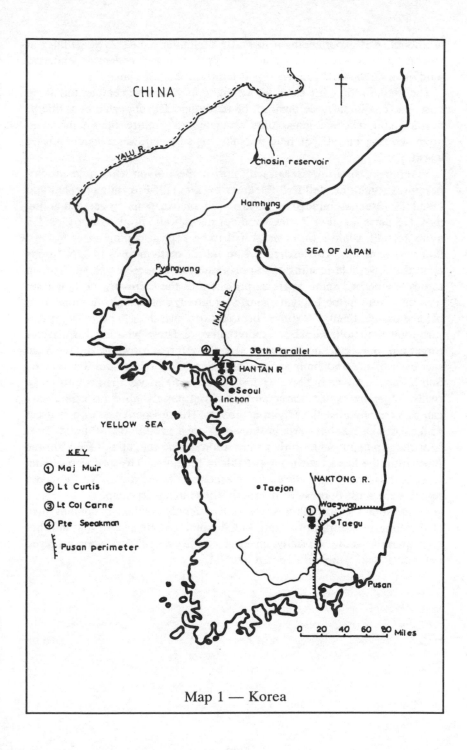

CHINA

YALU R.

Chosin reservoir

Hamhung

SEA OF JAPAN

Pyongyang

IMJIN R.

④ 36th Parallel

HANTAN R.

②①

● Seoul
Inchon

YELLOW SEA

KEY
① Maj Muir
② Lt Curtis
③ Lt Col Carne
④ Pte Speakman
Pusan perimeter

NAKTONG R.

● Taejon

① Waegwon
● Taegu

● Pusan

0 20 40 60 80 Miles

Map 1 — Korea

21

tal, Seoul, was experiencing a foretaste of similar scenes 25 years later in Saigon. Staff scrambled to burn heaps of documents, collect dependants, fend off unauthorized fugitives, and jump on the last plane out.

The soldiers of both sides who fought in Korea remember the same miseries. The infantry dominated the battlefield as, supported by artillery, mortars and machine guns, they struggled to capture or defend some unknown ridgeline. If you held the hills you survived, was a lesson quickly learnt.

Veterans of all armies recall with horror the Korean winter, when temperatures sometimes fell to 30 degrees below zero. Frostbite crippled and killed as often as bullets or bombs. Oil on weapons froze, cementing movable parts together if they were not periodically fired. Water took 1½ hours to boil, while a tin of meat had to be kept in boiling water for two hours to heat up. Also etched in the minds of thousands of UN troops were the miserable months of imprisonment in Chinese or North Korean camps. Some had spent years as prisoners of the Germans, or Japanese; now they were in the bag yet again. Starvation, degrading conditions, lack of medical treatment, beatings, brutality, brainwashing, and outright torture took their toll. Hundreds didn't survive. Those who lived will never forget the conditions they endured. Was the effort worthwhile, did the huge sacrifices of life and limb achieve anything? Ask these questions of any South Korean today and his response is an emphatic 'yes'. His country now rivals Singapore for economic and industrial power, while his capital city can successfully host the Olympic Games. His prosperity gives him great pride. Perhaps nowhere else in the world are a people still, 40 years later, so willing to express gratitude to the soldiers who fought and died to save them from the fate of their compatriots in the north. The iron grip of Kim Il Sung has not been relaxed by glasnost or perestroika; North Korea remains the most oppressive regime in the communist camp.

Of the four Victoria Crosses won in Korea only one holder remains alive at the time of writing; two were killed winning their award, and another died in retirement. Typically, in each case their gallantry was displayed defending some otherwise anonymous hill.

CHAPTER 1

Hill 282 — Korea,
23 September, 1950

MAJOR KENNETH MUIR VC
The Argyll and Sutherland Highlanders

'Neither the Gooks nor the U.S. Air Force will drive the
Argylls off this hill.'
Major Muir when lying mortally wounded on Hill 282.

Napalm is liquid fire. It is perhaps the most terrifying, most dreaded weapon in the modern tactical arsenal. Its use against all types of targets, from buildings to tanks or infantry, has been widespread by western powers since World War 2. Thousands of people have been burned alive by napalm in Europe and Asia in the last fifty years. In Vietnam the U.S. used it with devastating effectiveness in their search and destroy operations, sometimes incinerating whole villages.

It is jellied petrol, with various chemicals added to enhance its horrific properties. It is an ideal incendiary weapon. It flows, it clings, it is hard to extinguish, it burns with an extremely high temperature, and can be used without the need for pinpoint accuracy. Watch a bucket of water thrown over a floor — it rushes forward over a wide area, engulfing, swamping, and soaking all obstacles in its path. So with napalm. A canister of napalm launched from an aircraft ignites on hitting the ground, permitting no escape for anything or anybody it touches. It can destroy tanks 30 metres from impact, while infantry in the open are roasted alive. Even for those sheltered in trenches or bunkers the prospect of escape is small, as it flows over parapets, or is splashed through openings. Those who live suffer the agonies of third degree burns and deep shock.

At midday on 23 September, 1950, three U.S. F-51 Mustang fighter bombers took off from their base in South Korea on a mission to support the 1st Battalion the Argyll and Sutherland Highlanders (A&SH). They had been briefed that the Argylls were under heavy pressure from North Koreans, counter-attacking from hill 388, down on to the Argylls' position on nearby hill 282, a few miles SE of the town of Songju. It was only a short 15-minute flight and each aircraft had a full load of napalm, rockets and cannon shells. The Mustang, a single-engine piston plane, was a veteran of the Second World War. Indeed, it was still in use in a counter-insurgency role as late as 1968 in some South American countries. It was very reliable, had a range of 950 miles, a maximum speed of 437 knots, and could reach a ceiling of nearly 42,000 feet. It was no match for a jet, but in a non-hostile air environment it could operate at no greater risk than more modern aircraft, with the added bonus of its cheapness and versatility.

As the three Mustangs crossed the Naktong River the tangle of hills that was their target area was clearly visible below. The flight leader had no radio contact with the Argylls, but he could talk to his tactical air control officer, Captain Radcliff, at 27 Brigade Headquarters east of the river, but some 7-8 miles from the battalion. The pilots were responsible for locating the target by map reading, and spotting the ground identification panels that were put out by friendly troops around their positions. The crews were well aware that on that day the Argylls would be displaying vertical yellow panels. As they overflew the area for the first time the battle in progress on the hills was unmistakable, the large masses of troops, the smoke, and the explosions of bursting shells indicated where the Argylls were under attack. Nevertheless, the flight leader was confused. Hill 388 had some troops on it, but so did 282 where the fighting was concentrated. Both hills were close together and, at high speed from the air, it was far from easy to be certain which was which. Soldiers could be seen swarming on the slopes of 282, or was it 388? Then they saw the yellow panels in the midst of the battle, although they seemed to have been put out on what they thought was their target. Mystified, the three planes circled round while clarification was sought over the radio.

Captain Radcliff received the anxious message — there were marker panels out on what appeared to be the target hill. Radcliff, who could see nothing on the ground at that distance, turned to query the brigade staff. He was, apparently, informed that the enemy had overrun the position, so the panels could be ignored. With this information the Mustangs swooped down for their first run in, now using the panels as convenient aiming marks. Each aircraft would use its napalm on the first attack. None of the pilots noticed a tiny figure frantically waving a panel — it was Major 'Kenny' Muir.

Muir came from an Army family. His grandparents had named his father, who had fought in South Africa and the Great War, Garnet Wolseley, after the famous Victorian general. As a boy, Muir was accustomed to military life, and had been a lad of eleven at Malvern School when his father was appointed to command the Argylls in 1923. At 38, in Korea, Muir was a highly experienced soldier. On his battledress jacket were eight medal ribbons and an oakleaf for a MID earned during the latter part of the Second World War. Commissioned in 1932, his early campaigning had been in India. He was a subaltern on the N.W. Frontier from 1935-1938, which entitled him to both the Indian General Service Medals. The Frontier was a hard, unforgiving school for soldiers, through which every infantry battalion had to pass at some time. Its modern equivalent for the British Army, as a source of experience in a shooting environment, is Northern Ireland. Up there, in the mountains bordering Afghanistan, Muir learnt the rules of war — always occupy the hilltops; never let the enemy dominate you from higher ground; and never, ever leave behind your wounded. There can be little doubt that fighting in the Korean hills reminded him of his Frontier days.

During World War 2 he had risen from captain to acting lieutenant-colonel. Until July, 1943, he was attached to the Sudan Defence Force. He earned three campaign stars for service in North Africa, Italy, France and Germany, plus the 1939-1945 Star. For most of his time, however, he served on the staff, or was attached to the Military Police. Brought down to major again in 1946, Muir worked for a time in the Provost Marshal's branch of the War Office in Eaton Square, before joining the Argylls in Hong Kong as second-in-command. Few of his fellow officers knew him, as it had been eleven years since he had served with a battalion of the Regiment. He would never know that his three weeks service in Korea would add four more medals, including the VC, to his eight.

The Argylls went to Korea in a hurry. They belonged to 27 Brigade, under Brigadier Aubry Coad, which was Britain's 'fire brigade', always at ten days' notice to rush to any trouble spot. The battalion was warned on 19 August and sailed on the 25th. Holt's Wharf, at Kowloon, was the scene of an old-fashioned Victorian send-off for both the Argylls and the Middlesex Regiment, (the other infantry battalion in the Brigade). Bowed by the weight of their enormous loads, the sweat-soaked infantry filed slowly up the gangways to their ships, while thousands cheered, yelled, and waved flags. The bands of the KOSB and Leicesters, both in full dress uniform, vied with each other on the quayside. Muir was taking the Argylls to Korea as the CO, Lieutenant-Colonel Leslie Neilson, was to fly ahead with the advance party. He watched as the gangways were disconnected, then stood still as the boatswain's pipes shrilled, the Royal Marine buglers called the ship's companies to attention, and the bands played their farewell. From the Leicesters, the emotional 'Auld Lang Syne'; from the pipes of the KOSB, 'Will ye no' come back again?'.

Four days later HMS *Ceylon* with the Argylls, and the carrier HMS *Unicorn* with the Middlesex plus brigade headquarters, sailed into another tumultuous reception at Pusan. Again the crowds of well-wishers — South

Korean government officials, ambassadors, senior U.S. and Korean military officers, UN staff, together with hundreds of school children complete with a choir. Flags flew everywhere. A South Korean navy band and an American all negro brass band provided the musical entertainment. It was an historic moment. The UN forces had been pushed into the SE corner of the Korean peninsula. Now the first British troops were arriving, so everybody was out to ensure they had a memorable welcome. Muir, short, stocky, with a trim moustache, wearing tropical uniform under his web equipment, and carrying the Argyll officers' traditional long walking stick, was obliged to receive bouquets of flowers from several small schoolgirls in front of the press cameras before the battalion could leave the wharf.

The Argylls had just over three weeks before being committed to serious action as part of the UN breakout from the Pusan perimeter. It was a question of crossing the Naktong River to push NW up the road to Taejon and Seoul, down which the U.S. and South Korean armies had so recently retreated. In conjunction with General MacArthur's amphibious landings at Inchon, this offensive would eventually succeed in driving the North Koreans back to the Yalu — and in precipitating Chinese participation.

27 Brigade was nicknamed the 'Woolworth' brigade. It was short of manpower (with only two battalions), it had no supporting artillery and no administrative back up. It relied for all these things on the U.S. Army. American aircraft flew in support of it, American guns and tanks fired for it, while its men ate American rations, and eventually wore American winter clothing. The staff and officers had to learn U.S. methods of operating. The brigade major became an S.3, company commanders had to learn how to control U.S. artillery fire, radio procedures were different, the British took bearings in degrees, the Americans in mils, and their written orders took the form of map traces which became very inaccurate in reproduction. In accordance with British Second World War practice, Muir, as second-in-command, was banished to the rear battalion headquarters and echelon area, responsible for overseeing the Argyll's logistical needs. This was deliberate policy to keep the second-in-command away from the fighting so that he was immediately available should the CO become a casualty. It was not to his personal liking as he felt out of touch with the day-to-day tactical situation, although he made every effort to find out what was going on during his daily visits to the forward headquarters, when the company colour sergeants brought up the rations and ammunition.

On 16 September the breakout battle began. It was not a spectacular success. The U.S. formations were stale, they had been fighting bitter defensive actions for weeks, and their attack lacked spirit. One of the assaulting regimental combat teams (RCT) of the 1st Cavalry Division (an infantry formation), had been pushed back 1000 metres from its start line the day before. On D-day the massive carpet bombing in front of the U.S. localities was rained off, leaving it to the gunners to bombard the enemy positions. The advance never really got moving. The best effort came from the fresh troops of the 5th RCT who managed 1000 metres.

It was not until 22 September, when the 24th Infantry Division was put in, that progress was made. The 24th contained 27 Brigade, whose task was to protect the left flank of the U.S. advance. Seven miles over the Naktong lay the small town of Songju, a road junction on the route to Seoul. It was the objective of 27 Brigade, whose way was barred by a jumble of hills on both sides of the road. As in the N.W. Frontier it would be disastrous to use the road unless the hilltops overlooking it were secure. This was the first task of the brigade. The Middlesex would tackle two dominant features on the right (north) of the road, while the Argylls took those on the left.

A glance at Map 2 will help in understanding the brigade's intentions. First came the crossing of the Naktong, over a rickety pontoon footbridge that both battalions had to cross under spasmodic fire from self-propelled (SP) guns on the far side. The Middlesex led the way on the 21st, followed by the Argylls. Brigadier Coad watched, finding it 'very heartening to see these battalions moving across in single file. They never faltered, and we had relatively few casualties.' Ahead stretched some four miles of secondary road before the main barrier of hills, all of which were steep-sided and covered with scrub and fir trees. The two features on the right were slightly closer than those to the left, so the plan was for the Middlesex to secure these first, on the 22nd. The hill closest to the road was nicknamed Plum Pudding, while the other adjoining, but higher, hill was 325, afterwards known as Middlesex Hill. Division was sceptical about the enemy's intention to defend the hills and initially reluctant to allocate artillery support to the brigade, although some tanks of the Reconnaissance Company were moving forward with the infantry. B Company of the Middlesex took Plum Pudding, then D Company assaulted 325. Not until the final stages did they receive artillery support, the attacks moving forward under cover of the battalion's own machine guns and mortars. Substantial losses were inflicted on the North Koreans at little cost. By midday the Middlesex were firm, and it was the Argylls' turn.

The feature that directly dominated the road was 282, but it was joined to the SW by a ridgeline that ran up to a much higher hill, 388, about 1500 metres away. Some 1000 metres SE of 282 was point 148, an almost conical hill that acted as an outpost to the others. It had been Neilson's intention to attack on the 22nd, immediately after the Middlesex, but because of the lack of time he now modified his plan. Phase one would involve A Com-

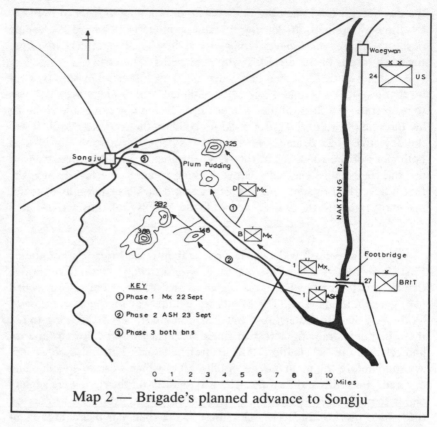

Map 2 — Brigade's planned advance to Songju

pany, under Major David Wilson, securing 148 that afternoon, while phase two would be the capture, at first light the next morning, of 282 by B and C Companies. Hill 388 was too far away to be included in the assault, but it worried Neilson because enemy on it would dominate 282, and the connecting ridge offered an ideal approach down on to the lower hill. It was never intended to occupy it, but it needed watching. Air reconnaissance had revealed nothing definite, so perhaps it was not occupied in strength.

Wilson received his orders around midday and by 2.00 pm his company was moving carefully down the road towards 148. He had no artillery forward observation officer (FOO) with him, but he contacted the troop commander of some nearby American tanks. The master sergeant, although not specifically tasked with assisting, agreed to co-operate. Wilson's plan was to move left, off the road and advance up the hill in the order 1-2-3 Platoons with the tanks shooting up some enemy positions spotted on the hill. The armour went into hull-down positions behind the road embankment and opened fire. Their shells scattered the North Koreans, permitting

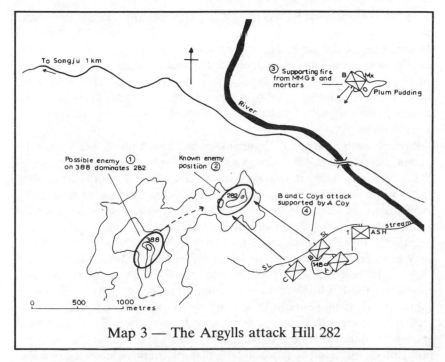

Map 3 — The Argylls attack Hill 282

A Company a virtually unopposed occupation. They spent the night digging in, protecting the start line for B and C Companies' forthcoming attack, and preparing to support their advance by fire as necessary.

Map 3 shows the details of the action for 282. The plan was that B Company (Major Alastair Gordon-Ingram) and C Company (Major Jim Gillies) were to move to a lying-up position near A Company during darkness, snatch a few hours rest, then move to the start line at 4.30 am on the 23rd, crossing it at 5.15. With luck they would time their arrival on top of 282 to coincide with dawn. It was to be a silent attack with the hope of catching the enemy by surprise. Once contact was made, covering fire would be available from A Company and the Middlesex on Plum Pudding. Both companies had American artillery FOOs accompanying them from their supporting battery. B Company would be on the right, C Company the left. The start line was a stream running at right-angles to, and left of, the road.

The companies were in their lying-up position by 8.00 pm, but the chill and tension prevented proper sleep. The move of the battalion's tactical headquarters to its position near A Company, from which Neilson could observe the attack, nearly caused a noisy, and potentially dangerous, breach of security. The intelligence officer (IO) was responsible for navigation and the daily issue of the password. 2nd Lieutenant Sandy Boswell was

29

extremely keyed up as he led the CO's party forward through the blackness on this his first operation[1]. As they were wading through the stream a challenge rang out from an A company sentry. Everybody froze. There was an ominous silence as the unfortunate Boswell desperately tried to recall the response. His mind was a blank. Just as the sentry must have been about to fire the situation was saved by a piper, Corporal Pitkeathly, who replied correctly. For Boswell it was to be the first of two instances of acute disquiet that day.

Precisely on time B and C Companies stood up to move forward over the stream, across the paddy fields, to start their stiff climb up the slopes of 282. Everybody strove to minimize the noise as they began the scrambling ascent in the darkness. They wanted to get as close to the summit as possible before they were discovered. In B Company, 4 Platoon was on the left under 2nd Lieutenant Peter Mckellar, and 6 Platoon, commanded by Sergeant John O'Sullivan, on the right. They were closely followed by company headquarters and the reserve, 2nd Lieutenant David Buchanan's 5 Platoon. It took under an hour to cover the 900 metres to the top and, incredibly, the North Koreans were caught unawares. It was just getting light as the leading platoons clambered up to the summit and, turning to their right to clear the spur, at last bumped the enemy. They were about to cook breakfast when the Highlanders suddenly appeared in the dim light. Firing broke out immediately and both platoon commanders fell wounded. Corporal Sweeney found himself leading the assault, which soon scattered the North Koreans, most of whom fled down the reverse slope leaving fifteen dead on the position. C Company had had an uneventful climb, so by 6.18 am 282 was taken — almost exactly an hour since crossing the start line — at a cost of only one killed and six wounded.

Now was the time to consolidate the position, to secure it from possible counter-attack. The vegetation was extremely thick, making it easy for enemy to approach under cover, and causing some problems with the Argylls' fields of fire, while the entire summit was overshadowed by 388. In the darkness one of B Company's platoons had made a slight navigational error, and it was found that 7 Platoon of C Company, under 2nd Lieutenant John Edington, was the forward platoon in B Company's area. It was also the nearest platoon to 388. The company commanders conferred, agreeing that 7 Platoon should come temporarily under B Company. The critical need was to co-ordinate defensive positions quickly. B Company now had four platoons on what was the largest feature of 282 (nicknamed Baker Ridge), and would bear the initial weight of any attack from 388. C Company, with only 8 and 9 Platoons, occupied the smaller ridge (Charlie Ridge). See Map 4 for the remainder of the battle.

Although it was not likely either company would remain on 282 for long,

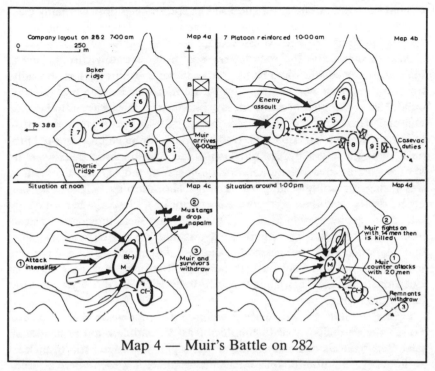

Map 4 — Muir's Battle on 282

as its occupation was only to facilitate the advance on Songju and beyond, the priority was to dig in, and to organize defensive fire (DF) tasks with the artillery, and the battalion's own support weapons. The difficulty with the digging was the hardness of the ground. Strenuous efforts were made, but scrapes of a few inches were the best that most could achieve. Attempts were made to build sangars, but they were hampered by a shortage of loose rocks.

Within half an hour of taking 282, the North Koreans began to shell and mortar the Argylls' positions causing several more casualties in both companies. It also slowed the digging. Both accompanying FOOs tried to locate the enemy guns without success. The two companies had no medium machine guns (MMGs) forward with them, and the battalion's 3-inch mortars were far to the rear, without vehicles to bring them forward to get within range at this stage. To add to the difficulties, it was discovered that B Company's 31 radio set, linking it to battalion headquarters, was not working. Gordon-Ingram left his second-in-command, Captain John Penman, in charge while he moved to C Company headquarters to keep in touch with the CO.[2] By 8.00 am 7 Platoon reported a group of enemy infantry endeavouring to approach its position from 388. Edington was told

31

to hold his fire until he got a good shoot, and to keep both company commanders informed. The struggle to hold 282 was beginning well before proper positions had been constructed.

After a slight lull of 45 minutes two significant events occurred. First, 7 Platoon reported that the enemy from 388 were getting closer; secondly, the two American FOOs came down from their observation posts to announce they were pulling out. Just as artillery support was about to become vital the officers responsible for co-ordinating it had been ordered to withdraw by their own headquarters. Both company commanders protested furiously over the radio to Neilson. Unlike the British system, there was no battery commander at battalion headquarters, so the CO was unaware he was losing his artillery support, or why. The attached FOOs took their orders direct from their own unit. Neilson spoke to the brigadier, who contacted the gunners, only to be told that the guns were moving on instructions from divisional headquarters. It was all part of 24 Division's belief that resistance would be spasmodic, and the consequential desire to regroup the artillery for the final push to Songju. There was nothing Neilson or Coad could do. The consequences of this decision led directly to disaster three hours later.

On the summit of 282 casualty evacuation had become an acute problem. To get the wounded back to the doctor at the battalion aid post necessitated a dangerous carry down the steep slopes — a round trip of at least an hour. A minimum of four men were required for each stretcher case. Although C Company sent a section to assist it proved inadequate, so a radio request was made for stretcher bearers and porters to be sent forward. This brought Muir into the battle.

He had come up to battalion headquarters with the usual daily supply of rations and ammunition, just as the counter-attack on 282 was developing. Anxious to play an active part, he asked the CO for permission to take the resupply party and stretcher bearers forward himself. Neilson agreed. He arrived at the joint B/C Company command post at around 9.00 am, and at once consulted with Gordon-Ingram and Gillies. Then, with the assistance of C Company's sergeant major, Tom Collet, Muir set about organizing the speedy evacuation of the wounded.

By this time mortaring and shelling had intensified. Next, 7 Platoon reported they were engaging enemy infantry at close range. The North Korean assault had begun in earnest. Edington could not call for supporting fire of any sort. His platoon had to rely entirely on their own weapons to drive off ever-increasing numbers, who were able to approach close to his position before exposing themselves. They began to infiltrate round to his left, and within a few minutes he was desperately calling for reinforcements. Gillies sent a section from 8 Platoon, followed by another from 9

Platoon. There was now not much left of C Company — 7 Platoon was fighting hard with B Company, a section was carrying casualties, and now two more sections had gone forward to Baker Ridge. Despite the extra men Edington was still in difficulties, and was himself wounded, along with his platoon sergeant. Buchanan was then sent forward with some of his men to this exposed position. By 10.45 am it was obvious that this area could not be held any longer, so after nearly two hours of bitter fighting the survivors were pulled back, bringing their wounded, into the main B Company locality.

With the platoons and sections so inextricably mixed, with both company commanders operating from a joint command post, and with Muir now the senior officer on the spot, it was decided to seek the CO's permission for him to take command on 282. Neilson agreed immediately.

Muir was about to earn his Cross. He started making fresh dispositions, tightening the perimeter, centralizing ammunition supply and distribution, supervising the continuing evacuation of casualties (which now totalled around 50), and walking around the positions. It was his dynamic personality that strengthened the Jocks' resolve. Utterly contemptuous of the risks to himself, Muir was everywhere. Resistance was redoubled. But without some heavy supporting fire on the build-up of fresh enemy reserves on 388 and the ridge running from it to 282, the defence was severely handicapped. Muir endeavoured to get the tanks to shoot, but, although they tried, it was ineffective, as their flat trajectory guns could not be brought to bear. The only remaining option was an airstrike.

At around 11.00 am Muir requested battalion headquarters to arrange the strike, indicating that the target was to be 388. At that stage of the war the only way to get air support was for battalion to ask brigade, and for brigade to ask the attached American air liaison officer. He then contacted the Air Force. It was a cumbersome and lengthy procedure, with no guarantee of aircraft at the end of it. Its greatest weaknesses, apart from the inordinately long time it took, were the lack of any direct communication between the aircraft and those on the ground they were supporting, and the inability of the air controller to see what was happening.

The Argylls had to hold on. It was to be over an hour before the three aircraft came in sight. The yellow marker panels had been put out in front of the positions, and Muir had spent the time on the summit of Baker Ridge where the fighting was most desperate. Here he directed fire, organized ammunition distribution and personally encouraged all who saw him by his disregard for the heavy automatic fire that was hitting the hilltop from several directions. The sight of the Mustangs wheeling round in the sky above was greeted with relief by the remnants of both companies.

The aircraft did not attack immediately, but came in low over the top of 282, circled round, had another look, then another. It was ominous — they made no attempt to strike 388. Then, as if finally making up their minds that the Argylls were the target, they turned together towards 282. Those on the ground could do nothing except fling themselves down into what meagre cover there was, and curse the pilots who must surely have seen the markers. Muir knew what was coming, but he did not dive for cover. He grabbed a panel and stood alone, frantically waving it in a last forlorn attempt to warn the aircraft.

It was useless. Each Mustang roared in low to release its load of napalm into the Argylls' position. The hilltop was engulfed with the terrible flowing fire that destroyed everything it touched. Clouds of black smoke and flames covered the top of 282. The aircraft returned again to strafe with rockets and cannon fire, before swooping down over A Company's position on 148, hitting them with bursts of cannon fire and several rockets. Fortunately for Wilson's men, and nearby tactical headquarters, they were well dug in, and the planes had run out of napalm, so they only suffered two casualties.

On 282 the results were appalling. Roughly 30-40 men, some of them already wounded, were killed or grievously injured. It was a shocking, hellish way to die, made worse by the fact that it should never have happened. It was a nightmarish mistake. Those that could had leapt off the hill to a position some 50 feet below the crest on Charlie Ridge.

Back at battalion headquarters Neilson had watched with impotent horror. Frenzied radio messages to brigade to abort the mission eventually produced results, but not until after the Mustangs had run out of ammunition and were on their way back to base. For the young IO, Boswell, it brought his second personal crisis of the day. It was his responsibility to ensure that all companies had details of the recognition panels to be used the next day. Two fluorescent panels were used, either red or yellow, in a combination of horizontal or vertical patterns. As Boswell revealed many years later: 'On the day in question the vertical yellow panel was to be used. When the air attack came in on us rather than the enemy, I had the most appalling doubts that I must have issued the wrong code for the day. We could see the single yellow panels clearly from Tac HQ, and I believe that during the height of the air attack, Kenny Muir even waved a panel round his head to try to warn the aircraft away. It was not until that evening that I could get back to Bn HQ to check the correct panel for the day — thankfully I had not got it wrong.'

Among the few who got off 282 unscathed were Muir, Gordon-Ingram, Penman, and Sergeant-Major Murray of B Company. They huddled together on Charlie Ridge, regrouped around C Company headquarters, stunned by events. Muir watched the flames and smoke die down on the summit, leaving charred and blackened ground upon which there could not possibly be survivors. Then, incredibly there was movement, indeed some firing from a small sector of the ridge. Although he could not know it at the time, it was Private Watt firing a Bren, with a handful of others, mostly wounded, who were continuing the fight. Muir also noticed that the enemy had not taken advantage of their unexpected support to occupy the hilltop, and he realized that there could be some injured still up there.

There is no doubt that had Muir requested authority to withdraw completely from 282 at that time he would have been given it, but that would have been totally out of character. With the help of the other officers Muir got together a group of 20-25 men to launch a counter-attack. The battle was far from over; the Argylls would keep the hill despite the North Koreans, and despite the Americans. Back at A Company and battalion tactical headquarters the spectators watched incredulously as a tattered line of tiny figures moved slowly up towards the smouldering crest. They could not hear Muir's shouts of encouragement, or the ragged cheer from his men, but it was a never-to-be-forgotten sight as, covered by Gillies and two Bren gunners, the remnants of the two companies once more gained 282. The price they paid was heavy. On the summit Muir was down to fourteen fit men, with the enemy now renewing their assault from three sides, and a number of wounded Argylls in critical need of evacuation. Ammunition was almost gone, the napalm having destroyed all reserve stocks, but Muir would not give in. He was utterly determined that the wounded should be got away, which necessitated a period of intense fighting to win time. His courage and leadership inspired everyone who saw him dashing round the tiny perimeter, now firing his sten gun, now handing out ammunition, now directing fire, now encouraging a wounded man. When his magazines were empty he seized a 2-inch mortar and began firing it to great effect, with Gordon-Ingram acting as loader. It was while operating the mortar that Muir was hit in the stomach and thigh by a burst of automatic fire. He retained consciousness for some minutes, and was still anxious that the crest be held. Not even the agony of his wounds could conceal his tenacity. At the very end his last words were typical of him — 'Neither the Gooks nor the U.S. Air Force will drive the Argylls off this hill.'

Gordon-Ingram assumed command of the ten or so soldiers still able to fight. With such numbers, and with only one magazine per Bren, he had no option but to rejoin what was left of C Company on Charlie Ridge. There, too, the lack of ammunition and the need to save the wounded made further resistance impossible. Neilson's response to the request to withdraw was: 'Damn well done. Now get out of it.' The withdrawal was authorized at 1.00 pm, and by 3.00 the twenty or so unwounded survivors had regrouped on 148. They had brought out all wounded, and the body of Major Muir slung in a groundsheet. The Argylls suffered 17 killed and 76 wounded or missing during this action — the equivalent of an entire company. The following day U.S. troops moved SW from Waegwan to take Songju.

It was clear to all who had witnessed the action on 282 that, but for Muir's outstanding gallantry and leadership, the effect of the airstrike would have been infinitely worse, with many injured men being left to die on the summit. The following day the adjutant, Captain John Slim, and the IO debriefed the remaining officers, NCOs and men[3]. Both company commanders discussed Muir's actions with Neilson. It was agreed that there was only one possible award — a posthumous VC. Statements were obtained, and the adjutant assisted the CO in compiling the recommendation, which Neilson took personally to brigade headquarters.

For the three hours or so that Muir was on 282 he held the defence together, eventually organizing a successful counter-attack in circumstances when all present considered it impossible. Muir was a military man, from a military family, whose traditions of loyalty, duty and courage had been cemented by his experience and training on the NW Frontier. You always held the hills, you always counter-attacked if you lost a position, and never, never, did you abandon your wounded to the enemy. Muir's supreme courage came from these unshakeable beliefs, from his intense loyalty to the regiment, and his sense of honour always to do what was right by his soldiers.

At the time the U.S. airstrike shattered the brigade's confidence in their allies. It so incensed B Company of the Middlesex, who had watched from Plum Pudding, that their company commander had great difficulty in restraining his men from leaving their positions to go and assist. In fact, many of the Middlesex came across to help carry the wounded, and it was heavy supporting fire from their machine guns that contributed to the Argylls' few casualties during their move back to 148. The American Air Force, particularly the pilots concerned, were devastated. Not only did the crews come forward by jeep to B Echelon of the Argylls to apologise — a brave act — but a generous cheque was given by the 93rd Bomber Wing for the families of those killed or wounded. This tragic error was not repeated. It led to a complete review of air-ground liaison and support, with the establishment of a U.S. Air Contact Team (ACT) at battalion headquarters. This facilitated the briefing of pilots as they approached, or circled the target, by people on the ground who could see what was happening. Time healed the rift. The Colonel of the Regiment, Lieutenant-General Sir Gordon Macmillan, was later able to end a letter to the Americans with the words: 'The Regiment's friendship with the United States Air Force personnel can never be impaired by having suffered on one occasion from the risks which are inseparable from operations in modern war.'

Perhaps appropriately, it was the Americans who were the first to honour Muir with the Distinguished Service Cross (DSC) in November, 1950. Then, on 6 January, 1951, Muir's award of the first VC of the Korean War was announced. His 75-year-old father's comment was: 'I am proud beyond all words. My son, my only son, was a soldier all the way.' Colonel and Mrs. Muir went to Buckingham Palace on 14 February, 1951, to receive the Cross from King George VI. It was the last time he was to present such an honour. It was the Argylls' sixteenth VC. All twelve of Muir's medals are today held by the Argylls' museum at Stirling Castle, while he lies buried in the Commonwealth War Graves Cemetery in Korea.

Exceptionally proud he undoubtedly was, but the death of his son broke his father's heart. The story ends with great sadness. Colonel Muir's grief undermined his health, bringing on bouts of acute depression. On 14 April, 1954, he was found on the floor of his bedroom in the White Hart Hotel at Frimley, Surrey. He had self-inflicted wounds to his throat and stomach, and a broken right femur. Colonel Muir was alive, and agreed to an operation on his femur, which was technically successful, but he died the next day after a collapse.

CHAPTER 2

Castle Hill – Korea
23 April, 1951

LIEUTENANT PHILIP KENNETH EDWARD CURTIS VC,
The Duke of Cornwall's Light Infantry,
attached to the 1st Battalion
the Gloucestershire Regiment

'We must take Castle Site'
Lieutenant Curtis, although grievously wounded, a few moments
before his solitary charge on a Chinese machine gun.

It was shortly after first light on the morning of 25 April, 1951, that Private Sam Mercer was hit.[1] Fragments of mortar bombs landing nearby struck him in the head, eye and leg. He crawled, agonisingly, into a small bivouac tent where a comrade desperately sought to stem the flow of blood. Gratefully, Mercer allowed the balm of blackness to sweep over him. When he regained consciousness all seemed strangely quiet. The roar and crash of battle had gone. Now, as he struggled to sit up, Mercer reluctantly acknowledged the pain of his wounds, and the fact that he and the other injured lying nearby had been seemingly abandoned. The few companions left in A Company of the Glosters had disappeared, except for those like himself who could not walk. One of these he recognized as Sergeant Eames, who had won the MM only two months earlier for his dashing leadership, when he took command of a platoon of C Company, in an attack on the heavily defended Hill 327. Eames was badly hurt now and could scarcely stir.

Mercer was near the summit of Hill 235, to which the remnants of A Company had withdrawn two days ago from Castle Hill. On 235 the battered battalion had made its final stand. Now Mercer could hear the shrill chatter of approaching Chinese. Three soldiers were scouring the slope, dark brown eyes peering out from under their long peaked caps as they examined the wounded and discarded debris of war. To Mercer they were a familiar sight. Cheap cotton khaki uniforms, with cloth ammunition bandoliers slung round their bodies, rubber-soled canvas shoes on their feet. One carried a burp gun, the others rifles, one of which looked like an

American Garand. They seemed intent on sorting out the wounded into those who could walk and those that could not. The Chinese soldier looking down at Sergeant Eames quickly made up his mind. He murdered him with one shot into the body. Mercer was then confronted by the soldier with the Garand who gesticulated and yelled at him. Mercer got the message – he was to stand up. Painfully he got to his feet with his back to the Chinaman. Instantly, a sledgehammer blow struck him in his thigh, and simultaneously he heard the crack of a rifle shot as he pitched forward onto the ground. Rolling over, he looked up into the muzzle of the rifle, as he cursed and raved at the man he thought was to be his executioner. The Chinaman showed no emotion. Then, for no apparent reason, he turned away and left Mercer with a smashed leg – the bullet having come out through his knee. He dragged himself tortuously down the hill towards the ambulance wagon where the Gloster's Medical Officer Captain Hickey RAMC, was trying to cope with the casualties. Mercer made it, although he was later to lose his leg and the sight of one eye. Despite his condition he subsequently recalled getting wry satisfaction from watching an unsuspecting Chinaman trying to eat a packet of Colman's mustard powder.

A Company had had a particularly rough time at the Imjin battle, which included the determined defence of Castle Hill during the night of 22/23 April, followed by 48 hours on Hill 235. The severity of the action is reflected in the casualties and the awards made later. Not a single officer or man from the company escaped becoming a casualty. Of the 109 men that started the battle on Castle Hill, all were either killed, wounded or taken prisoner. For their gallantry during the fighting, or in captivity, members of A Company won 1 VC, 1 GC, 2 DCMs, 1 MM, and 6 MIDs. Of the officers, the company commander, two platoon commanders, and the attached artillery FOO all died on Castle Hill. The other platoon commander, 2nd Lieutenant Waters, died in circumstances of outstanding courage as a prisoner.[2] Only the company second-in-command, Captain Wilson, who did not join the company until it deployed on Hill 235, was eventually repatriated. The struggle for Castle Hill was the opening round of what became known as the Glosters' Imjin battle, an epic example of a battalion fighting against immense odds although completely surrounded, and despite crippling casualties.

Like the rest of the battalion, A Company was a strange mixture of men hastily assembled to go to war in Korea. On Castle Hill only the company commander, Major Pat Angier, and the newly joined subaltern commanding 2 Platoon, 2nd Lieutenant John Maycock, were regular Glosters. Angier was a quiet, unassuming officer, but competent, unflappable, and experienced, having seen action in the Second World War when he had been wounded in North Africa. The din of battle was to blame for his slight deafness. Lieutenant Phil Curtis, commanding 1 Platoon, was 24 years old, but a reservist officer from the Duke of Cornwall's Light Infantry (DCLI), while 3 Platoon was under 2nd Lieutenant Terry Waters, a reinforcement officer originally from the West Yorkshire Regiment. Of the 100 soldiers in the company on that hill only about a third were regulars, mostly the NCOs, while another third were reservists and the remainder national servicemen, including a number of special Korean volunteers.

Private Mercer was in 1 Platoon, under Curtis, and like the rest of the platoon had a great respect for his officer, although Curtis had only joined the company in early March. During those few weeks Curtis established a reputation as being a highly professional soldier. He was thorough and had impressed his men with his tactical knowledge and ability, particularly during patrols across the Imjin. On one such occasion a group of American Rangers were incorporated into a patrol led by Curtis. Afterwards the Ranger 1st Sergeant summoned up his impression of the young British officer with the words, 'Gee, that guy sure knows his stuff.'

Curtis came from Devonport, and had grown up during the war years. As a teenager during the blitz on Plymouth he had volunteered as a messenger for A.R.P. wardens. Desperately keen to get into the Services before it was all over, he tried to enlist in the RAF, but was rejected because of his age. In 1944, however, when he was eighteen, he was accepted into the Army but was not posted overseas to an operational theatre. In May, 1946, he was given a Regular Army Emergency Commission in the DCL1, although he never actually served with any battalion of that Regiment. After service, attached to the RASC, at HQ Middle East he was demobbed in 1948, and placed on the Reserve of Officers, with the honorary rank of captain.

While still a soldier he had married a local Devonport girl, Joan Haynes, and they had a daughter, Phillipa Susan. After leaving the Army Curtis secured a job with Roneo, the duplicator firm, but found life exceedingly dull after the excitement of the previous four years. Then, just as Curtis had settled into family life, disaster struck. His young wife died suddenly, leaving a grieving husband with a tiny child to bring up. Not long after this tragedy fate intervened again in the form of the Korean war, and the urgent need for officers and soldiers to fill out the depleted ranks of the infantry. There was no way that regulars and young national servicemen could meet the immediate requirements, so the government resorted to recalling reservists. With much grumbling they came trooping back into depots to don battledress once again. They were sent, not necessarily to their old Regiments, but to where they were needed, to units already in Korea, like the A&SH or the Middlesex Regiment, or those destined to go, like the Royal Northumberland Fusiliers (RNF), the Royal Ulster Rifles (RUR) and the Glosters.

When Curtis received his recall papers it put him in a quandary. As a young widower with responsibility for a small daughter there is little doubt that he could have claimed exemption. He thought long and hard about where his duty lay. In his heart he felt the pull of Army life, his country wanted him back, there was fighting to be done, he had enjoyed the adventure and travel in the past, while his present life at home was full of sad memories, and his civilian routine was humdrum. The only problem was Susan, his little girl. When his wife's mother, Mrs Beatrice Haynes, undertook to look after Susan, Curtis was persuaded that he could follow his orders with a clear conscience. He rejoined the army, made known his desire to get to Korea and sailed on 17 October, 1950.

On arrival in Japan there were delays. Curtis pestered the American authorities to get him to Korea. The UN counter-offensive was under way, and it could all be over before he arrived. He had missed the excitement of pushing the Germans out of France, now he might be too late to help push the Chinese out of Korea. After several frustrating clashes with bureaucracy, Curtis joined A Company, the Glosters, on 3 March, 1951.

1 Platoon were impressed with their new officer. His former platoon sergeant, Norman Tuggey, still remembers his first appearance: 'Dressed in well-tailored battledress, wearing his SD (Service Dress) cap and carrying a walking stick, quite tall, 5' 10" to 6', and sporting a thin black moustache. His first priority was to work the platoon up on patrols at which he was exceptionally good.' Tuggey, who was to survive the coming battle and retire from the Army as a Warrant Officer Class I in 1975, got on well with his new officer. They made a good team. Curtis discussed things with his sergeant, considered his advice, while Tuggey for his part quickly got to respect his commander's competence. By the time A Company clambered up Castle Hill for the first time, 1 Platoon reflected the keenness and ability of its leaders.

A short distance up the eastern re-entrant of Castle Hill was the remains of an old Korean temple (see Map 5). Nearby were one or two small, deserted houses. At this site A Company had established an administrative area. Only 200 metres from their positions around the summit, it was sheltered from prying eyes over the Imjin. Here, when the situation permitted, the platoons were able to take turns enjoying the luxury of a centrally cooked meal. It was brought up from 'F' Echelon area, several miles to the rear, by Colour Sergeant Buxcey, who doled out the inevitable stew to the shout of: 'Come and get it. Lots of grub; half a ladle.' Anything was better than mess tin cooking in the trenches. Here also bathing arrangements were improvised, using large Korean pottery jars which the locals normally used for pickling vegetables. A number of these

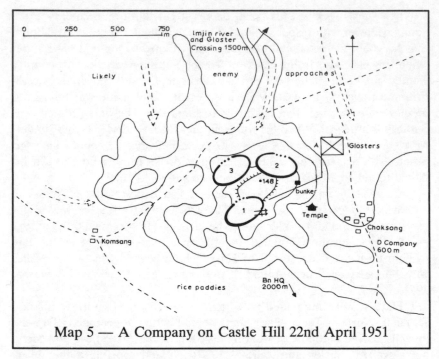

Map 5 — A Company on Castle Hill 22nd April 1951

had been liberated from the nearby houses. With care it was possible to immerse oneself up to the waist.

The morning of Sunday, 22 April, was fine and bright. A lovely spring day after a cold, clear night. Down near the temple Padre Sam Davies was setting up a makeshift altar for a Communion Service he intended to hold for those members of A Company who could be released from their duties and wished to attend.[3] With the sloping tiled roof of the temple gateway in the background, Davies positioned a large wooden crate as a table. A small crucifix attached to a board was propped upright against his chaplain's field communion case at the back of the crate. A piece of cloth, upon which was placed the chalice, was put in front of the crucifix. On either side was a candle. Four or five soldiers, an NCO, and two subalterns came to the service. The officers were Phil Curtis and Terry Waters. For the participants it was a moving experience. Reports had started to arrive of enemy activity over the river; the whole battalion was on alert, with 25 per cent stood-to at all times. These young men were facing battle for the first time. They wanted to make their peace with God. The Padre sensed the feeling of apprehension. As the two officers knelt quietly to receive the bread and drink the wine, they were both spiritually strengthened. Neither could know that it was to be their Viaticum — Holy Communion given to the dying, or those in imminent danger of death.

Angier's task was to hold Castle Hill (Map 5). Within the battalion defensive layout A Company was the left forward company, some 2,000 metres south of the Imjin River, opposite a ford that would afterwards be known as Gloster Crossing. If an attack developed it would be likely to push southwards over the ford, following a track through the village of Choksong immediately east of Castle Hill, and then disappearing into the tangle of hills towards Seoul, 30 miles further south. The CO, Lieutenant-Colonel 'Fred' Carne, had made it quite clear that A Company must hold the hill to block Chinese progress along the track.

The hill itself was 148 metres high at its highest point in the north. On the top, centuries ago, a castle had stood. In 1951 nothing remained except the hint of walls where low mounds encircled the summit. This part of the hill was called Castle Site. To the north, a long, thin spur pointed like an outstretched finger towards the river. Five hundred metres out, a small hillock, like a knuckle, sat on top of the spur. This finger ridge sloped down towards the Imjin for 1,000 metres and could offer a narrow but relatively gentle route up to Castle Hill.

On the much shorter eastern spur, overlooking Choksong, was a rectangular bunker, built during an earlier military occupation and recently refurbished by American engineers as an OP. From this bunker the Army Commander, General Matthew Ridgway, was scheduled to observe the hills north of the river. He never visited the site, but the bunker was to play a crucial part in the drama that followed.[4]

To the right rear of A Company, across the track, on another slightly higher hill some 1,200 metres away, was D Company. It was Angier's nearest neighbour. Behind Castle Hill, about 1,000 metres of rice fields, crisscrossed with footpaths, separated it from the mass of mountains which stretched across the horizon, restricting passage southwards except through the defile now guarded by the Glosters.

In the west another narrow spur ended in a low knoll 600 metres from Castle Hill; beyond it, 2,000 metres away, was the river again. This spur was worrying to Angier as, like the finger in the north, it offered a possible enemy approach to his main position.

Units of the 1st Republic of Korea (ROK) Division were somewhere to the west, but a long way off, and in no position to give much protection to A Company's exposed left flank. Angier was uncomfortably isolated. If the enemy crossed the river they would bump his company first. The nearest infantry company (D Company) could at best give fire support on his right (eastern) flank. The remaining companies were 3,000 metres away to the east and south-east, in no positon to assist if things became difficult.

When the Glosters had arrived two weeks earlier the feeling was that the halt was temporary, that the general advance would continue to roll forward across the Imjin. The Brigade Commander, Brigadier Tom Brodie, had written of the previous weeks: 'Today we have ... pushed right up to the river with little opposition, through the most terrific country I've yet met, hills for miles ... striking right across country into the blue ... It is an amazing war — jets, napalm, porters, and load-carrying bullocks all in a brigade area at the same time.' The CO of 45 Field Regiment RA, whose guns supported the brigade, was not in a defensive mood either. He later wrote, 'When we joined them (the Brigade) all was serene. The enemy had been pushed back right along the line and, though as far as we knew no plans were cooking, we were still mentally in forward gear.'

The problems facing Angier were familier ones — how to reconcile conflicting factors. Was he to spread his company to hold the spurs to the north and west, which seemed likely enemy approach routes, or should he keep concentrated on the main feature? Was he to deploy on to the forward, northern slopes of the hill, thus giving his platoons excellent fields of fire and view up to, and over, the river, but equally exposing them to observation and fire? Would it be better to pull back from the crest on to the reverse, or southern, half of the hill, sacrificing a long-range shoot for concealment? How could he position his platoons so that they would mutually support each other, and at the same time give all-round protection? From which directions would an attack be likely to develop and, as he knew the Chinese invariably attacked at night, where were the likely places that they would form up prior to their assault?

Angier carefully walked the ground before deciding — then issued his orders to the assembled platoon commanders.

———————————

A Company Commander had decided that he would keep his platoons within supporting distance of each other on Castle Hill, and that the advantage of the long field of fire from the top and forward slopes outweighed the disadvantages. There would be two platoons forward along the northern side of the hill, with one platoon held back on the southern slope in reserve, giving depth to the position. This meant that the spurs running north and westwards would not be occupied, but they could be covered by fire.

The right-hand forward platoon belonged to Maycock and directly faced the northern spur, Gloster Crossing, the track south, and overlooked Choksong village. He was responsible for the defence of Point 148, or Castle Site, which, as the highest area, was vital ground. If this locality was overrun the rest of the company positions could prove untenable. Because of the excellent view north the artillery FOO, attached to the company to direct the fire of the supporting battery of 25-pounder guns, located his OP with 2 Platoon. This was Lieutenant Bruce Hudson from 70 Field Battery RA. Like the other platoon commanders Maycock had just over thirty men div ided into three sections, plus his own small headquarters. The only problem with siting his section trenches, or in allocating fields of fire, was whether to occupy the bunker. It was located down the eastern spur, but to incorporate it in his position would mean stretching his sections more than he considered wise. It was left empty, although some barbed wire was put between it and the nearest trenches.

Forward on the left was Waters with 3 Platoon, on the higher part of the spur running NW and then west. His responsibility was from the NW round to the SW, where a deep reentrant came up from the tiny hamlet of Komsang in the rice paddies at the foot of the hill.

In reserve was Curtis. His platoon was 250 metres south of 148 on a small spur pointing due south. From this location Curtis could cover the rear and both flanks, and would be able to act as the counter-attack force should either of the forward platoons be forced to withdraw. 1 Platoon was also responsible for the close protection of Number 3 Section of the MMG Platoon. This consisted of two Vickers MMGs with their teams. These guns were belt-fed, water-cooled, mounted on tripods and capable of firing 500 rounds per minute up to ranges of 4,000 metres. Together with artillery and mortars, these machine guns were the war-winning weapons of Korea. To see the almost slow-motion, gracefully arching streams of tracer bullets reaching out through the darkness, and listen to the never-ending tac-tac-tac-tac-tac of 40, 50, or 60-round bursts was immensely reassuring to the soldier in his trench. Because of their long range and curved trajectory, which produced an elliptical beaten zone of bullets at the receiving end, these guns were often used on indirect fire tasks, that is, they could bring their fire to bear on dead ground that the gunners could not see. At night they were locked on to predetermined fixed lines, usually across the front of another company position. In this case the main task of the MMGs with Curtis was to shoot NE and east across D Company's location, while another two guns with D Company reciprocated by covering A Company's flanks and rear.

Angier positioned his headquarters close to 1 Platoon. From his trench he would control the battle. Field telephone lines were laid to each platoon, thus duplicating communications within the company. There was also a radio and telephone link to battalion headquarters, and the FOO had his own radio net to the guns and his battery commander, Major Guy Ward, alongside Colonel Carne.

During the preceding ten days defensive positions had been dug among the scrub and stunted oak trees on the hillside. Fields of fire had been cleared, trenches camouflaged, trip flares positioned and tin cans with stones inside tied to the wire for early warning. Defence stores were scarce: while there was barbed wire there was no abundance of it, certainly not sufficient to erect a dense barrier, or even to cover the whole perimeter. An import ant task of the company commander was to agree the DF tasks for the guns with the FOO, Hudson. Likely lines of Chinese advance, dead ground and possible forming-up places were plotted on officers' maps, given numbers and registered by the guns. This system was essential if supporting fire was to be readily available on a particular target in the heat of battle. A number given over the radio was sufficient to ensure shells arriving on a particular spot with minimum delay. The most dangerous potential target was designated the DF/SOS task. The 25-pounders would be loaded and laid on this target when not otherwise engaged. The artil lery could often respond to a DF/SOS in seconds. All the platoon commanders had been trained to control artillery fire if necessary.

An identical system was used with the mortars. A Company could call on either the battalion's own 3-inch mortars or on the 4.2 inch mortars of C Troop, 170 Independent Mortar Battery RA, whose base plate positions were near battalion headquarters. The beauty of mortars was that with their very high-angle fire they could be positioned behind steep slopes or in gulleys and still hit targets in dead ground. In Korea the 4.2 was highly regarded. Its bomb packed the same wallop as a 105mm shell. An American officer described it as 'a beautiful weapon. With a fast and well-trained crew, and with all eight mortars [a battery] firing, we found it possible to put 96 rounds in the air before the first one burst.'

For Curtis and his men the days leading up to 22 April had been relatively quiet. Of the enemy there was little sign. Even patrols up to nine miles beyond the Imjin had failed to locate him. Air reconnaissance revealed nothing significant, although this was not surprising as the Chinese were normally invisible by day. They had a healthy respect for allied aircraft, so most movement was carried out at night, including attacks. Curtis spent his time supervising the platoon with the routine of defence. Posting sentries, manning OPs, going on night patrols, feeding, cleaning weapons, improving trenches, sleeping, and standing-to at dusk and dawn were the daily chores. After a week or so of this Curtis was beginning to think nothing would happen and that they would be on the move again shortly.

What Curtis could not know was that while he was receiving Communion late that Sunday morning 9,000 men from the 187th Division of the 63rd Chinese Army were poised to march south over the Imjin that night. In their way was A Company and the remainder of the Glosters. Their move had started on the evening of the 21st and it was that night that a three-man listening patrol at Gloster Crossing, under Corporal Cook, had the first clash with Chinese advanced patrols. At around 10.00 pm movement over the river was spotted and, under the glare of parachute illuminating flares, fourteen of the enemy were seen wading across. Cook, Drummer Eagles and Private Hunter fired their rifles so rapidly that the adjutant thought they had a bren gun with them. Three dead disappeared downstream, four more were dragged away by their comrades.

At midday on the 22nd a patrol from C Company that had been over the river was due back and the MMG section from Curtis' platoon area was sent forward to cover them across. While they were there a small group of ten enemy soldiers were seen to the west, but on the north bank, near the village of Sindae. The two guns swung into action at a range of over 3,000 metres. Several long bursts scattered the Chinese, some of whom were seen to fall. The machine guns stayed forward until just before dark, when they retired to 1 Platoon's locality and prepared for the anticipated night's shooting.

During Sunday afternoon extra ammunition was distributed, platoon and section commanders busied themselves checking all was ready, and the guns and mortars fired a few rounds to check DF tasks were accurately registered. Down at the crossing were Carne, his IO, Lieutenant Henry Cabral, and the adjutant, Captain Anthony Farrar-Hockley. Lying on their stomachs, peering through binoculars, they spotted no less than four small parties of Chinese in the hills on the far bank. It was decidedly odd. The enemy never showed themselves by day, so why now? Why alert everybody? The adjutant wondered if it was a deliberate deception. The CO thought not and ordered a section of mortars to come forward to discourage further activity. No. 1 Section drove up to the river at around 4.30 pm; the mortars coughed several times, and after a long pause tiny flashes and puffs of black smoke were visible on the distant hills. The Colonel ordered a strong fighting patrol to be in position at the crossing after last light.

There was an air of tension at the dusk stand-to. Everybody was at his battle position, peering into the gloom, as platoon commanders and sergeants came round to visit the trenches, whispering words of encouragement or advice to the riflemen or bren gunners, crouched over their weapons. After half an hour — nothing. Fifty per cent of the men stepped down to try to get some rest. At 1 Platoon Curtis and Tuggey conferred in low tones, agreeing a roster for staying awake between the two of them.

At 10.30 pm the watchers on Castle Hill suddenly saw a series of flashes from the area of Gloster Crossing, followed by the noise of bursts of heavy automatic firing. The C Company patrol was under attack. Soon the fighting was continuous. Then came the pop, pop, popping of illuminating shells bursting high up in the sky, adding their glare to the moonlight as they floated lazily down. Next, the battalion's mortars and the artillery joined in, hammering the north bank of the river. The clear night air brought the faint yells and screams of combat to the ears of the fully alerted company. Four times the little battle raged fiercely; four times it died down. The Glosters pulled back from the river around midnight, leaving scores of dead Chinese behind them. Miraculously not one of the sixteen men had been scratched. It was an action that earned the young officer in command, Lieutenant Guy Temple, an MC. Sergeant Eames, his platoon sergeant, had been left behind with the third section in C Company's position.

For Curtis and his men the long hours of early morning darkness on 23 April were spent, for the most part, as spectators of the struggle for Castle Site and 3 Platoon's position. For hour after hour they witnessed and heard the roar of battle only 200 metres away. Night was transformed into day, with the flash of exploding shells and mortar bombs, and the eerie light of the never-ending umbrella of illuminating flares. Tracer rounds by the thousand criss-crossed the hill. On the platoon 88 sets the frantic voices of operators, and the two forward platoon commanders, yelled for more and more supporting fire. Curtis heard his friends, John and Terry, reporting the critical situation as the endless waves of Chinese clambered up the slopes. Casualties mounted, particularly in 2 Platoon. The fighting became hand to hand, with burp guns, bayonets and grenades being used by both defenders and attackers as they grappled with each other for possession of each trench. Time and again the flood receded, time and again the shouting and blare of bugles announced a renewed assault. For nearly six hours it continued. As dawn approached it was clear to Angier that, despite a magnificent defence, 2 Platoon was in serious trouble, with part of their position over run, ammunition low, and only a fraction of the defenders unscathed. The enemy had established one or more machine guns up near the crest of Castle Site and were able to cover their attacks with heavy close-range fire. If Castle Site was lost, all was probably lost. At around 5.00 am during a slight lull, Angier summoned his platoon commanders for an 'O' group (orders group).

Quickly Angier told Curtis that he was to mount a counter-attack on to Castle Site at first light, stressing how crucial it was that 2 Platoon's position be held if A Company was to retain Castle Hill. Curtis nodded; his platoon was still intact, so such a task was expected. Waters was to keep holding, as were the remnants of 2 Platoon, until Curtis made his attack. The officers dispersed back to their positions. It was during his walk back up the hill that Maycock was killed outright by a burst of machine-gun fire. Sergeant Frank Cottam was now in command of what was left of 2 Platoon. After the 'O' group broke up Angier spoke to the adjutant on the radio, stressing the perilous situation, explaining the intended counter-attack and the

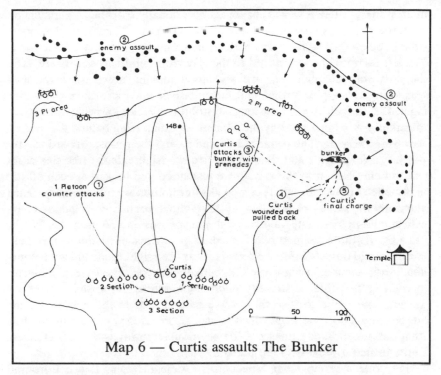

Map 6 — Curtis assaults The Bunker

urgent need for reinforcements. Above all, was A Company expected to hold Castle Hill come what may? Carne was summoned to the set. 'You will stay there at all costs until further notice,' he said. Farrar-Hockley spoke again, wishing Angier good luck, to which he responded, 'Don't worry about us; we'll be all right.'

Curtis explained the situation to Tuggey and his section commanders. At dawn the platoon would advance across the 250 metres to Castle Site in extended line. Number 1 Section under Corporal Halpin, to which Mercer belonged, would be the right forward section; on the left 2 Section, with Curtis, his runner, and radio operator, in between them. Slightly to the rear would be Sergeant Tuggey, and behind him the reserve, 3 Section. As the ground dipped down slightly between 1 Platoon and Castle Site supporting overhead MMG fire would be available initially (see Map 6).

At first light Curtis got his men out of their trenches to form up and lie down. Strangely, it was relatively quiet, with no firing on either Castle Site or 3 Platoon's area. Curtis looked left and right, shouted 'fix bayonets', paused briefly as the thirty or so bayonets clicked on to rifles, then stood up to give the order 'advance'. Steadily the two lines moved forward. A time-honoured vignette of British infantry — advancing at the walk, five metres apart, rifles lowered, bayonets occasionally catching a glimmer of light, their officer in the centre, out in front. Sergeant Tuggey has described what happened: 'Daylight was with us as we moved through 2 Platoon ... The left forward section moved to the NW ridge, and I went forward with them. It was all quiet, and we just stood looking down the slope and wondering, I suppose, what had created such a shindig throughout the night. It's difficult to say how long we stood there, not knowing quite what to make of it, when suddenly the Chinese stood up from behind the bushes they were carrying. The distance between us and their most forward troops was just a few yards, and their numbers quite frightening. I find this difficult to believe even to this day — we just stood and looked at each other, in disbelief I think, for what seemed like ages. Then we all seemed to react at exactly the same precise moment, hitting the ground and engaging them with small arms at first, followed with phosphorus and 36 grenades.'[5]

To Curtis there seemed two immediate problems. First the danger that enemy would quickly infiltrate round his exposed right flank and get behind him; and, second, Ridgway's OP bunker was occupied by a Chinese machine gun, firing at virtually point-blank range. He dashed across to Tuggey telling him to take the reserve section over to the right of Castle Site, to find a position from which to engage any enemy coming up the hill from the direction of Choksong. Tuggey doubled away with the section as Curtis turned to deal with the bunker.

Gathering a group from 1 Section, including Halpin, Lance Corporal Mairs and Mercer, Curtis worked his way, under intense fire, to a fold of dead ground only 20 metres south of the bunker. The machine gun was clearly visible through the apertures, as were the gunners inside. Curtis began to hurl grenades at the bunker which were passed to him by his men, his .38 revolver being useless in the circumstances. The response from the machine gun was immediate. It poured burst after burst of fire into the area of 1 Section forcing them to crawl back to better cover. Not so Curtis. He remained, continually exposing himself to throw more grenades, even trying to get closer so that he could lob one directly through the opening. It was while doing this that he was hit. The bullet struck him in the head, knocking him over, to lie exposed within a few metres of his objective. Gallantly two of his men wriggled up to him to drag him back under cover. Curtis was still conscious, although his face and head were covered with blood. A soldier was despatched to fetch the medical NCO, Corporal Papworth RAMC, while others bandaged his head with a field dressing.

Curtis's men, including Halpin, Mairs and Mercer, sought to restrain their platoon commander. 'Don't worry sir, you'll be OK; the medic's on his way; lie still sir; keep down.' The company commander, who had followed up 1 Platoon with the FOO, tried to reassure him, but Curtis was a

5. Lieutenant-Colonel J. P. Carne. *(The Rev. S.J. Davies, MBE)*

6. Lieutenant-Colonel J. P. Carne, VC, DSO, with his wife and stepson, just after receiving his Cross at Buckingham Palace. *(Imperial War Museum)*.

7. Gloster Hill, seen from the reverse (southern) slope of Castle Hill. Note the track disappearing into the entrance to the ravine the Glosters defended. *(Imperial War Museum)*

8. Padre Sam Davis conducts a service for a small group of officers and men from the Glosters' battalion headquarters, prior to the Chinese assault. The battalion command-post truck is visible to the rear. *(Imperial War Museum)*

9. A defensive post of 'The Hinge'. *(Regimental Headquarters, The King's Own Scottish Borderers)*

resolute man. 'We must take Castle Site,' were the words he used as he strove to get up, Several hands held him down; one soldier reported to sitting on the wounded officer, so desperate were they to restrain him. From some hidden reserve of strength Curtis summoned the effort to break free, to resume his single-handed assault on the bunker. Hurling grenades, he lurched the last few metres towards the still-firing machine gun. As Private Ward said in his sworn statement long afterwards, as a witness for the award of Curtis's VC: 'He moved into the attack for the second time, again throwing grenades. A few yards from the bunker he was mortally wounded by a burst of machine-gun fire in the stomach.' Corporal Masters from 2 Platoon later stated: 'As this grenade left his hand he fell, mortally wounded. I noticed that after the explosion of this last grenade he threw, the machine gun did not fire again. The bunker was now sufficiently subdued to enable the rest of Lieutenant Curtis's platoon to clear Castle Site.'

Curtis was carried back to shelter by his men, still alive, but only just. Papworth arrived but there was nothing he could do to save him. He died in the arms of his soldiers who had brought him down the slope.

Angier quickly realized that, despite the temporary success on Castle Site, it could not be held much longer with so few men. Using the slight lull gained by Curtis's destruction of the machine gun, a withdrawal back to the area of company headquarters was arranged. Tuggey was puzzled by the message to return with his section to 1 Platoon's original position. On his arrival Angier told him he was now in command of the platoon, showing him Curtis' body wrapped in a sleeping bag. Within a few minutes Angier himself was struck down, killed outright by a burst of automatic fire through his mouth and head. Hudson, the artillery FOO, died at the same time. Now the only remaining officer on Castle Hill was Waters, still fighting to keep the Chinese attacking from the west from overrunning his position.

At about 8.15 am Carne gave permission for the fifty-four survivors of A Company to pull back 3,000 metres to Hill 235. With artillery, mortars and MMGs from 235 pummelling the hilltop it fell to Sergeant-Major Gallagher to organize the withdrawal. This he did with a competence and coolness that would earn him the DCM. With the exception of the company commander, all dead bodies had to be left on the hill. Later that morning the padre read a brief burial service over Angier's body which then was placed beside a stream under an overturned assault boat.

Curtis's body, along with those of the other dead on Castle Hill, was not recovered for six weeks, and it was not until December, 1953, that his posthumous award was gazetted. The long delay was due to the living witnesses being held as prisoners of the Chinese for over two years, in particular Carne, who instigated the procedure for the VC on his own repatriation.

There is no doubt that Curtis's actions resulted in the destruction of the machine gun in the bunker, which in turn enabled the Chinese attack on Castle Site to be driven off for sufficient time to permit the withdrawal of the company. Had the enemy occupied the high point of the hill while the remnants of Angier's men retreated across the open rice paddies many more casualties would have been inflicted. Curtis's sacrifice was far from in vain, but why did he do it when, with a serious head wound, he had more than fulfilled his duty already? Mercer recalled: 'We soon realized that he was inclined to lead from the front with a rifle, if he could get one, rather than a revolver. Within the platoon it was generally felt that the first trouble we hit we would lose him.' Curtis was a proud and determined man, proud of his platoon, proud of his position as its leader, and determined that both he and it would excel when the test came. His was a spur-of-the-moment example of battlefield bravery, when nothing seems important except achieving the immediate objective. For a few brief minutes all thought, all feeling, all effort, is focused on one goal. Such a state of mind is not uncommon. In Curtis's case it produced exceptional results.

It was not until 6 July, 1954, the day before what would have been his 28th birthday, that the Investiture took place. Attending to receive the Cross were his mother, Mrs Florence Curtis, his seven-year-old daughter Susan, and his wife's mother, Mrs Beatrice Haynes. For Mrs Curtis it was her first visit to London and the party were staying at a hotel as the guests of the *Daily Express*. She was immensely proud and sad, but the passage of over three years since her son's death had done a little to heal the initial shock and grief. When interviewed, the white-haired lady with bright blue eyes said, 'It has been a sad day of memories for me. This medal is very nice, but it doesn't bring him back... I am going to be sensible and not get upset. This is my first visit to London and I'm going to enjoy it.'

At the Palace, as is the practice with posthumous awards, the Queen held a private audience with the relatives to give the Cross to Susan before the main Investiture. Just before 11 o'clock they were told the Queen was coming. Susan had to put her doll down on a nearby couch. Through the double doors stepped a smiling Queen, in a fur stole over a lemon silk, cap-sleeved dress. Susan, also wearing a yellow dress and matching bonnet, came shyly forward, followed by her two grandmothers. Her Majesty took Susan's left hand and handed her her father's Cross with the words: 'Susan, I present you with your father's Victoria Cross. We all had great admiration for what your father did'. Susan took the medal, remembered to curtsey, and murmured: 'Your Majesty'. The Queen, turning to the ladies, said: 'I am glad to hand this to you personally. We are all very proud of your son'. After watching the remainder of the Investiture they went outside, where Mrs Haynes pinned the Cross to Susan's dress. The little girl's comment was: 'The Queen was wearing a lemon dress too. We both had the same colour.'[6]

Over 20 years later, at Sotheby's auction rooms, Curtis's VC was sold for the then record price for any gallantry award — £7,200. It was purchased by Mr John Hayward, a medal dealer, after some keen counter-bidding by the representative from the DCLI museum. Lieutenant-Colonel John Fry, the curator, was disappointed that the £5,200 that he had raised to keep the Cross in the Regiment was not enough.

The seller was Mrs Susan Griffin, Curtis's daughter, who now had a small son, named Philip after his grandfather. The decision to sell had not come easily. As she explained to *The Daily Telegraph:* 'My father was not able to do anything for me. I had a working class upbringing without any luxuries. It was an awful decision to make, but I knew that my father would have wanted me to do something for the grandson he never saw. I started to think about selling it as soon as my son Philip was born 15 months ago. I naturally wanted to give him more security. This money should mean quite a nest egg by the time he is 21. I plan to invest almost all the money for him. Ideally I would have liked the medal to have gone to my father's Regiment, but having put it up for sale I wanted the best price possible.'

She need not have worried. The purchaser generously agreed to re-sell the Cross to the Regiment for £6,200, thus in effect giving £1,000 towards it himself, provided other donations amounting to £1,000 could be raised. This was quickly accomplished by a Canadian and a British businessman, and English China Clays of St Austell, Cornwall. Within a few days the VC was safely in The Keep at the barracks in Bodmin.

With his Cross in the Regiment, and the money saved for his grandson, Philip Curtis must surely rest content.

CHAPTER 3

The Imjin River – Korea
22 – 25 April, 1951

LIEUTENANT-COLONEL JAMES POWER CARNE,
VC DSO DL
The Gloucestershire Regiment

'Oh, just shooing away some Chinese.'
Colonel Carne's description of personally shooting at several
Chinese who had infiltrated to within a few metres of his com-
mand post.

On the 21st day of March every year the Glosters celebrate Back Badge
Day. All members of the Regiment, the old 28th Foot, have the unique
privilege within the British Army of being able to wear a small replica of
their cap badge at the back of their headdress. This distinction was granted
for their defeat of the French at the Battle of Alexandria in 1801. At a critical moment, when the battalion was charged in the rear by three ranks of
cavalry with sabres drawn, the senior officer, Lieutenant-Colonel Chambers, gave the order: 'Rear Rank, 28th! Right about – Face!' Back to back,
the battalion beat off assaults from both directions simultaneously. Almost
exactly 150 years later, their descendants, the 1st Battalion, the Gloucestershire Regiment – The Glosters – performed the same feat in Korea. On
this occasion they were outnumbered by 10 to 1, and completely surrounded, but continued to fight on from an ever-shrinking perimeter until,
with all hope of relief gone and ammunition exhausted, they sought to break
out to rejoin the UN forces to the south. Very few succeeded; most survivors were destined for over two years as prisoners of the Chinese.

That battle, in defence of the Imjin river line, has passed into military
history as an epic defensive action, or last stand, of equal fame as the Spar-
tans at Thermopylae, the 7th Cavalry at the Little Big Horn, or the South
Wales Borderers at Rorke's Drift. Now, serving members of the Glosters
are entitled to wear the emblem of the US Presidential Unit Citation. The
piece of dark blue, watered silk ribbon, enclosed in a gilt metal frame, can
be seen at the top of each sleeve of all ranks, in addition to the second cap

badge won at Alexandria. Each year when the Regiment's Colours are paraded for Back Badge Day, the US Battle Streamer, with the words Solma-Ri (the name of the Korean village near the battle site), is attached to the staff. Awards to individuals were exceptionally high. For outstanding performance of duty by the Glosters, and attached artillery and medical personnel, no less than 2 VCs, 2 DSOs, 1 MBE, 4 MCs, 2 DCMs, 8 MMs, 3 BEMs, and 48 MIDs were conferred, a record that has never been equalled by one battalion during a three-day battle.

The CO of the Glosters during this action was Lieutenant-Colonel Carne, who only two months before had earned the DSO for his skilful leadership of the battalion when it attacked and secured Hill 327. Carne had the inevitable nickname of Fred, from 'Fred Carno's Army', which he accepted with great good humour. It stuck; to thousands of people he was always Colonel Fred Carne; many never realized it was not his proper name. His command of the Glosters in Korea, at the age of 45, had come as a surprise to him. It was to be the fourth time he had been a CO, having commanded the 26th battalion of the King's African Rifles in Burma, another after the war in British Somaliland, and then the 5th Glosters, a Territorial Army unit. His appointment to the 1st Battalion on active service was as unexpected as it was welcome. It was, and still is, the pinnacle of a regular officer's career – no matter how high he may go later. For an infantryman the command of the battalion one joins as a young subaltern is the ultimate goal. Carne had joined the Army in 1925 and 20 years later, after a world war, he had only four medal ribbons. After Korea he added five more.

Of the eleven VCs described in this book Carne's is the most unusual. The great majority of acts that gain this exceptional award are clear-cut examples of an individual's physical courage. Most winners of the VC charged an enemy position single-handed, defended a post despite grievous wounds, saved others by sacrificing themselves, or some other combination of such deeds. It is comparatively simple, after the event, to pinpoint the moment when the Cross was won; the heroic act stands out as happening at a specific time, or times. Not so with Carne. He did not storm a machine gun, he did not lead a desperate charge, or rescue wounded men under fire – he himself was not even wounded during the battle. This does not mean that he was not a brave man – he was, as the story of his actions will show – but it is one of the rare cases where the VC has been given, not just for personal gallantry, but for quite outstanding leadership at a senior level.

Carne provided the coolness, the control and the inspiration, that held the Glosters together during 72 hours of intense and seemingly endless action. Without his example, without his influence, it is highly probable the Chinese would have overrun the defences and poured southwards, with perilous consequences for the whole UN line along the Imjin. The pressure and stress of battle did nothing to alter his normal outward confidence and calmness. He never raised his voice, never swore, never appeared unruffled, was always there when needed, always with his pipe clamped firmly between his teeth, giving him a father-figure image that was immensely reassuring to his soldiers. All this was in addition to his physical courage. During the battle he frequently exposed himself to heavy mortar and machine-gun fire, particularly in the latter stages on Gloster Hill, as he tramped the battlefield to encourage, assist and advise his men. At the end, when he knew that any hope of relief was impossible, that his battalion had been sacrificed to save the rest of the brigade, or indeed the division, Carne continued to foster the will to resist among his troops. As his citation was eventually to state, 'Lieutenant-Colonel Carne showed powers of leadership which can seldom have been surpassed in the history of our Army. He inspired his officers and men to fight beyond the normal limits of human endurance.'

In retrospect it seems almost certain that the Chinese attack in late April, 1951, caught the UN high command off balance. The weight, ferocity and location of the main thrust was unexpected, and but for the bitter determination of the units of 29 Brigade and the ultimate sacrifice of one complete battalion − The Glosters − it might have penetrated as far as Seoul. As it was 29 Brigade was ultimately routed, with the RNF, RUR and a Belgian battalion severely mauled, being compelled to run the gauntlet of enemy ambushes from the hillsides as they streamed south at the end of the battle. For the Glosters there could be no retreat; they were completely cut off. At last they were ordered to break out if they could in small groups. The struggle of 29 Brigade on the Imjin was a tactical defeat, but a strategic victory; the Chinese intentions were thwarted, not by superior plans or manoeuvres, but by the indomitable spirit, and sheer fighting ability, of the infantrymen and gunners. Artillery gun lines were subjected to close attack, guns were fired over open sights, company and platoon positions were surrounded and sometimes overwhelmed, one CO was shot dead in an ambush, and in the end the Glosters' wounded had to be abandoned to the mercies of the enemy.

Was it a bungled battle? Was is an unnecessary battle? The answer of history will probably be yes. Despite the heroism and hard fighting which prevented disaster, the Imjin battle was mishandled at divisional and brigade level.

It was the intention of the 8th Army Commander, General Van Fleet, to push the whole UN line further north, over the river, the pause on the Imjin being a temporary one. During this halt it had been difficult to pinpoint any large concentration of Chinese forces. Daylight air reconnaissance and mobile patrols of tanks and infantry had reported nothing significant. For up to 15 miles north of the river all seemed peaceful. For the units halted on the Imjin this period of over two weeks was a relaxing one compared with the frantic days of retreat in January, followed by the advance in March. It was a time for enjoying plentiful rations, washing clothes, cleaning weapons, sleeping, and undertaking the not-too-strenuous routine activities of manning a defensive position. Certainly patrols and sentry duty were frequent and trenches had to be dug, but there was no driving urgency, nobody was shooting at them, no enemy could be seen, patrols returned with nothing to report and most officers were waiting for the order to resume the advance. This attitude was not dispelled by higher command. Units in the line dug defensive positions, but there was no elaborate trench system in the hills, no deep bunkers, and above all very little barbed wires and no mines. Defence stores were scarce so the obstacles in front, and to the flanks, were thin, with large gaps.

The Glosters were part of 29 Brigade, under the command of Brigadier Tom Brodie. He reported to Major-General Searle of the US 3rd Infantry Division, which was part of 1 Corps. 29 Brigade had the nickname of 'The Old Men's Brigade' due to the large proportion of reservists in its ranks, which brought the average age up to 30. At least a third of all ranks had seen active service during the Second World War, so there was a wealth of experience with which to leaven the green young national servicemen. The units within the Brigade were the Glosters, the RNF, the RUR, a Belgian battalion, C Squadron, 8th Hussars, in Centurion tanks, 45 Field Regiment RA, (45 Field), and 170 Independent Mortar battery RA, with 4.2 inch mortars. Although Brodie had four infantry battalions, the Belgians only had three rifle companies, instead of four, and the RUR had not fully recovered from the 200 casualties inflicted on them when they had been ambushed during the January retreat.

With the UN line stretching from coast to coast every formation was responsible for areas so wide that large gaps were unavoidable. The 29 Brigade front along the Imjin was nine kilometres across. To the right was the US 3rd Division, to the left the South Koreans of 1 ROK. Brodie's defensive task, if it ever materialized, was to hold the two road routes south, which passed through narrow defiles of the four-mile-deep belt of mountains south of the river. These roads led to more open ground, and thence to Seoul (see Map 7). If Brodie had seriously been expecting an all-out Chinese attack he would hardly have adopted the deployment he did. It suffered from several defects. He chose to position three out of his four battalions, his artillery, the tanks and his headquarters, on the right hand (eastern) road, leaving the left (western) one entirely to the Glosters. Not only this, but the weak Belgian battalion was posted north of the river, on relatively low ground, with the Imjin to its right and rear as the river looped

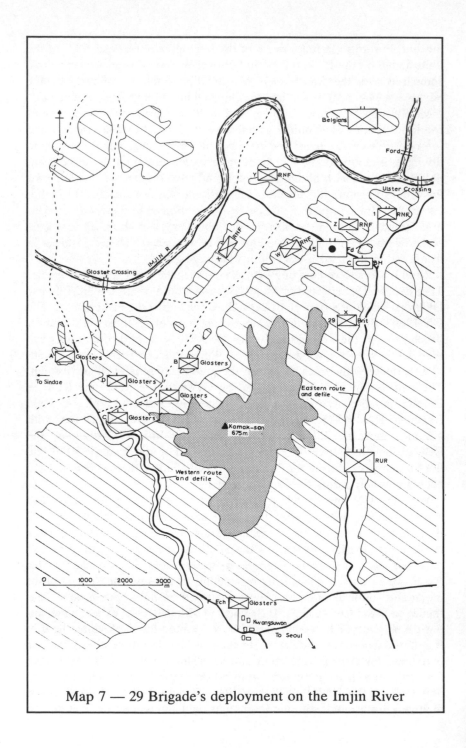

Map 7 — 29 Brigade's deployment on the Imjin River

north. Behind it were two fords over the Imjin and the Hantan, near where these two rivers joined. Neither of these fords were held. It is difficult to explain this unbalanced layout from a defensive point of view. Seemingly Brodie's thoughts were more concerned with pushing north, with the right-hand route as the main axis for the brigade. In which case a battalion bridge-head north of the river would be convenient.

Brodie attempted to cover his front with three battalions forward near the river, and one in reserve − the RUR. Had he put these more or less in line south of the Imjin he could just have covered the ground − but he did not. The Belgians were isolated north of the river, while the central battalion, the RNF, were stretched to such an extent that two miles separated company positions. Immediately behind the RNF was the only suit-able ground for the guns of 45 Field. The artillery was virtually in the front line from the start, with the battery supporting the Glosters facing SW, as the infantry positions of that battalion were further south than the gun lines.

Even with the Fusiliers so scattered, there were three miles between themselves and the nearest Glosters' company. Although a track joined the two routes just south of the Imjin, if the RNF had to pull back from it, there was no other lateral communication between the roads until they joined south of the mountains. To reinforce either route quickly from the other would be impossible, with the 2000-feet-high Kamak-san sitting cen-trally between them. The brigade positions invited infiltration, isolation and defeat in detail. A sounder scheme would have been to have two battalions on each route, the northern ones concentrated in mutually supporting com-pany positions where the roads entered the defiles and the other two a mile or so further back in reserve. In case of a local withdrawal being necessary, the forward battalions could have retired through the reserves to final blocking positions at the southern exits of the defiles. The artillery could then have covered all units from south of the mountains. That such a solution was not adopted was due, almost certainly, to no serious defence of the positions being contemplated until 24 hours before the assault started − too late to rectify shortcomings.

Overall command of the Chinese People's Volunteer Armies rested with General Peng Te-huai.[1] He had not, at the outset, been enthusiastic about Chairman Mao's decision to slip the leash on the Chinese dragon and send it over the Yalu, as he foresaw logistic problems with the poorly equipped army. But now he was determined, once again, to roll back the UN line.

It was the Chinese 63rd Army that was tasked with breaking through to Seoul via the two roads defended by 29 Brigade. H-hour, the time for the general advance over the Imjin, was 8.00 pm on 22 April. The Korean

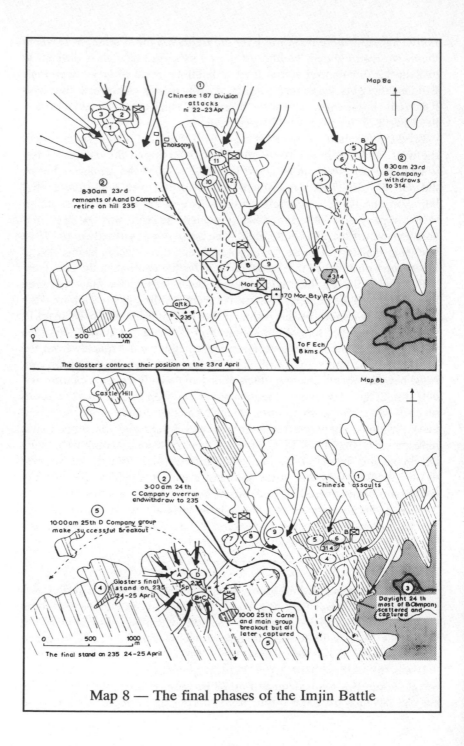

① Chinese 187 Division attacks ni 22–23 Apr

② 8·30am 23rd remnants of A and D Companies retire on hill 235

Choksong

② 8·30am 23rd B Company withdraws to 314

3 2
1
A

D
11
10 12

B
5
6

1

C

7 8 9

314

Mors

C ✠ 170 Mor Bty RA

a/tk
235

To F Ech 8 kms

0 500 1000 m

The Glosters contract their position on the 23rd April

Castle Hill

① Chinese assaults

② 3·00 am 24th C Company overrun and withdraw to 235

⑤ 10·00am 25th D Company group make successful breakout

C

7 8 9

B
5 6
314
4

5

④

A D
15p 235
B+C

Glosters final stand on 235 24–25 April

③ Daylight 24th most of B Company scattered and captured

⑤ 10·00 25th Carne and main group breakout but all later captured

0 500 1000 m

The final stand on 235 24–25 April

Map 8 — The final phases of the Imjin Battle

capital was to be captured by the morning of the 24th. Thirty-six hours to march over 30 miles and sweep aside UN resistance was optimistic planning. The commander of the 63rd Army, General Yang-Teh-Chi, was confident as he briefed his divisional commanders. In all some 30,000 men from the 187th, 188th, and 189th Divisions were arraigned against 3,000 men in the fighting elements of 29 Brigade.[2] The Chinese had no aircraft and little heavy artillery; they relied mainly on mortars and machine guns for fire support, and overwhelming numbers of infantry attacking by night to carry the day. Yang-Teh-Chi planned to pierce the UN front with the 187th leading the way, striking south over the ford opposite the western route (Gloster Crossing), closely supported by the 188th and 189th, who were to pass through the 187th after the defile had been secured. To the west the Belgians and RNF would also be pushed aside, or bypassed, to open the second road.

Carne's task was to hold the western, left-hand, route (see Map 7). This meant that, although his positions might be outflanked, he was to sit tight, unless given authority to withdraw, and ensure that Chinese vehicles, supplies and reinforcements could not use the road through the defile west of Kamak-san. To do this he must hold some of the hills on either side of the road, so that he could actually shoot at troops moving along it. Carne was worried about the huge gaps that would separate his company positions, and the Glosters, from their neighbours – the South Koreans on the left and the RNF on the right. He partially succumbed to the temptation of spreading his companies to cover as much ground as possible by deploying three companies forward (A, D and B), with C Company, Support Company and his headquarters further back at the entrance to the defile. While not as far apart as the RNF, 1500 metres between companies did not permit effective mutual support, except by long-range weapons such as the MMGs. In retrospect a tighter layout on the hills at the mouth of the defile would probably have been wiser from the outset.

If the battle ended on Gloster Hill (235), then it started at Gloster Crossing. It was an ancient ford over the Imjin which was, at that point some 200 metres wide and too deep to wade except at the ford. Both the Glosters and the Chinese knew of its existence and, indeed, its importance, so the former were lying in wait for the latter when they arrived on the far bank at about 10.00 pm on Sunday, 22 April. Lieutenant Guy Temple had positioned sixteen men from his 7 Platoon on the south bank, with a good view over the moonlit water. The leading Chinese were allowed to splash across, with the icy water surging round their waists in midstream, until they got within five metres of the ambush. Temple tapped the shoulder of the bren gunner beside him, and the first stage of the Imjin Battle had started. Again and again scores of screaming Chinese were cut down in the water, their bodies disappearing downstream. Flares lit the night sky, the gunners had their first shoot, so too the mortars.

It was nearly midnight. At the river Temple was in contact by radio to battalion headquarters, located just behind C Company's hill in the mouth of the defile. Here, in the command vehicle, Carne took the message from Temple that his ammunition was exhausted and made his first decision. He looked up, took the pipe from his mouth, and quietly said: 'Tell them to start withdrawing in three minutes. One last artillery concentration on the crossing, then the shells will come down south of the river.'

While the Chinese had been delayed and badly cut up at Gloster Crossing, not so elsewhere. The Glosters were unaware of the fords to their west, opposite Sindae, and 200 metres further south. Crossings there were unopposed and the leading companies padded swiftly SE and east up the long spurs that led to Castle Hill. Further east, opposite B Company and the RNF, more enemy crossed the river to start the process of infiltration. North of the river the isolated Belgians were under attack from all sides.

The first stage of the Gloster's battle continued until 8.30 am on Monday, 23 April — St. George's Day. Throughout the night endless waves of Chinese had hit A and D Companies. Again and again the effect of shells, mortars, MMGs, brens, rifles and grenades had blown them away; but always more followed. A Company's action has been described in detail in Chapter 2. The story of D Company was similar — mounting casualties, Chinese getting round their flanks, machine guns brought up close for point-blank fire, hand-to-hand fighting with grenades and bayonets, ammunition running low, and the increasing danger of encirclement.

Calmly Carne listened to every report, assessing the situation, speaking to Major Ward RA, the battery commander, about adjusting the gunfire, talking to his company commanders on the radio or field telephone, pondering what daylight would bring. Shortly after dawn the priority was to get casualties back from the forward companies and evacuated to the rear, while at the same time restocking ammunition. The MO organized the former, the adjutant the latter, using the Oxford carriers of Support Company. Carne now made up his mind to withdraw all three of his forward companies.

Dawn had brought a slight let-up from the assaults, as the Chinese were worried by the threat of airstrikes and observed artillery fire. If any adjustments were to be made it must be by day; in the dark movement would be too confusing and supporting fire could not be properly adjusted. Carne's concern was that, already, after one night's fighting, the enemy had filtered through the gaps between his positions and those on his flanks. A and D Companies had been attacked from their flanks, and the vital ground within A Company around 148 had been lost. The troops were exhausted; to leave them in these exposed positions for another night would invite disaster. Carne gave the order to pull back early, and by 8.30 am A and D Companies withdrew to the area of battalion headquarters, where they sank exhausted to the ground to await a welcome hot breakfast brought up by Colour Sergeant Buxcey. Drummer Eagles later recalled seeing a group of four men plodding wearily back across the rice fields under mortar fire. Too tired to take any avoiding action, they ignored the bursting bombs until one landed in among them, blowing them over. Eagles thought they were finished and was amazed to watch all four clamber slowly to their feet and continue trudging back as though nothing had happened.

B Company, on the right, had had a relatively quiet night, so the company commander, Major Denis Harding, was surprised to get his order to withdraw 1200 metres to point 314, immediately east of C Company (see Map 8a). Already Chinese patrols were occupying his new position; he would have to fight to secure it.

With A and D Companies relocated up on 235 (Gloster Hill) to the left of the entrance to the defile, and C and B Companies on the long spur leading up to 314 and thence to Kamak-san, on the right, Carne had deployed his battalion in a much-reduced perimeter. Mutual support was easier and the route south was still firmly blocked.

Through Carne's skilful handling of the mounting crisis on the left-hand road, all was still under control on this part of the Brigade front. On the right, however, a serious situation had developed by morning on the 23rd. The Chinese assaults on the Belgians and RNF had been ferocious and sustained. With the Belgians, the enemy had almost surrounded their positions during darkness, and the folly of their being north of the river with unsecured fords to their rear became glaringly obvious to Brodie. He had realized the error late the previous night and had ordered up a battle patrol, in carriers, from the RUR. Under Lieutenant Hedley Craig they crossed the river at what later became known as Ulster Crossing, only to run straight into a Chinese ambush. Far from securing the crossing the hapless patrol was scattered in confusion. Six men escaped, with Craig taking two days to get back to his unit.

The RNF were quickly in trouble. The Chinese dragon swiftly infiltrated through the huge intervals between the companies, each one of whom manfully took on the role of St George, wearing red patches in their caps. Before dawn X Company, nearest the river, had to withdraw, while more Chinese bypassed Y Company to capture a hilltop position dominating the road junction at the head of the defile leading south. The defenders, Z Company, were soon in dire straits, and after a magnificent fight were also compelled to pull back.

The scattered deployment of the RNF, the extensive infiltration of the enemy, and the withdrawal of the forward companies, quickly exposed the guns of 45 Field to direct attack. Because of crest clearance difficulties in the hilly terrain, they had been forced to position themselves much further forward than was tactically prudent. Now, up front, just to the rear of the RNF, the gunners found themselves repelling an infantry attack by firing over open sights. Had they not succeeded in driving off their attackers the story of the Imjin battle would have been one of total disaster. Of this incident the artillery CO, Lieutenant-Colonel Maris Young, wrote: 'It is worthy of record that the one and only prisoner captured by the brigade in the whole of this battle was taken by 70 Battery at the cannon's mouth. This was no robust character. On being rounded up he was promptly and violently sick.'

Brodie was sufficiently alarmed by developments that first night to commit his reserve early on the 23rd. The RUR received their orders at 7.20 am − to counterattack northwards and clear the high ground east of the road. The advance, when it materialized, was confused and weak. Weak, because B Company had to be left in the old position to guard the road, and in the middle of his 'O' group the CO was ordered to detach another company with some mortars and MMGs to go to the Glosters' assistance. It was confused because the gun lines, and the 8th Hussars assembly area, were under fire, the valley was full of smoke and their objective was far from clear. The two companies of the RUR decided to make for Hill 398, but they were not firm on it until dark on the 23rd, when they were joined by C Company who had failed to reach the Glosters.

Meanwhile, that morning, the Belgians had to make a rapid withdrawal over the two fords, almost literally firing over their shoulders. The intention was to position them well back down the road on the hills east and SE of Kamak-san. They could then re-form as the reserve unit, but it would take a long time before they could complete the march. The three companies were weary and depleted; by the time they reached their new position they would be exhausted.

The second stage of the Glosters' battle began with the withdrawal of the three forward companies (see Map 8a) and ended some 24 hours later when it merged into the final phase on top of Gloster Hill. It was during this period that the last opportunities for fighting a flexible engagement occurred. If any sort of organized withdrawal was to be made it had to be on the 23rd. If the Glosters were to be reinforced or relieved, then the 23rd was the time to do it, before Chinese forces cut the road behind them in strength. By mid-morning parties of the enemy had reached the road three miles south of the Glosters, attacking and dispersing 'F' Echelon. Thus their line of communication was severed at the southern end of the defile, a mere 12 hours after the Chinese had first attacked at Gloster Crossing. It meant that supplies could not be got up by road, nor casualties evacuated — except by helicopter. If the Chinese were allowed to consolidate their grip on the Glosters' life line a substantial force would be needed to effect their relief.

Brodie was constrained by his instructions to hold on by his American superiors. The US high command appreciated that, if 29 Brigade broke, the whole of 1 Corps would be at risk, with Seoul exposed to yet another occupation. But they failed to understand the need to support 29 Brigade strongly on the 23rd, or even on the 24th. Certainly the whole UN line was under pressure, but the main attack was taking place on 29 Brigade's front and that was the area that demanded attention. Brodie was, perhaps, not as forceful in making the situation as clear as he could have been, but there was no excuse for not a single airstrike being made by US aircraft in support of the Glosters during daylight on the 23rd or 24th. With no medium artillery support, no minefields, no wire (in the new company positions) and no airstrikes, it is not to be wondered at that the Glosters' own resources, and those of 45 Field, proved inadequate to stem the tide for ever.

During daylight on the 23rd the Glosters had a relatively quiet time. The enemy occupied their old positions and brought mortars and machine guns to bear on their new ones. Some casualties were evacuated early by road, and some by helicopter. The company seconds-in-command had come forward with the colour sergeants, bringing the daily resupply of rations and ammunition. They were unable to rejoin F Echelon, as by noon the Chinese held the road to their rear. Major Grist, the battalion second-in-command, only escaped by running the gauntlet in a jeep, during which he was shot through the wrist.

It was not until late afternoon that Carne was informed that an attempt would be made to reinforce him the next day (the 24th), but in the meantime he must hold out for another night. By 10.00 pm the Chinese offensive was resumed. The 187th Division had been replaced by the 188th and 189th. Chinese losses had been crippling, but there were plenty more men behind. This time the assault fell on B and C Companies. For hour after hour the din of battle, the blare of bugles and the screams and yells of men in combat ebbed and flowed around these two companies. Wave after wave of infantrymen clambered up the steep slopes of Hill 314 and its western spur, only to be swept away by the fire of the defenders.

By 3.00 am on the 24th weight of numbers won the day on C Company's position. The field telephone jangled in the command post. The adjutant picked it up. Major Paul Mitchell explained: 'I'm afraid they've overrun my top position (9 Platoon) and they're reinforcing hard. They're simply pouring chaps in up above us. Let me know what the Colonel wants me to do, will you?' Carne made his decision immediately: 'Pack up the headquarters and get every one out of the valley up between D Company and the Anti-Tank Platoon position. I'm going to withdraw C Company in ten minutes, and I shall move B over to join us after first light.' (Map 8b)

The Chinese had got up on to the ridge, into the gap between C and B Companies, turned right, or westwards, and, pouring down the slope, had overwhelmed 9 Platoon. Next came 8 Platoon. As Carne appreciated, this could be disastrous. The enemy now held the high ground 250 feet above battalion headquarters, and were only 200 metres away. While it was imperative C Company moved, Carne calculated that B Company should remain until daylight. They were not so hard-pressed as to have them risk a night withdrawal. Daylight would facilitate the coordination and observation of supporting gunfire; to blunder around in the dark with the Chinese between them and Gloster Hill would invite catastrophe.

Carne was contracting his position again, but this time B Company would be on their own for at least four hours, with no hope of assistance from the other companies, then some 1500 metres away to the west (Map 8b). Between dawn and 8.15 am B Company was subjected to seven separate attacks from their front, and from the old C Company position slightly lower down the ridge. Time after time it was the guns that saved them. As Harding later recorded: 'All of them [the attacks] were pressed home with the utmost vigour, with complete disregard for the casualties sustained. The pattern was the same − groups of enemy forming up about 100 yards from the position and then rushing forward in mass, screaming, throwing grenades, and firing wildly with their automatics . . . it was only by bringing artillery fire within 30 yards of the company position that [they] could be driven back.' By the time of the last Chinese charge it was too late, and the enemy too close, for any coordinated withdrawal. 4 Platoon were pushed over the ridge, company headquarters became involved in hand-to-hand fighting as the word was passed to pull out. It was virtually every man for himself in a mad scramble down the hill; contact was lost between platoons and sections; the Chinese were everywhere; it was left to individual officers and NCOs to break through to the final battalion position as and when they could. Eventually only the company commander and fifteen soldiers made it to Gloster Hill, where they were combined with the remnants of C Company to form two weak platoons. The gamble of a daylight withdrawal in some sort of order had not come off.

The final 24 hours of the drama was about to be played on the summit of Hill 235. It was now too late for the Glosters to attempt an orderly withdrawal, even if one had been sanctioned. The enemy were all round in great numbers. Encouraged by the lack of airstrikes, they swarmed over the hills and down the valleys. The Glosters' strength had shrunk from nearly 800 to around 500, including wounded. Their only hope was the reinforcing column that was supposed to fight its way up the defile on the morning of the 24th.

It was a little after 7.00 am that the adjutant's doze was disturbed by rifle shots and exploding grenades. On investigating, he saw a group of soldiers 'all watching the Colonel. Armed with rifle and grenades he was completing the rout of a group of Chinese who had crept forward along the ridge . . . it was already over. Two Chinese lay dead about 40 yards away and, a minute or so later, the Colonel was walking back, slinging the rifle over his shoulder as he came along towards me filling his pipe. "What was all that about, Sir?" I asked. He looked at me for a moment over the match that lit the pipe. "Oh, just shooing away some Chinese", he said.'

Shortly after this Farrar-Hockley was called to the rear-link radio to speak to the brigade major. The counterattack force was on its way. A Filipino battalion, with some light tanks, supported by Major Huth's Centurions, were to push up the defile. Regrettably, it was much too little, much too late. Within a short distance the leading Filipino tank was brewed up, blocking the road, and the infantry had no stomach for the Chinese on the hills.

During the afternoon Carne spoke on the radio to brigade as he wanted to know if he could call artillery fire down on his own vehicles, abandoned in the valley, to destroy them. Brodie came on the set to explain yet again that the Glosters must hang on. Carne replied: 'I understand the position quite clearly. What I must make clear to you is that my command is no longer an effective fighting force. If it is required that we shall stay here in spite of this, we shall continue to hold. But I wish to make known the nature of my position.' Brodie understood, but could say nothing other than emphasize the need to stay put. Tomorrow, the 25th, another attempt would be made to break through, this time by a Regimental Combat Team with tanks − perhaps by 10.00 am.

Hill 235 was an obvious place for a last stand (see Map 8). Its summit was roughly triangular in shape, about 300 metres in length, and protected on all sides, except the SE and NW, by precipitous slopes. It completely dominated the defile below. While it was held the road route south could not be used. This was Gloster Hill. Up there Carne was to inspire his men again and again as he strolled the perimeter, oblivious to bullets and bombs, unlit pipe in his mouth, imperturbably encouraging and directing his Glosters. If Colonel Fred could do it, so could they. When he had climbed the hill earlier, he had passed some mortarmen, now fighting as riflemen as their ammunition had gone, and explained to them that he was going to bring the whole battalion up on to their hill. A West Country voice replied, 'Us'll be all right, zurr. T'will be laike the Rock of Gibraltar up yere.' Such a comment, at such a moment, touched the Colonel deeply.

Just before dark on the 24th an attempt was made by light aircraft to free-fall-drop critical supplies. Brens, batteries, and ammunition were tumbled out, but only a small proportion landed where they could be retrieved. Then, at last, there was confirmation of an airstrike for the next morning. Just after dusk Carne tightened his perimeter for the last time. Trenches were few and shallow as picks and shovels were scarce. But for the 25-pounders' support they would have been overrun at the first assault. Some 350 men were on top of that hill, many of them injured. Artillerymen and mortar crews, anti-tank gunners and drivers, cooks and signalmen, officers and senior NCOs, all had become riflemen for the final act. All were determined to hang on; perhaps, just perhaps, the relieving force might get through if only they survived until daylight. Survive they did – just.

One incident, for example, of the defiant, determined, spirit of the survivors on Gloster Hill stands out in the memory of veterans today. It was the clear, nostalgic, notes of a bugle. It was heard over the shouts and yells, above the exploding grenades, and above the rattle of small-arms fire, just as dawn was breaking. Not everybody could see the bugler, but all heard his familiar calls. The music seemed to float above the battle, above the hill, silencing the Chinese trumpets and bringing forth a roar of cheering from every Gloster throat. The magical music went on and on – Long Reveille, Short Reveille, Defaulters, Fall In, Cookhouse, Fire Call, Officer's Mess Call, Lights Out, and others – but no Retreat. They were beautifully played.

The soldier reponsible was the drum major himself. Standing upright and unflinching, Drum Major Buss gave the recital of his life. The adjutant and the colonel had been discussing the endless discordant blaring of the Chinese trumpets. Carne wondered if anybody had a bugle, so the adjutant shouted to the drum major. He did not have one, but Drummer Eagles did. He handed it to Buss. Afterwards, when the survivors left the hill, Eagles destroyed the bugle with his last grenade. A pity – it might have become a priceless memento of a famous action, but he feared he would lose it to the Chinese.

By 10.00 am it was all over. Despite no less than seven strafing runs by aircraft, which checked the Chinese with napalm and rockets, what was left of the Glosters had to abandon their hill. The rest of the brigade was pulling out, the supposed counterattack force had failed to cross their start line, and the brigadier had come on the set to tell Carne he had permission to break out, or surrender if that was impossible. He stressed how magnificently the Glosters had done, but that the rest of the brigade was withdrawing and the faithful artillery could no longer help them. Carne held his last 'O' group. It was every man for himself; they had to try to get through on their own, and there was no way of taking out the wounded. The MO,

Captain Hickey, remained with them, as did Padre Sam Davies, Sergeant Brisland, and Corporal Papworth. Only forty-one men under Captain Mike Harvey of D Company made it back to safety; the rest went into Chinese prison camps.

As the brigade log recorded, in Brodie's handwriting, 'Only the Glosters could have done it'.

Some nine months later Colonel Carne, Major Harding, and Colonel Brown (the senior US Officer), with three American majors, were put on 'trial' by their Chinese captors. The scene was the lecture room in the officers' P.O.W. Camp No. 2, at Pi-Chong-Ni near Korea's Manchurian border. Commander Ding, known as 'Snake-eyes', presided. Always well-groomed, with a cold, pale face and elegant slim hands, Ding lived with his wife and small daughter just outside the compound, only entering the camp to carry out inspections, or deliver his regular three-hour political lectures — in Chinese. His interpreter was a young man with a squeaky voice called Wong. His nickname was 'DP' because of his repeated tirades against the American habit of having pictures of pin-up girls in their wallets. These Wong regarded as 'dirty pictures'. Often 'DP' was infuriated when his remarks were greeted with great hoots of mirth. Padre Sam Davies remembers some: 'No man can be sick without getting permish'; 'When the Commander speaks, no man can joke, and make the strange noises.'[3]

There was no laughter now among the officers squatting shivering on the floor, as their leaders were brought in under heavy guard. All the accused looked filthy, unshaven and numb with cold. Harding's wrists had noticeably dropped. This 'trial' was assembled to hear 'confessions' to crimes of so-called 'subversive activities', of 'plots against camp authorities', or 'preventing the junior officers from learning the truth'. Carne had also recently forbidden the prisoners to sign a Christmas greetings card, addressed to General Peng Te-Huai, which had particularly incensed Ding and his political commissar, Comrade Sun. In other words the Chinese were exasperated beyond measure with the steadfast refusal of the senior officers to submit to their pressure to collaborate. Their leadership and example was infuriating their captors, so they had been singled out for special treatment.

One by one the six senior officers, led by Colonel Brown, came forward to read his 'confession'. These amounted to nothing more than admitting they had been doing their duty as leaders, in 'intimidating' the younger officers to ensure non-cooperation. They were worded in such a way that they satisfied their captors, but to the British and US officers it was perfectly clear that the whole process was meaningless. All the accused had been subjected to beatings or torture in the days preceding the trial. All would have died of their treatment, or gangrenous frostbite, if they had not agreed to concoct the bogus confessions. Harding had been strung up to a beam by his wrists in such a way that he was forced to stand on tip-toe. For two successive nights he was left in temperatures of 35 degrees below zero. Every four hours Comrade Sun would return to see if he had agreed to confess. As a result of Carne's 'confession', he was led away to start nineteen months of solitary confinement.

Carne's integrity and example had been a major factor in sustaining morale within the camp for many months before his 'trial'. Today this period is often remembered as the time during which he carved the famous stone Celtic cross, which now has a place of prominence in Gloucester Cathedral. Sitting on the steps of his hut, frequently with frozen fingers, he worked laboriously away with a makeshift hammer and two rusty nails. It stands 10 inches high, mounted on a rough-hewn plinth, with the arms of the cross joined, like a Cornish cross, by a circle of stone. When it was finished, just before Christmas, 1951, Carne handed it to the padre to use at services in the camp. Sam Davies was delighted with it, and in his prayer of blessing said: 'May all who look to it with faith and love be given grace to endure unto the end'. Carne endured his endless months of solitary confinement until he was finally released in late August, 1953, having lost three stone in weight, and suffering from poor eyesight. When his name was called for release in the Kaesong transit camp, it was greeted with spontaneous cheers and clapping by the American prisoners. On arrival at the Commonwealth reception centre in Japan, Gloster soldiers seated their CO in an armchair, lifted him on to their shoulders and carried him to the officers' mess. Ever one to belittle his own achievements, and possessing a dry sense of humour, which his months of suffering had failed to suppress, his response to questions on his captivity by the communist correspondent Wilfred Burchett was typical: 'The food was rotten, and I was damned bored'.

The day following his return to England his award of the VC was announced. It was 2½ years exactly since the struggle on Gloster Hill. The Investiture followed four days later, on 27 October, 1953. He was the first of 250 recipients of honours, going forward to receive both his VC and his DSO at the same time – an almost unheard-of event. In replying to the Queen's question about prison conditions, Carne modified his previous answers, given to Burchett, – but only slightly: 'They were not too bad, ma'am. The worst part was the boredom'. Her Majesty told him: 'We at home thought a lot about you all'. Shaking his hand, she said, 'I wish you all very good luck'. His next Investiture was at the US Ambassador's residence in Prince's Gate. There Mr Winthrop Aldrich pinned the DSC to his uniform. It was the highest military award the US can bestow on a foreigner. Carne, who was a man of great modesty and few words, publicly stated that he had accepted the VC on behalf of all the officers and men of the Glosters. To him they had won it; he merely wore it for them. A typical gesture of Fred Carne.

On 21 November, 1953, the Imjin Glosters formed up on a car park in Gloucester for their final parade. 'This is our last parade all together; let's make it a good one,' were Carne's words before taking his position at the head of the column, to march through the city to the cathedral. In drab battle dress, unarmed, except for the officers wearing swords, and without Colours, the Glosters set off behind their Colonel. Led by the band in full dress, the companies wound their way through streets lined with cheering, flag-waving, citizens. Bringing up the rear were men in civilian clothes, soldiers who had been discharged, proudly wearing their medals on their raincoats. The Thanksgiving Service started with the handing over into safe-keeping of Colonel Carne's Celtic cross, which had survived the rigours of the prison camp. Appropriately, it was handed over to the Dean by Major Harding, flanked by Captain Farrar-Hockley and Regimental Sergeant Major Hobbs. It remains on prominent display in the cathedral to this day.

After the service the battalion paraded again for the march to the Guildhall, where Carne was to receive the Freedom of Gloucester, and to a civic luncheon for all ranks at the Wagon Works Assembly Hall. As they started out six Vampire jets, flying in a double V formation, screamed overhead in salute.

More honours followed. Freedom of his home town, Falmouth, in January, 1954; promotion to full colonel in April, 1954; and, after retirement, appointment as Deputy Lieutenant of Gloucestershire in 1960.

His retirement was quiet and secluded in the tiny village of Cranham. For eighteen years he and his wife, Jean, attended the village church where he was a churchwarden. The tall figure, bent a little with age, suffered from severe back pain. Perhaps his constitution had been undermined by those terrible months of privation, but his last few years were dogged by ill health and suffering. He became more taciturn, more withdrawn, but still loved to welcome his old regimental friends to his home. Just after his 80th birthday he suffered a fall and was taken to hospital. Within two days the gallant old soldier had faded away. It was 19 April, 1986, almost 35 years to the day since his epic fight.

Padre Davies came from his parish near Exeter to give the funeral address on 25 April, the anniversary of the last day of the battle. Five days later Davies spoke again at the Service of Thanksgiving: 'Colonel Carne's per-

71

sonal courage, coolness, and intrepid leadership inspired others, and were a source of great moral strength ... modesty and reticence were hallmarks of his character. This concealed a resolute inner strength: as our text this morning says, "He took his share of hardship like a good soldier of Jesus Christ". To serve with him in time of danger and crisis was to know a commanding officer who imparted reassurance, and the will to fight on.'

At the time of writing (May, 1989) his widow still lives at Cranham, and his stepson, Brian, works in Scotland. In 1988 Mrs Carne gave his VC and other medals to the Regimental Museum of his beloved Glosters.

CHAPTER FOUR

'United' – Korea,
4 November, 1951

PRIVATE WILLIAM SPEAKMAN VC,
The Black Watch,
attached to the 1st Battalion
The King's Own Scottish Borderers.

'It was a fair old go'
Private Speakman's description of the intense close quarter
fighting that won him the Cross.

Ask people if they remember anybody who won the VC in Korea and, of those that can, nine out of ten will say Speakman. Colonel Carne is occasionally recalled, but Major Muir and Lieutenant Curtis are rarely mentioned. 'Big Bill' Speakman has become a legend in his lifetime. The publicity he engendered for months, if not years, afterwards has imprinted his name on the public memory more than any other post-war VC winner.

The media has been partially to blame for perpetuating a number of myths about Speakman, which, despite attempts to dispel them, remain to this day. *The Daily Telegraph,* as recently as July, 1982, headlined an article on his medals, 'Beer Bottle VC'. This was a reference to the story that circulated after the battle that Speakman had been drunk at the time and threw as many empty beer bottles at the enemy as he did grenades. It is an entirely false accusation. Speakman was not drunk during his four-hour fight with the Chinese. The daily ration of beer per man in the line was one bottle. Its consumption was carefully supervised and Speakman was at company headquarters, under the eyes of his company commander and sergeant-major. There was no opportunity to accumulate the amount of beer to make a soldier his size drunk, even in the unlikely event of his having the time to consume it. His former sergeant-major, 'Busty' Murdoch, is quite emphatic — Speakman was sober. This does not mean that he never threw the odd bottle. Towards the end, the stock of grenades was running out, so both he and others, resorted to hurling rocks, ration tins and the occasional beer bottle.

Another erroneous belief is that Speakman belonged to the Gloucestershire Regiment and that his actions were a part of the Glosters' Imjin battle. The attention given to Speakman and the Glosters has, over the years, mistakenly linked the two together in the public mind. It is a fallacy. Speakman never served in the Glosters; when they fought their battle, he was with the Black Watch in Germany.

Then there is the story that Speakman, after being wounded, left the company position to descend the hill to the aid post and that, after he was treated, the sight of a medical orderly being killed nearby so enraged him that he went back up the hill to resume the fight. Here the truth has been embellished. He was wounded, but he had his injuries dressed in the company position and then carried on the battle.

It is sometimes claimed he gained his award in a gigantic bonfire night battle that would have put Guy Fawkes to shame. Not true; Speakman fought his action on 4 November, 1951.

All this does not mean that Speakman was not sometimes at the centre of controversies. He was, and to some extent still is, but there can be no doubt that his VC was richly deserved. Speakman is a giant of a man, 6 feet 6 inches tall, with a powerful frame to match. Today, at 63, he is still trim and, although his hair has greyed, he is not hard to recognise from photographs of his younger days. He keeps fit, enjoys climbing, and has qualified as a light aircraft pilot.

Speakman was the first private solider to be awarded the Cross since the Second World War, and no other has received one since. He was the first person to be invested with any decoration by Queen Elizabeth and he represented the Army when the Services broadcast their tributes to King George VI, a week after his death, in a programme entitled, 'The Commonwealth mourns the King'. There was just a hint, which nobody appeared to notice, of the Speakman roguishness and willingness to cock a snook at authority at his Investiture. His battledress jacket had six medal ribbons on it, when he was only entitled to three. His enlistment in August, 1945, meant that he did not qualify for the Defence Medal or the War Medal, while he earned his General Service Medal, 1918-64, in Malaya in 1953.

Speakman was not a Scot; he came from Altrincham in Cheshire, where he was brought up in a working class home, and later, at fifteen, joined the 1st (Cadet) Battalion of the Cheshire Regiment. He was an enthusiastic cadet, determined to join the regular Army as soon as he was eighteen. On 10 August, 1945, he joined the Black Watch, completed his basic training, then served with the 1st Battalion for a while, before being detached for duties at Brigade Headquarters in Trieste. Service in Hong Kong followed, where his height and size made it impossible for Speakman to remain anony mous for long in the bars of Wanchai and Kowloon, or at the China

Fleet Club. His company and regimental conduct sheets lengthened considerably. He built up a reputation, not so much for starting fights, but, once embroiled, for winning them. His pals also remember his sense of humour, and ability to entertain with his singing — albeit unprintable Army songs.

He was back in Germany when the call for volunteers to transfer to battalions in, or destined for, the Korean War was made to the Black Watch. Speakman stepped forward. He had only the vaguest notion of where Korea was, but he craved action. Initially he was destined for the A&SH but by the time he arrived they had completed their tour, so he and his batch of reinforcements were posted to the KOSB. He never returned to the Black Watch. He joined his new unit in time for the one and only divisional attack by the 1st Commonwealth Division, under the command of the future Field-Marshal (then a Major-General) Jimmy Cassels. Cassels was a former Seaforth Highlander, who had commanded the 51st Highland Division in the World War at the remarkable age of 32. He was, a few months later, to pin the VC ribbon on Speakman's chest.

By the summer of 1951 the western end of the UN line was comfortably secure in the hills south of the Imjin, dug in on the same slopes that had witnessed the spring battles during the Chinese offensive. The enemy was over the river, holding a broad belt of mountains some 6-8 miles away. In between, just north of the river, was a no-man's-land of low hills and valleys, unoccupied except for patrols from both sides. In early September the comparative tranquillity was to be disturbed by a limited advance of the 1st Commonwealth Division, as part of a general push forward by 1 Corps. The reasons for assuming the offensive are somewhat nebulous, but had to do with wanting to get the UN line closer to the 38th Parallel, give the vacillating and intransigent Chinese negotiators at the peace talks a sharp shock, and forestall a possible enemy advance.

The division consisted of the 28th Commonwealth Brigade with the 1st Battalion KOSB, 1st Battalion the King's Shropshire Light Infantry (KSLI) and the 3rd Battalion Royal Australian Regiment (3RAR).[1] They had the initial task of establishing a bridgehead over the Imjin. This they accomplished on 8 September. Next, on the 11th, came Operation Minden which saw the other two Brigades (29 British and 25 Canadian) close up to within 2 or 3 miles of the Chinese main defensive positions. The third phase, scheduled for early October, was Operation Commando, a major assault on a number of key hill-tops. 28 Brigade, under Brigadier George Taylor, who had won two DSOs in NW Europe, was given the toughest objective. It had to seize Kowang-san and Maryang-san, the former referred to as Hill 355, the latter as 317 (see Map 9). Both these features had been held by the Chinese for months, giving them plenty of time to convert them into

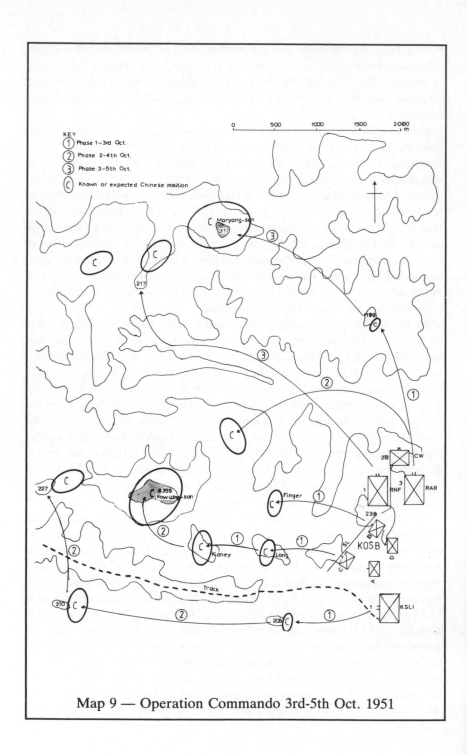

KEY
1 Phase 1–3rd Oct.
2 Phase 2–4th Oct.
3 Phase 3–5th Oct.
C Known or expected Chinese position

Maryang-san
317

217

199 C

C

C

217

3

3

2

1

C

28 CW

227 C

355 Kowang-san

1 RNF 3 RAR

Finger 1

C

238

2

KOSB

1 C Kidney 1 C Long 1 C Sly

D

C

Track

210 C

2

208 C 1

1 KSLI

Map 9 — Operation Commando 3rd-5th Oct. 1951

76

strong-points. Both dominated the surrounding hills, their peaks bare and black against the sky.

Speakman had joined B Company of the KOSB, under the command of Major Philip Harrison, a Second World War veteran in his late thirties, who selected Speakman for his headquarters. His enormous bulk had impressed his company commander, so he assumed the official task of company runner, although this entailed other responsibilites such as acting as a bodyguard, batman, brewing tea, and undertaking more than his share of digging for his seniors.

Speakman's baptism of fire in a large operation took place during Operation Commando. The KOSB were to seize Point 355. It was a barren, austere pile of rocks, thrusting over a thousand feet above the paddy fields. It was guarded by several lower hills and ridges between the KOSB start line, some 2000 metres to the east, and itself. By moving at night and lying concealed by day, the KOSB had managed to get to their forming-up place undetected. Throughout the hot afternoon of 2 October Speakman and his comrades lay on the scrub-covered hillside waiting for darkness. The following dawn was H-hour. It had the elements of a First World War infantry attack. Under a heavy concentration of softening-up fire by 120 guns and mortars, which started at 5.00 am, and which was to include the smoking-off of the summit of 355, the long lines of infantry would move forward in daylight in a frontal assault on prepared enemy positions.

Lieutenant-Colonel John McDonald, the CO of the KOSB, had planned his advance in two phases. The first was to get his left-hand assault company, C Company, on to an intermediate ridge nicknamed Long and his right-hand company, B Company, on to another spur called Finger. From these positions they would support the final attack on 355. Shortly before 7.00 am B and C Companies stood up to begin their advance. Up over the ridgeline walked the leading two platoons of B Company, followed by company headquarters, with Speakman a few metres from Harrison and his radio operator. Then down into the valley for 400 metres before the stiffish slope up to Finger. The noise was the most striking feature of the attack for Speakman: the continuous crash and crump of shells, the banging of mortar bombs, the crisp crack of the tank guns, and the endless, slow rattle of the MMGs. Much to the satisfaction of the men in the assault companies most of the fire was friendly. Resistance to B Company was slight, so they were soon able to consolidate on Finger ridge.

C Company, however, got into difficulties on Long, which was strongly defended by at least a company of well-prepared Chinese. Their battle was slow and hard, platoons got strung out, ammunition expenditure was high, casualties occurred, confusion developed, and the enemy counterattacked. After three hours A Company was brought up from reserve to assist. By early afternoon a fresh attack by A and C Companies was ready. With strong artillery and mortar support, coupled with fire from B Company in the north, and inspired by the skirl of a lone piper playing them in, the attack succeeded by 3.30 pm.

The next day, 4 October, saw 355 fall to D Company attacking from the SW, and B Company making a diversionary advance from the east. The 355 feature fell with a whimper rather than a roar. Although such a dominating position, the shells and smoke screen that shrouded its summit effectively blinded the defenders. On the first day the Chinese OP on top had sent a frantic radio message: 'I cannot see anything. All my signallers and mortarmen are dead'. The casualty count was light for the KOSB. Seven killed and thirty-four wounded was not devastating, while the enemy's was about three times as severe.

By 7 October Operation Commando was successfully concluded. 28 Brigade, with the help of 1 RNF, had secured both 355 and 317 (Maryangsan) 3000 metres to the north, at no great cost. On the 28th the KOSB lost their commanding officer, Macdonald, who was suddenly made the acting brigade commander. Major-General Cassels had fired Brigadier Taylor. The reasons remain a closely guarded secret, secure in confidential files within the Ministry of Defence, but it was a controversial removal of a senior officer in the field. Taylor, who felt his career in jeopardy and the action unjustified, appealed to the Army Council. He later commanded another brigade in Kenya, but was never promoted again.

By the end of October Speakman found himself doing a lot of digging. The KOSB, now under the command of Major Dennis Tadman, had relieved 3 RAR up on the 317 feature and its subsidiary spurs and ridges to the west and south. The line now occupied by the division was to be held. It was necessary to dig in, and quickly, before the sub-zero winter temperatures made such work impossible. Deep trenches were required, with thick overhead cover to withstand shellfire; bunkers must be built for platoon and company command posts; weapon pits for mortars and machine guns needed to be constructed; thick belts of barbed wire had to be erected around each position; field telephone lines had to be buried between headquarters; and ammunition reserves must be stocked up. But despite the burrowing Cassels was far from happy. The problem was the length of his divisional front – nearly 20,000 metres – which together with the wild nature of the country had compelled him to spread seven of his nine ballations in a thin line. It invited attack and penetration. Operation Commando had taken a large bite out of territory considered vital by the enemy. The Chinese had lost face as well as ground – a dangerous combination.

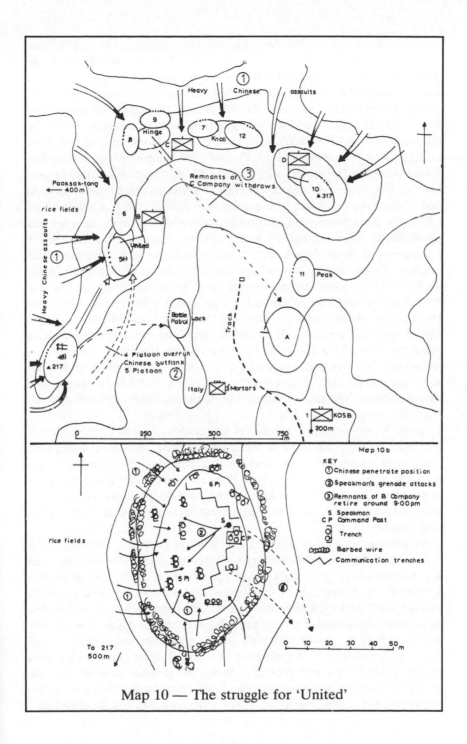

Map 10 — The struggle for 'United'

To understand the battle about to unfold it is necessary to refer to Map 10. Tadman had to deploy his battalion to defend a long, arrowhead-shaped ridge, which pointed roughly NW towards the enemy. At the eastern end was 317, the highest point, with sheer sides to the SW and north. From 317 a long, narrow spur ran south for 500 metres; this spur was nicknamed Peak. Hill 317 and Peak were the responsibility of D Company. About 400 metres west of 317 the saddle rose up to a small hillock called Knoll. Here 12 Platoon of D Company and 7 Platoon of C Company shared defensive duties. Another 200 metres west was the tip of the arrow − the Hinge, a hill with C Company headquarters and two platoons posted on its northern and western slopes. Running due south from Hinge a long spur formed the left side of the arrowhead. Four hundred metres from Hinge, the ridge rose up slightly to form another distinctive hilltop, nicknamed United. Here B Company was to be found, with 5 and 6 Platoons, plus company head-quarters, facing west. This was Speakman's location. Here he would win his VC. From United the spur sloped down, losing height for another 500 metres as it swung SW. At the end, out on a limb, was Point 217, occupied by 4 Platoon of B Company, reinforced by a section from 5 Platoon with a pair of MMGs. Behind or SE of United, a very narrow ridge ran south for 500 metres. At the northern end the Battle Patrol, a strong platoon, was entrenched. Its position was called Lock, while the southern end of the spur was named Italy. From the Peak round to 217 nine platoons were strung out over 2000 metres. In reserve, on the southern extremity of Peak, was A Company.

As the KOSB prepared themselves they could not know that the Chinese had selected their positions as the main objective of a divisional attack. Some 6000 infantrymen were ordered to retake the 217-317 ridge. It was to be the scene of some of the most intensive hand-to-hand fighting of the war so far. The three companies in the forward positions mustered, at most, 400-men. They were to face an onslaught by at least twelve times their number.

B Company's trenches mainly faced west, down into a 500-metre-wide valley filled with rice fields, and the scattered village of Paoksok-tong. This was no-man's-land, with the Chinese positions in the hills beyond the valley. On the northern side of United was 6 Platoon under 2nd Lieutenent Brooks, while to his south, just over the highest point, was 5 Platoon, less one section, commanded by 2nd Lieutenant Thomson. Then came the 400-metre gap before 217 with 4 Platoon, the extra section, and the two MMGs, all under Lieutenant McMillan-Scott. The majority of the trenches were on the forward slope, with several shallow crawl trenches twisting their way over the crest line to permit movement between the forward and reverse slopes without undue exposure. There were wire barriers all round each platoon position and a much thinner belt along the western edge of the saddle joining United to 217 (see Map 10b).

Company headquarters was dug in on the reverse slope of United behind 5 and 6 Platoons. From the command post bunker Harrison would control the battle by radio and telephone, assisted by his operators, by Company Sergeant-Major Murdoch, and by his runner, Speakman. It was in here that Murdoch kept his ammunition reserve, a vital responsibility of the CSM being to ensure that nobody ran out once the battle started. Part of his stock was a pile of wooden boxes containing over 200 extra 36 grenades.

Last minute preparations were stepped up on 2 and 3 November, when it appeared that a build-up of enemy troops was taking place. The whole ridgeline became the target for sporadic shell or mortar fire, which looked suspiciously like pre-attack ranging shots. During the morning of the 4th the shelling increased until by 4.00 pm the foward companies were cowering in their trenches under a furious bombardment. From the battalion headquarters 'the whole ridgeline became an inferno of smoke, dust, flame, and explosions: with awe we wondered how anyone could remain alive under this avalanche of fire and fury. Our own artillery and mortar fire was brought down, and our aircraft called in to do what they could in the failing light'.[2] At least nine Chinese tanks were spotted from Hinge, adding their shells to the weight of metal pummelling the positions.

B Company were suffering particularly from precision shooting by SP guns that were hitting the slit trenches on the forward slope with unnerving accuracy. It was later estimated that the KOSB received 6000 shells in an hour, the most intense bombardment of the war to date.

The infantry assault started while it was still daylight. Shortly after 4.00 pm around 1500 Chinese began their advance across the paddies below B Company, moving close behind their own artillery fire. Their objective appeared to be the forty-five men with Lieutenant McMillan-Scott on 217. Simultaneously the enemy attacked all along the line in great strength, with complete disregard for the casualties inflicted by the defenders' artillery, mortar and MMG DF tasks. The Chinese soldiers were equipped with satchels full of grenades, and many carried nets and pole charges to blast their way through the barbed wire. Unfortunately for the KOSB the preliminary concentrations of shellfire had blown away much of this obstacle, so there was little to check the rush once the attackers got to within throwing distance of the trenches. Some Chinese were seen to advance right into their own barrage, taking casualties from it, in their eagerness to get up the slopes of 217, United, Hinge, Knoll and 317. To some defenders they seemed dazed or doped. Many in the forefront had submachine guns. As fast as the defenders blew them away more sprang up to replace them. Three rifle companies were in the way of a full-scale divisional attack, supported by all the firepower the enemy could bring to bear.

In B Company command post Harrison was receiving radio reports of hand-to-hand fighting on the forward slope. On 217 the situation soon became critical, with the defenders being overwhelmed and pushed back over the ridge on to the reverse slope. There, with the reserve section, the remnants deperately fought to keep the crest clear with grenades or bren guns firing from the hip. It was the sort of fighting where weight of numbers was the winning factor.

CSM Murdoch had organized Speakman and others to start breaking open the grenade boxes. With frantic haste they began to prime each grenade ready for use. This was a time-consuming task, involving the removal of the base-plug with a special tool, inserting the primer, and then replacing the base-plug. At the same time the surplus preservative grease had to be wiped off, to ensure the working parts were not clogged at the crucial moment. The 36 grenade, which resembled a tiny pineapple, was a most effective weapon. Anybody within a 20-metre radius of an exploding grenade was likely to become a casualty from the flying rectangles of jagged metal of the casing. If hit by the solid lump of the base plug, which made a distinctive whine if it passed nearby, the victim was unlikely to get up. Speakman began to stuff primed grenades into his pounches and pockets.

By 5.30 pm it was all over on 217. McMillan-Scott, who had been decorated a few weeks before by Cassels with an MID, and twenty-two of his men were never seen again. Only a handful of survivors crawled away to join the Battle Patrol on Lock. The Chinese were now able to infiltrate behind United, and, more importantly, attack NE up the fairly gentle saddle that separated 217 from 5 Platoon. To the north, on Hinge, C Company too had lost the summit. After savage, close-quarter fighting first 8, then 9 Platoon, had succumbed to the impossible pressure and fallen back. After two hours Tadman gave them permission to withdraw to A Company's location on the southern end of Peak. Now the enemy could pour down the spur from Hinge on to 6 Platoon. B Company was reduced to two weak platoons and company headquarters facing assault from three directions, and outnumbered by 10 or more to 1.

It was about then that Speakman decided to take a hand in things (see map 10b). He heaved himself towards the entrance of the bunker. 'Where the hell do you think you're going?' demanded Murdoch. 'Going to shift some of them bloody chinks, sir,' grunted Speakman as he disappeared outside. It was on his own initiative that he resolved to have a go; nobody had ordered him to assist, but Speakman had heard the frantic messages coming in over the radio, the noise outside was stunning, and he realized that 5 Platoon in particular were in dire need of help, as they had started

10. Private W. Speakman, VC, shortly after he had been presented with the ribbon of the VC by Major-General Cassels. *(Imperial War Museum)*

11. Private W. Speakman, VC, outside Buckingham Palace just after his Investiture. His mother is on his left, and the other couple are the Mayor and Mayoress of his home town, Altrincham. *(Hulton Picture Library)*

12. Captain Rambahadur Limbu, VC, MVO, with his son, Bhakte, then a corporal, on the day he retired from the British Army. *(Soldier Magazine)*

13. Warrant Officer Class 2 K.A. Wheatley. *(Australian War Memorial)*

14. Warrant Officer Wheatley's funeral in South Vietnam. The coffin is flanked by fellow Team comrades, as a South Vietnamese general places Wheatley's Vietnamese decorations on it. *(Australian War Memorial)*

the battle with only two sections. The platoon headquarters trenches were very close to the command post so Speakman did not have far to go. The Chinese were a mere 20 metres away, over the crest of the hill. The whole scene was lit by parachute flares and the continuous flash of explosions, bullets cracked all around, and enemy shells were still thumping the ridgeline.

Speakman joined 5 Platoon headquarters and the survivors of the platoon nearby. He yelled across to the platoon sergeant, 'Dolly' Duncan, who was firing the 3.5 inch rocket launcher, an anti-tank weapon, against human targets. Then he started to hurl his grenades. Being such a tall man Speakman was a conspicuous target even when standing in a trench, but his powerful shoulders gave him the strength to throw grenades as though they were marbles. An average soldier lobbed a grenade 20-25 metres; Speakman could almost double that. Pull the pin, right arm back, then heave with a motion similar to a bowler at cricket, duck down briefly to await the roar four seconds later, then up again to repeat the procedure. Steadily, calmly, and without flinching, Speakman continued to unburden himself of his stock of grenades, sometimes throwing at a group of the enemy coming forward, sometimes at the muzzle flashes of their weapons, sometimes in the direction of their screams and shouts, and sometimes just over the crest line into the dead ground on the forward slope.

Speakman's example was an inspiration to all who saw it. Several soldiers nearby joined in, including Corporals Wilson and Wood and Private Buchanan. The showers of grenades checked the Chinese assault and 5 Platoon gained a momentary respite. Speakman rushed back to replenish his stock from Murdoch who was still hastily priming more. Once again, with pockets, pouches, and shirt front bulging, Speakman renewed his efforts. This time he decided he must clear the crest properly and keep it clear, so he charged up the slope hurling as fast as he could pull pins. Shouting encouragement to the others who had joined him, Speakman stood and threw, and threw, and threw, seemingly oblivious to the close range machine-gun fire or the bursting mortar bombs. It was impossible to know the number of Chinese getting killed or maimed by his efforts, but it was considerable. Within a few minutes, with all his stock gone, he was back at the command post for more.

Speakman's performance was repeated again and again. At least ten times he charged the crest. During this period, mortar fragments struck him in the left shoulder and thigh. 'It felt as if a stone had hit me,' he explained afterwards. His wounds had no effect on his actions, although somebody, he cannot recall who, ordered him to get medical attention. This entailed the application of field dressings in the company area – nothing more.

During the struggle for United the situation was so critical, with the

Chinese so close, that Harrison decided he must call down artillery fire on his own location to try to clear it. By radio, and yelling, the message was conveyed to the remnants of B Company to crouch down in their slits. Moments later the summit of United was engulfed in flame and smoke as the 25-pounder shells of the supporting New Zealand guns pounded the position. It helped, but not for long. The desperate situation, and the incredible ammunition expenditure, is well illustrated by the KOSB's 3-inch Mortar Platoon. During the night of 4-5 November well over 4500 bombs were fired. This meant some 600 for each tube; it is little wonder that they became so hot it was unsafe to drop bombs in them for fear of a 'cook-off'. The mortarmen resorted to pouring beer down the barrels in an effort to keep them cool.

For hour after hour the dwindling perimeter around United held. With enemy assaulting without respite from all sides, and with the other companies already forced back, it looked as though B Company would be swamped. The Sergeant-Major had finished priming grenades and had left the bunker to join in the melee with Speakman, but his pile was exhausted. Ammunition of all types was almost gone, fighting was hand-to-hand, soldiers, including Speakman, were grabbing anything to hurl at the enemy — ration tins, rocks and beer bottles. At around 8.45 pm what was left of B Company got permission to withdraw to the Battle Patrol's location at Lock. But with both sides engaged in combat at such close range this was no simple operation. In the event Harrison got them away under cover of a last grenade charge by Speakman, Murdoch, and several others, which cleared the crest for the last time. Then, as the company made its way back, Speakman and Murdoch, who had also been wounded, assisted each other down the hill to the aid post. For them the battle was over, and it was the first stage of their journey back to hospital in Japan.

Murdoch received the DCM and Speakman the VC. Speakman had spent between three to four hours exposed to intense point blank fire, tossing over 100 grenades, which killed dozens of the enemy. He ignored his own wounds, and he encouraged others by his example. That he was only lightly injured is little short of miraculous. Speakman was a fighter. Whether it was a bar room brawl or on an unknown hill, 'Big Bill' was a daunting opponent to face. On his own, like many men of his stature, he was normally quiet and unassuming, seeking to avoid the spotlight. But once roused, once angry, he was a hard man to stop. Up there, on that barren hill, Speakman was fighting mad, his efforts being instrumental in the company holding its position for so long, after neighbouring platoons had withdrawn. He broke up attack after attack and his heroism, as his citation stated, was 'deserving of supreme recognition'. Despite their magnificent defence the KOSB had been pushed off 217 and 317. Chinese face had been saved — at a price of over 1000 dead and countless wounded.

While Speakman was recovering from his wounds he received a summons to brigade headquarters. If the brigadier wanted to see him, to Speakman that meant trouble. Brigadiers only asked to see privates in exceptional circumstances. He was shattered when the brigadier said: 'Speakman, you've been awarded the VC'. On 30 December, 1951, in the courtyard of a Korean school, with snow-covered hills all round, a special parade had formed up. It was the coldest day of the winter. The six kilted pipers had had to keep their bagpipes heated by a fire all night to ensure they played that morning. Major-General Cassels was to be the inspecting officer. It was a parade at which the ribbons of some of the awards made for the November battle were to be presented. Major Harrison was to receive the DSO, 2nd Lieutenant Brooks the MC, Sergeant Major Murdoch the DCM, and Private Speakman the VC ribbon. Speakman listened as the citation was read out, then strode forward, saluted, stood at attention as the General, himself a six footer, pinned the tiny crimson ribbon on his bare combat jacket. That night Speakman celebrated with his mates, assisted by a liberal ration of whisky, rum punch, and beer. His comments on the whole affair were typically modest. 'I did not really lead anybody. There were lots of chaps who did what I did. I did what anyone would have done. I was mad at them — it's natural.' When asked if he would like more leave he replied, 'No Sir, I want to rejoin my company right away.'

Nevertheless, within a few weeks Speakman was flown home for the Investiture at Buckingham Palace. It was then that the realization of what he had become — a celebrity, a national hero — hit him. His action was the last in the Korean war to earn a VC, but he was the first to receive his award. Major Muir was dead, and so was Lieutenant Curtis, while Colonel Carne was in solitary confinement in a Chinese prison camp. Until he was released, a VC for Curtis and Carne was not contemplated. The British people wanted a hero — Speakman was it. Always shy of his exceptional height, always one to avoid the limelight, never a good public speaker, Speakman now found himself at the centre of the stage, with the full glare of the spotlight on him. His name was in every newspaper, on the radio, and the press pestered him without let-up. Everybody wanted to see him, photograph him, hear him speak, or get him to attend some celebration, with his every action the subject of public comment. For Speakman it was an ordeal infinitely worse than dealing with the Chinese on United. He did his best, although throughout the weeks of parties, concerts, handing over cheques to pools winners, attending official receptions, such as that given for him by his hometown, Altrincham, he vowed he would escape back to his comrades at the earliest opportunity.

His chance came four weeks after the Investiture. Although given the option of a posting at his Depot, Speakman insisted on returning to Korea. He had had enough. The daily mail delivery at his mother's house filled him with dread. Letters invited him to football matches, darts matches, shows, contests, and bazaars − some sought marriage. Most said they would be honoured by his presence, a few admitted he would attract a crowd. He struggled to answer them all, dutifully promising to come if he could. Wherever he went he was instantly recognized and led away for more rounds of drinks, more backslapping, and more publicity. Sometimes he missed engagements he had agreed to attend, which caused anger and unpleasantness. Many people genuinely organized functions for charity, or were honoured to shake his hand, but others only wanted to bask in his glory themselves.

To Robin Glenton of the *Sunday Express*, Speakman exploded. 'Look; I'm just one of the lads. I've been made up to lance corporal and corporal, and I've been busted for not behaving myself. I'm an ordinary man. The Victoria Cross gives you pride. I'm a regular soldier and I'm happy as one. I want to do my job as well as I can. That's why I'm in the Army ... like my father was. The bad side to winning the Cross is that people make you into something like a freak. They won't let you be normal. And all the time they are watching you to see if you get above yourself. You have got to watch yourself.'

Speakman rejoined the KOSB in Korea and put a lance corporal's stripe on his sleeve, but he did not rejoin B Company, nor was he involved in further action. From Korea the KOSB moved to Hong Kong, where Speakman, ever conspicuous for his size, was now doubly so. Visits to the clubs, bars, and indeed the Peninsula Hotel, soon cost Speakman his stripe. There was no way he could avoid trouble. A normal night out with the lads was impossible. Speakman attracted attention and trouble as a magnet attracts metal. When his troopship called at Singapore on the way home it was a similar story. His shore leave involved too much celebration, and this time the ship's engines were running before Speakman made the gangway. The rest of the journey he was under arrest in the brig.

Speakman's seven-year engagement with the Army was up soon after his return to the UK. He decided to give civvy street a try, but within a month or so he was back. He had not been able to find a job he liked, he missed his pals, and he missed Army life. He volunteered for the Malayan Scouts, formed to operate deep in the jungle against the Chinese Communist terrorists. He was accepted, received parachute training at Aldershot, and in

June, 1955, sailed once again for the Far East. Speakman joined a squadron of the SAS, but spent most of his time as a lance corporal in charge of the armoury, rather than on operations. When, in late 1955, the KOSB arrived in Malaya Speakman rejoined them. On New Year's Day, 1956, Lance Corporal Speakman married a Women's Royal Army Corps Private, Rachel Snitch, at St. George's garrison church in Singapore.

His wife, family responsibilites, which eventually included the arrival of six children, and promotion to the rank of sergeant, all had a steadying effect on Speakman over the next few years. With his family at home, and the RSM in barracks and the Sergeants' Mess, to steer him around some of the pitfalls which had beset him in his younger days, Speakman concentrated on the responsibilities of his job. Tours in Aden, Radfan and Brunei followed, with Speakman's duties being largely confined to administrative rather than operational matters. He served for much of the time as the battalion's PR sergeant and photographer. Back in Edinburgh in 1967 he became a recruiting sergeant, but there he was no longer with the battalion, no longer under its tight control and discipline. His marriage and home life was not the haven it has once been, so he allowed himself to slip back into some of the wilder ways of his youth. The climax came in April, 1967, when he appeared in the Sheriff's court to plead guilty to the theft of a purse containing £104 from a house in Edinburgh. The Court took cognizance of his great gallantry and the immediate repayment of the money to give him an absolute discharge. His Regiment hastily posted him to Germany.

In early 1968 Speakman's 22-year engagement ended. At 40 he could no longer be a soldier. The prospect of civilian life did not appeal. He had no idea of what to do. With his large family his pension would not stretch far, so work of some sort was essential. Rachel Speakman summed up his feelings when she explained: 'The Army is the only life he has known since he was a boy. I don't know what he can do. He has no qualifications for another job. Really, he didn't want to leave the Army ... He loved the life and will miss it a lot.'[3]

Speakman moved into a house at Wyton, near St Ives in Huntingdonshire, which had once belonged to his wife's parents. It was in a bad state of repair, but he did not have the capital to put it right. Speakman then made a decision that was at once controversial, and possibly ill-considered, and it certainly brought the media back to badger him – he went to London to sell all his medals, including the VC, to a dealer for £1500. Although he was told they would be permanently in a private collection this was not the case. The medals changed hands many times, on each occasion at a greatly inflated price. In July, 1982, Sotheby's had them up for auction. The buyer was a dealer acting for an English private collection.

He paid £20,000 for the six medals, but they did not remain in this country. As recently as 1986 the Scottish United Services Museum purchased them for an unspecified amount from overseas. They hang on display to this day in Edinburgh Castle.

Speakman tried a variety of jobs, night cleaning work, gas conversion, and warehouse manager, but nothing suited him until he moved to Torquay. There he secured a post as an assistant master-at-arms on Union Castle liners sailing between Southampton and Cape Town. This was much more to his liking. He could travel, he was in a semi-service environment, and was responsible for maintaining discipline. It was not so good for his marriage. As his wife explained: 'He was away most of the time ... just coming home for a few days at a time. I could see that things were not going to improve between us ... so I asked him for a divorce .... We parted in 1971 and we were divorced in June, 1972, on his petition. He said it was on the grounds of two years separation and irretrievable breakdown. I did not contest his grounds ...'[4]

In 1972 Speakman made a break with the past — he settled in South Africa. For many years he found the anonymity he craved, deliberately cutting himself off from his former Regiment, the VC and GC Assocation, and most of his family. He changed his name to Speakman-Pitt, moved from Cape Town to Durban, then back to Cape Town, remarried and had another daughter. It is only comparatively recently that Speakman has started to renew contact with his family in England. He has visited London some three times, the most recent occasion being in October, 1990, when he stayed with two of his daughters in their flat. They were impressed with his appearance and his cooking; his old humour was still sharp, and he was obviously settled in his security job with the Cape Town Divisional Council.

As to the future of the only living British postwar VC — who knows? [5] There are indications that Speakman would like to return to England, the possibility of his becoming a Pensioner at Chelsea Royal Hospital has been hinted at. If that is what the old soldier wants then let us hope the authorities can find a way. For Speakman, whose gallantry on that Korean hill almost 40 years ago was unsurpassed, it would make a fitting home for a man whose attitude to life is perhaps encompassed by Sir Walter Scott's famous verse;

> 'Sound, sound the clarion, fill the fife!
> To all the sensual world proclaim,
> One crowded hour of glorious life,
> Is worth an age without a name.'

PART TWO

Borneo

On a hot sticky day in December, 1962, Rifleman Nainabahadur Rai of the 1st Battalion the 2nd Gurkha Rifles (2 GR) was standing alone in an overgrown rubber plantation in the Sultanate of Brunei, the tiny oil-rich enclave on the NE coast of the island of Borneo. His closest comrades were 100 metres away in the process of flushing out rebels, who had recently attempted a coup against the Sultan. Suddenly he saw four of them between himself and his comrades. He was unable to fire for fear of hitting his friends, although the four were moving directly towards him as he stood behind a tree, rifle raised. At 30 metres they saw him and charged. At 15 metres Nainabahadur fired, hitting the leading rebel in the chest. The round passed through his body and struck his second attacker. Both fell dead. The remaining two dived for cover, and a gun battle developed during which Nainabahadur wounded one and captured the other. He earned the first of his two MMs.

Gurkhas were the first troops to arrive from Singapore to rescue the Sultan of Brunei in late 1962, and they were the last out, in 1966, at the end of the four year 'confrontation' with President Sukarno of Indonesia. Although numerous British battalions served in Borneo, the Gurkhas were a permanent feature, providing the great majority of troops, and an expertise and continuity in jungle operations that was vital to the eventual defeat of the Indonesians. It marked the start of a special relationship between the Sultan and the Gurkhas that continues to this day, with a battalion of for-

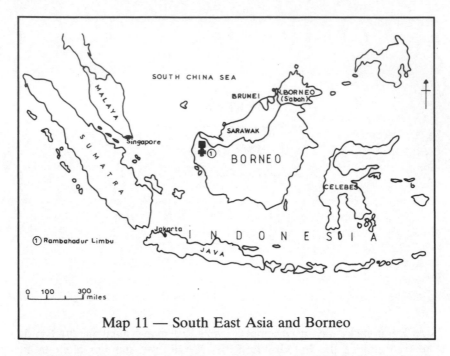

Map 11 — South East Asia and Borneo

mer Gurkha soldiers now serving on contract in the Gurkha Reserve Unit. It has special responsibility for the protection of the Sultan, and key points in Brunei.

Borneo is huge. Some 287,000 square miles of inaccessible mountains and jungle make the island one of the wildest and most unexplored places on earth. The southern two-thirds previously belonged to the Dutch, but had been inherited by Indonesia and called Kalimantan. The 1000-mile frontier between Indonesia (Kalimantan), Brunei and the two British territories to the north was marked on maps but seldom on the ground. In 1962 the northern coast of Borneo was divided unequally into three small countries. The largest was Sarawak in the west, where most of the military operations would take place. In the NE was British North Borneo (later known as Sabah), while between them was the tiny Sultanate of Brunei. In the early sixties there was every likelihood that all three territories might opt to join the proposed Federation of Malaysia. The attempts of Sukarno to prevent this by fomenting rebellion, and later outright military aggression, was the cause of the confrontation.

Virtually all operations were in deep jungle, and of a type that mirrored the twelve-year Malayan emergency that had ended three years earlier. The campaign was to last just under four years, with the maximum number of Commonwealth troops deployed being 17,000. The Commonwealth units, which included Malaysians, Australians and New Zealanders, as well as the British and Gurkhas, suffered 114 killed and 181 wounded. Indonesian killed exceeded 600. Hardly a major conflict, but as the Labour Secretary of State for Defence, Denis Healey, said in the House of Commons: 'In the history books it will be recorded as one of the most efficient uses of military force in the history of the world.'

Every unit of the Brigade of Gurkhas took part in the campaign, adding to the enormous debt of gratitude owed by Britain and the free world to these sturdy soldiers from Nepal. For almost 175 years Gurkhas have fought alongside the British in countless wars, campaigns and skirmishes around the globe. From the Pindaree War in India, in 1817, through to the Falklands in 1982, these remarkable little men (average height 5 feet 4 inches) have gained a fighting reputation second to none. In the two world wars alone they suffered 43,000 casualties. After the Battle of Loos the 8th Gurkhas fought to the last, and in the words of the Corps commander: 'Found its Valhalla'. At Sari Bair, in Gallipoli, they were the only troops to reach the ridgeline and look down into the Straits — the final campaign objective. In the Second World War no less than 40 Gurkha battalions saw service — over 250,000 men. Gurkhas marched, fought and died in Syria, Greece, the Western Desert, Italy, Malaya, Singapore and Burma. When Britain stood alone in 1940 the Prime Minister of Nepal put the entire Nepalese Army at the disposal of the British Crown. Some of its regiments went to India for internal security duties, and others fought in Burma at the Battle for Imphal. Seldom has a country had such a generous and stalwart ally for so long.

By late 1965 the campaign in Borneo had swung in favour of the British, to the extent that operations were taking place inside Indonesia along the majority of the ill defined, mountainous frontier. The war had become known as the 'secret war', as the frequent incursions of Gurkha and other troops into Indonesia were steadfastly denied. These cross-border operations were launched under the codename 'Claret'. They had the backing of the British Labour Government, but were never hinted at in any press release. It could never be admitted that Claret raids were taking place for fear of worldwide condemnation of an 'invasion'. Each raid was initially planned and conducted under the so called 'golden rules'. These included every operation being authorized by the Director of Operations; only jungle-experienced troops to be employed; the depth of penetration limited to 5000 metres (later extended to 20,000); absolute security, with the troops even leaving their identity discs behind; and on no account allowing any dead or wounded to be captured by the enemy. The first troops to be used were Gurkhas.

The story that follows, of how a young lance-corporal won the thirteenth

Gurkha VC, is of a Claret operation. Because the action took place inside Indonesia the eventual citation for the Cross had to be fudged, so that the exact location was not identified. Three years were to elapse before the truth was officially admitted.

CHAPTER 5

Gunong Tepoi, Indonesia
21 November, 1965

LANCE-CORPORAL RAMBAHADUR LIMBU VC MVO
2nd/10th Gurkha Rifles

'It is a miracle he is alive'
The words of Rambahadur Limbu's company commander, Captain Maunsell MC, when asked to comment on his young NCO's actions that won him the VC.

On a windy winter evening in 1954 two boys timidly tapped on the door of a large house in the foothills of Eastern Nepal. Both were barely 15 years old, though neither was certain of his exact age. Both shivered miserably in the gathering darkness, both looked grimy, their young faces drawn and tired, and both were suffering from severe hunger pangs. When an old man opened the door, Rambahadur Limbu begged for shelter for the two of them. There could be no refusal on the part of the owner, as needy strangers are treated as welcome guests by most Nepalese, but the man's first question concerned their caste. As Limbus the two boys were of medium caste, whereas the house owner revealed that he was of a lower one. In those days this created a difficult problem for Rambahadur and his friend, as their religion forbade them to accept hospitality from a person of lower caste. The man offered shelter, but the boys hesitated despite their distress. Then, noticing a stable nearby, they readily accepted to sleep there, rather than in the house. Blankets were provided, but the offer of food was at first refused. Later the kindly wife appeared with uncooked rice, vegetables, and the means to cook them. The two ravenous boys set to to fill their empty bellies, although years later Rambahadur could not see the logic in refusing cooked food but accepting uncooked. 'After all it was their food I ate'.[1]

What they did not explain to the owner was their real plight. They had recently deserted from the Army.

Rambahadur had not had a happy childhood. Life for most Nepalese was usually one of grinding poverty, endless labour for the basics of existence, frequent bouts of sickness, and the physical struggle against the environ-

93

ment. Nepal is breathtakingly beautiful, but it is also cruel and unforgiving. Only the fit can survive the rigours of the Himalayas. Even in the foothills, where numerous tiny villages hang precariously from the ridges, the people can only eke out a hazardous existence as farmers and grazers of sheep or cattle. Water, food and firewood are the essentials. To get each requires daily exertion. Even obtaining water, which is plentiful, can involve climbing down into gorges hundreds of feet deep, while tending cattle on the steep, treacherous slopes is never without danger. The characteristics these conditions foster in the people make for exceptional soldiers. Their stamina, both physical and mental, is unrivalled. Years of carrying heavy loads up hillsides at high altitudes gives the young men powerful legs and lungs. To watch them race down a mountain side is to see them fly. The Gurkha, short, stocky, olive-skinned and almond-eyed, is an immensely resilient, resourceful and proud man. There is about him a dependability, an openness and an unshakeable loyalty. These qualities are linked to an enthusiasm for soldiering that, as all British Gurkha officers admit, makes the Gurkha one of the easiest of men to train and lead.

Rambahadur's father fought the Japanese in the Second World War and, like thousands of others, had returned home to show his scars and recount his stories to his children. Rambahadur's boyhood was abnormally hard. His father died when he was about eight. Then, within a year or two, sickness decimated his family of ten, leaving only three — himself and two brothers, the youngest of whom was too small to work. Responsibility for keeping the family farm fell on the older of the three, but Rambahadur was obliged to assist, spending his time toiling in the fields, with scant chance of schooling. As he himself described his childhood — 'The years passed by, but not with comforts and happiness. I had always been a lazy farmer who never wanted to work in the fields because I was always restless. I had to work to eat, and to live. I struggled to live until I was nearly fifteen. I then began to make plans to leave the village and to join the Army.'[2]

Like so many young Gurkha boys Rambahadur had dreamt of becoming a soldier. It was a profession that would give him everything he could want. Freedom from farming, the opportunity for travel, excitement, a smart uniform, good pay, and maybe, one day, medals and a pension. But above all he would be proud of himself. He would be joining a profession that would entitle him to great respect among his peers. Many young men wished to be soldiers, to escape into a new world, but not all succeeded as vacancies were limited and the medical standards high. Rambahadur knew that, although he was not yet fully grown, he could, with luck, join as a boy soldier.

The problem was that his elder brother would never consent. How would he manage with just the youngest boy to help? Rambahadur planned to slip away without permission. He discussed it with his cousin and another young friend. They agreed to go together, to creep out of the village before dawn. On the chosen day, with a few coins and some old clothes, the trio escaped unobserved on their long trek to the recruiting depot at a place called Pashpati.

Rambahadur's cousin was not accepted for health reasons, but he and his other friend became boy soldiers. Within a few days, however, both started to become disillusioned with their life of two meals a day and few physical exercises. Nothing exciting happened. There was no mention of moving to Malaya, not even any training with weapons, or a proper uniform to make them feel like soldiers. Apart from their shorn hair they looked and felt like any other Gurkha boys, although now they were far from home. A feeling of impatience and annoyance was soon coupled with pangs of loneliness and homesickness. Rambahadur discussed his feelings with his friend, and both agreed to sneak out of the depot at the first opportunity, just as they had secretly left their village a few weeks before. Once again nobody noticed.

They quickly realized that what they had done was shameful. How could they return home and admit to being deserters? Who would accept such worthless boys, who had so quickly rejected such an honourable career? They had no money and few clothes so they quickly resorted to begging for shelter or food as they wandered aimlessly for weeks, hoping that something would turn up to save them. It did not. Eventually Rambahadur persuaded his companion they must return and face their families. It could not be worse than their present plight. In the event, although Rambahadur's brother voiced the expected anger, he was secretly delighted to have him back. As Rambahadur described it, 'He needed me in the house, if not in his heart'.[3]

For two years Rambahadur worked as a farmer for his brother, but his heart was never in it. The restless yearning for a better, less tedious life soon returned. 'I would unwillingly go to the fields to work. I preferred to take the cattle out on the pastures than to work in the fields. Leaving the cattle on their own I could idle my days, sitting and thinking about so many things . . . Most of the time I would curse myself for deserting the Army . . . I could not go back to the recruiting depot again to join the Army. They would not accept a deserter . . . they would certainly arrest me and put me into jail . . . To become a soldier, therefore, was out of the question for me.'[4]

Fortunately this was not the case. Nevertheless, it was to be another two years before Rambahadur finally made it back into the Army. At seventeen he wandered off once more, this time to Darjeeling, in India, and then to the tiny mountain kingdom of Sikkim, where he worked for a timber company. Here he met a girl and fell in love, but refused to consider marriage despite her coming from a well-to-do family, as he himself was ashamed he could not afford to keep a wife. They quarrelled. The problem was solved by the appearance of his elder brother to persuade him to return home. But still he could not adjust. He wanted to marry his girl and bring her home; surely, he thought, she would come if she really loved him. He would go and fetch her.

This decision coincided with his younger brother departing to try to enlist, and with the local recruiter (Galla Wala) gathering together his quota of potential recruits for the journey to the depot. The Galla Wala was the first step in the annual recruiting exercise. He was an old soldier who was given a number of likely boys to bring to the special 'Hill Selection'. He might be required to visit up to 30 villages but have only a quota of 60 vacancies. Rambahadur's Galla Wala had 22, but at the start of the journey was still one short. Rambahadur was going to Sikkim, but to begin with he travelled with the others. The Galla Wala tried repeatedly to persuade Rambahadur to enlist. Repeatedly he refused. The recruiter, however, was a shrewd old soldier, and like his counterparts not so many years ago who managed to persuade reluctant civilians to accept the 'King's shilling', he resorted to strong drink to soften Rambahadur's resistance. He became generous with 'rakshi', the local rice wine. As Rambahadur admitted: 'In one of these drinking sessions I must have gone out of my mind when I said, "Yes I'll join the Army". Once the Galla Wala had my word he never left my side, and after a few days I found myself at the Jalapahar Recruiting Depot, Sikkim and the girl all forgotten.'[5]

Rambahadur had arrived at 'Hill Selection', where a two-man team of retired Gurkha officers would select the best candidates for the next stage. Only about one in six or seven would filter through, so there was a tremendous feeling of apprehension, of nervous excitement. Before crowds of interested and vocal spectators, the process of elimination takes place, each candidate's physique being carefully examined – height, weight, build, eyesight, hearing and age. The latter is often tricky as it is difficult to tell the age of a young Gurkha, who usually does not know himself, and if he did would be likely to lie about it to ensure he got through. It is recorded that once a father and son were recruited together at the same selection. How was this possible? The father later explained that, 'he shaved in hot water that morning', and that his son had stood on tiptoe while being measured. Not only are physical standards checked, but each person is interviewed by the recruiters to assess their general suitability. Full details of each successful applicant are recorded so that he can be easily identified at the next stage of the recruiting process. This is a necessary precaution as disappointed candidates or relatives commonly try to infiltrate substitutes into the system.

Despite his concern that somebody might recognize him from his earlier enlistment nobody did, so Rambahadur found himself back in the Army at nineteen. He was enlisted at Lehra on 11 November, 1957. He took the oath of allegiance in the Gurkha manner. In front of the assembled recruits was a table, draped in the Union Jack, on top of which was a framed portrait of Her Majesty. Behind stood a Gurkha officer in ceremonial uniform. In pairs the young men came forward to place their right hands on the flag. Then they repeated the oath while gazing at the Queen's picture. It was the start of 27 years exemplary service to the Gurkhas and The British Army, during which he gained the VC, and rose to be a captain, Queen's Gurkha Officer (QGO). An outstanding record for an outstanding man.

Captain 'Kit' Maunsell, commanding C Company, 2/10 GR, was lying on a constricted path running up the narrow, almost vertical-sided ridge only 60 metres from the centre of the Indonesian hilltop position. Crouched with him were the leading scouts of 7 Platoon, while immediately to his rear were his three Gurkha platoon commanders. Behind them, a long single-file snake of 100 men sweated and waited in the dense trees and scrub. It was early afternoon on a sweltering day, the uniforms of all the soldiers lying on the hillside were black and sodden with the efforts of the previous six hours spent approaching the enemy. The operation had reached its climax; the company had succeeded in getting within striking distance without discovery. Luck had played its part, as well as skill, as no sentry seemed to have been posted on this obvious approach, not even at the two barriers of dead trees blocking the track that the leading Gurkhas had just crossed. Maunsell could see an atap-thatched roof some 50 metres up the hill, which looked to be covering a trench. As he watched, wondering how they could best set about completing their mission, which was to snatch a prisoner, an Indonesian soldier stepped out from under the roof and began to walk directly towards him. Perhaps this was the sentry who should have been guarding the path. The man came steadily forward, oblivious of the soldiers crouched in wait. At ten metres, when it seemed certain he would walk into the Gurkhas' arms, he halted, stared, then started to unsling his rifle. Maunsell, instantly aware they had been spotted, yelled 'Fire', at which the Gurkha scouts opened up with several quick shots. The Indonesian collapsed, dead. The battle for Gunong Tepoi was joined. It was to be the largest and longest action of the campaign.

It was late November, 1965, and Rambahadur, now a lance-corporal, had been with the 2/10 GR for eight years. During this time he had become familiar with jungle operations in Malaya. While on his first long (six months) home leave in 1961 he had married, although not to the girl from Sikkim, and started a family. His battalion was now based in Singapore, and after his second leave Rambahadur was able to bring his wife and small son to join him in the unit lines in Blakang Mati. In November, 1964, he left his family to join his unit in Borneo. He was posted to 7 Platoon of C Company. His platoon commander was Lieutenant (QGO) Ranjit Rai, a veteran of many years soldiering, and jungle operations in particular. Rambahadur was put in charge of a bren gun group in a section of about ten men under a full corporal. Within the section Rambahadur was responsible for ensuring the bren gave covering fire in support of the riflemen in action. Even in the close-range fighting inevitable in dense jungle, the heavy weight of fire that could be produced quickly by the bren was a critical element in the tactics of a section. Rambahadur's task involved the selection of good fire positions, directing the fire, moving the gun team, passing on the orders of his corporal, and supervising all the activities of his two-man team. If the section commander fell he took command. His two gunners were Kharbakahadur Limbu and Bijuliparsad Rai, one of whom carried and fired the bren, while the other carried the spare magazines and assisted in reloading the gun in action. Their tasks were interchangeable. The group had trained and lived together for many months before the Gunong Tepoi operation and were close friends.

By late 1965 virtually all operations were of the Claret type. This was despite the fact that Major-General Walker, and his recent successor Major-General Lea, could not count on more than 14,000 troops to cover a frontier of 1000 miles − fourteen men to a mile of some of the most remote and inaccessible terrain in the world. A combination of skilful strategic planning, the concentration of available resources in critical areas, a first-class intelligence network involving local inhabitants, the maximum effective use of limited air transport for deployment and resupply, the high level of jungle skills of the infantry and the seizing of the initiative to take the fighting over the frontier were winning the war.

In November the 2/10 GR were deployed to cover a huge area of the key First Division, around the town of Bau, at the western extremity of Sarawak (Map 12). This had always been a crucial district due to the proximity and vulnerability of the capital, Kuching, which was only 40 miles from the border. It was a tempting target for the Indonesians, not only for cross-border incursions, but for stirring up insurrection within the township. This area had seen an intensity of operations unusual in other localities. Twenty miles of frontier had to be covered, with battalion headquarters co-ordinating activities from Bau, 20 miles back from the border. There were four rifle companies and support company (Recce, Mortar and Assault Pioneer

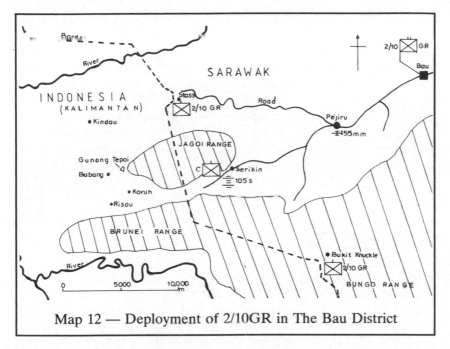

Map 12 — Deployment of 2/10GR in The Bau District

Platoons) available, together with some artillery support from a few 105mm and 155mm guns. The method of operating was to have three companies forward, with bases only a short distance behind the frontier, each with their specific area of responsibility. From these bases companies and platoons would take the war over the border to the Indonesians. By patrolling, harassing, ambushing, the aim was to keep the enemy off balance and frustrate any attempted offensive moves on his part. It was a company and platoon commanders, campaign where initiative and high standards of low-level leadership won the day.

Since 16 November Maunsell's C Company had been reinforced by the addition of the Recce and Pioneer Platoons to an overall strength of nearly 150 men. For months the company had been in the vicinity of the border in the centre of the battalion's area. The company main base camp was at Serikin (Map 12) where there were 2 x 105mm howitzers in support, 4000 metres from the frontier. To the NE, at Pejiru, a solitary 155mm gun was available, while there were other infantry company bases at Stass in the north and Bukit Knuckle to the SE. Maunsell was accompanied by the artillery FOO, Lieutenant Douglas Fox, whose task it was to control the firing of the guns by radio. C Company had been given the task of crossing into Indonesia to establish the layout of the enemy positions in the Risau-Babang complex. Weeks of careful patrolling had brought results, although

99

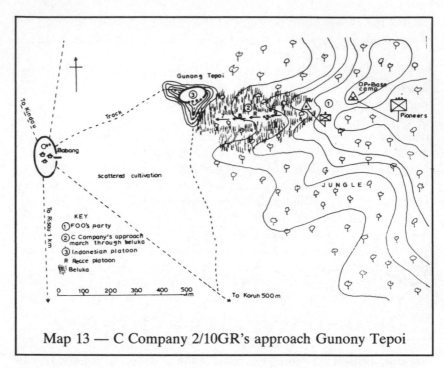

Map 13 — C Company 2/10GR's approach Gunony Tepoi

an ambush operation had been compromised by local inhabitants. Reconnaissance in October had identified what looked like a platoon position on a hill close to the village of Babang. This was Gunong Tepoi. What was needed was a prisoner who could be interrogated for information on which to base another ambush. Maunsell felt a 'snatch' on Tepoi looked promising.

On 18 November permission was given for Maunsell to plan and mount the new operation, codenamed Time Keeper. The company group moved nearer to their objective to establish a forward base just inside Sarawak, 4000-5000 metres east of Tepoi. From there an excellent OP was found, across the border, only 1000 metres from the objective. It offered a clear view of Tepoi and the nearby hamlets of Babang, Koruh and Risau. From this OP Maunsell and his platoon commanders could study the enemy's activities, and devise a plan of attack (Map 13).

Maunsell was looking down into the relatively low-lying area at the western end of the Jagoi range of mountains. Here were a few scattered villages and areas of shifting cultivation. Tepoi was an isolated hill at the western tip of the range. It was in the locality of what was called the 'J' battalion of the Indonesian Army, which had troops with mortars in Babang, Koruh and Risau. The previous Gurkha patrol clashes and ambushes had

100

alerted the enemy, so it was going to be difficult to achieve surprise. The aim was to grab a prisoner and get out without disturbing the whole hornets' nest.

Tepoi was about 500 feet high, the top relatively open with scrub and a few trees, while the sides were covered with dense beluka and tangled secondary jungle. Beluka is giant fern, which grows, thickly matted, to heights of 10-12 feet. It is one of the most difficult obstacles to penetrate. Not only does it hold the heat like an oven, but it is resistant to hacking with machetes. One method of progress is for the leading soldier to hold his rifle in both hands above his head and fall forward, the beluka bending beneath his weight. This is repeated again and again, with the leading man being changed every few minutes. Both chopping it and falling on it are noisy, which prohibits their use near the enemy. Whatever method is used is agonisingly slow and can be dangerously dehydrating. Maunsell estimated there would be 800 metres of beluka and secondary jungle on their approach march.

Another problem was the hill itself. The word 'gunong' means a hill with precipitous sides, and Tepoi was aptly named. It was a vaguely T-shaped feature with all approaches, except three, seemingly sheer and impossible to climb without early discovery (Map 13). Two exceptions were up steep tracks that climbed the razor-sharp ridges forming the NW arm and southern stem of the T. The former led down to Babang, some 500 metres away, the latter to Koruh, about twice that distance from the hill. As Maunsell appreciated, these were the routes that the garrison on the hill used and so would surely merit sentry posts. Perhaps they could snatch a sentry. The third possibility was the right (eastern) arm or ridge which did not carry a path, but pointed towards the border. This being the obvious enemy approach, and not used by the Indonesians, meant that it could well be mined. For this reason Maunsell discounted it. Careful observation indicated that there were probably 30-40 men on the hill. The afternoon seemed to be the quietest period and some troops had been seen disappearing into a patch of primary jungle still standing between Babang and Koruh ridges during that time. Perhaps they may have been going to wash in the stream at the foot of the hill.

Maunsell considered that it was the Babang ridge track that was the most heavily used by the enemy, as the village was close and it was probably the company based there that supplied the platoon on Tepoi. This left the Koruh ridge track as the best approach route, but, like the others, it was so narrow there would only be room for three or four men abreast. The whole strike force would have to advance in single file.

The plan envisaged taking all the platoons, except the Pioneers who would remain to protect the base camp, up on to Tepoi. The order of march would be scouts, followed by Maunsell and his four platoon commanders, (so that they were immediately to hand to receive orders), then 7, 8, Recce and 9 Platoons. Three light 2-inch mortars and three general purpose machine guns (GPMGs) would travel with the last platoon, to be ready to form a fire support base as required. The FOO would come forward to a suitable spot from where he could watch events and control the gunfire. Pre-arranged targets of known or likely enemy positions in and around the villages were agreed and on immediate call. Although only a raid to take a prisoner, Maunsell was venturing into a battalion defensive area and had no way of knowing if he could achieve surprise and succeed without arousing strong opposition. This was the reason for taking over 100 men.

The intention was to move on a compass bearing from the OP area to hit the Koruh ridge track near the foot of the hill, then follow it cautiously upwards to the enemy. The plan could only take them thus far. What happened then would be dependent on what they found on Tepoi. The worst part of the operation would probably be getting through the beluka. This had to be done slowly and silently. The two leading soldiers would each have a pair of garden secateurs with which carefully to clip the fern to make a narrow tunnel. Creeping along behind would be the entire force, stretching back for almost 200 metres. To allow sufficient time to arrive in the early afternoon of the 21st meant starting out at dawn.

Like many Gurkhas, Rambahadur has a fatalistic streak in his character and believes in the significance of dreams. During the night before this battle he dreamt he was leading his men when they were confronted by an arc of fire his section shrank from entering, but Rambahadur was drawn forward into the heart of the heat, feeling nothing. The next morning his two gunners seemed abnormally subdued over their breakfast brew of tea. Bijuliparsad, who was a big eater, just picked at his food saying he felt unwell. Rambahadur recalled: 'I clearly noticed something was wrong because he looked unusually sad and uncomfortable.'[6] He wondered whether his dream had been some sort of premonition.

The company had started out at 6.00 am and halted for a light meal in the jungle near the OP position. Here the Pioneer Platoon, under Sergeant Dhankarna Rai, was left to form a rear base and to act as a radio relay station, while the bulk of the force continued for another 400 metres to a suitable spot for the company RV. This was the place at which the assault platoons, or individuals, would rally if things went badly wrong and subunits became scattered. There was a good view over the area of operations, so the FOO and his party remained here with a section from 9 Platoon for protection, under the command of CSM Indrahang Limbu.

Rambahadur and his bren group were part of the leading section of 7 Platoon, so near the head of the column as it began the exhausting task of cutting through the beluka. Progress was painfully slow — a pace or two, then halt while the men at the front clipped a passage, then another few steps. The heat was horrific, and once inside the tunnel the air dry, dusty and furnace-like. Pores opened; sweat flowed in streams. The Gurkhas needed all their stamina, especially those carrying radios, machine guns and the extra mortar bombs. To make 150 metres an hour was good going through beluka.

At around 1.30 pm they struck the Koruh ridge track near the base of the hill. The navigation had been spot on, as had the estimate of time and distance. At this stage Maunsell whispered to Lieutenant (QGO) Puransing Limbu, commanding 9 Platoon and the fire support group of mortars and GPMGs, to bring his men up and occupy a position on the end of the ridge, with the mortars located at the end of the tunnel. It was his task to take on any counter-attacks from Babang, Koruh, or elsewhere. Only when this platoon was firm could Maunsell continue towards the enemy. As the remainder filed silently past the mortars those Gurkhas carrying extra bombs gratefully shed their load.

Maunsell had been right about the narrowness of the ridge. There was barely room for four men abreast, so any flanking move or deployment, before they reached the Indonesian position where the summit levelled out, was impossible. Along this steep path through the secondary jungle an uphill frontal charge by a handful of men was the best they could do. Thus far the plan had worked perfectly — from now on Maunsell had to play it as it came.

As they crept warily up the hill the enemy position was only 100 metres away. Within a short distance the scouts bumped a barrier of dead trees blocking the ridge. As they started to work their way through, a noise of rustling leaves beyond made them freeze into the undergrowth. They waited tensely for somebody to appear, Maunsell hoping he would, as it could provide an ideal opportunity to grab a prisoner and thus complete his task. After some twenty minutes the noises ceased and the Indonesian could be glimpsed through the trees and scrub making his way back to the summit. Maunsell signalled to advance again. There was a second barrier of trees, on which the enemy soldier had been working, just beyond the first. Shortly after this a second man was seen to leave the hut and approach. A moment later the shots that started the battle rang out.

Surprise had gone. Maunsell ordered Ranjit to assault the hut immediately to the front, which he did, storming uphill with four soldiers, hurling grenades as he went and killing the occupants. Maunsell, with his radio operator, moved forward to a position just beyond the captured hut to control the battle. By now heavy fire from rifles and machine guns was coming from the more open ground around the hilltop and the leading Gurkhas

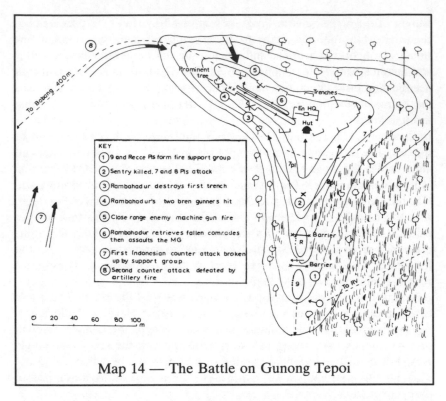

KEY

1. 9 and Recce Pls form fire support group
2. Sentry killed. 7 and 8 Pls attack
3. Rambahadur destroys first trench
4. Rambahadur's two bren gunners hit
5. Close range enemy machine gun fire
6. Rambahadur retrieves fallen comrades then assaults the MG
7. First Indonesian counter attack broken up by support group
8. Second counter attack defeated by artillery fire

Map 14 — The Battle on Gunong Tepoi

had to take cover (Map 14). Realizing instantly that the company could achieve nothing bunched up on the narrow ridge, Maunsell shouted to Ranjit with 7 Platoon to take the left and for Lieutenant (QGO) Bhagatbahadur, with 8 Platoon to go right. The wisdom of having his platoon commanders to hand was apparent. One of 8 Platoon's riflemen caught a full burst of automatic fire, killing him instantly; another fell wounded. There was a pause in the attack as platoon and section commanders strove to get their men forward, while the enemy fire intensified. Maunsell yelled for covering fire, and began to crawl towards the wounded soldier, reached him, and dragged him back down the slope to the right, before returning to the hut. Their company commander's gallantry inspired a determined effort from both the forward platoons. Bhagat's men surged forward on the right, firing from the hip, to secure some trenches on that flank.

On the left Ranjit had ordered Rambahadur's section forward, towards several trenches and a troublesome machine gun. Seeing the machine gun, Rambahadur, with his two gunners, charged forward and silenced the gun with a well-placed grenade into the trench. His assault produced a storm of firing from at least two more machine guns further up the hill. The

104

weight of this fire forced Rambahadur and his bren group to take cover in the trench. He appreciated that the machine guns were the key to the enemy defences on this part of the hill, so he resolved to attack them. Yelling 'Come on' Rambahadur leapt from cover and the three men dashed towards a large tree some 25 metres away. Near the tree another trench was seen and one of his comrades dropped a grenade into it as he passed. At that moment their luck ran out. An Indonesian in the trench, too scared to show his head, raised his automatic rifle above the trench and fired a wild, blind, burst, before dying in the roar of the exploding grenade. Unfortunately his shots struck Bijuliparsad and Kharkabahadur and they both fell.

Rambahadur later described his feeling at that moment. 'Bijuliparsad was on my right hand side . . . I saw blood on his face. As soon as I saw his blood, my own blood began to boil. I swore that the enemy would pay for this with their blood . . . for a few moments I could think of nothing else.'[7] Then he realised he should inform his platoon commander what had happened. The noise of battle drowned his shouts, and anyway Ranjit was fully occupied in the centre of the position. Rambahadur, with bullets clipping the ground around him, started to crawl towards the hut, but suddenly checked himself. What about his two gunners? They were lying bleeding and totally exposed; he must try to rescue them, get them out of the line of fire. He tried crawling towards them. This drew fierce fire from point-blank range. He realized that to continue crawling was certain death. To reach his friends required speed, to give the enemy marksmen a fast-moving target. He stood up and dashed forward, snatched up one of the bodies, turned and half-ran, half-staggered across some 50-60 metres of bullet-swept ground to the hut. Then, without the slightest hesitation, he ran back for the other soldier. Once more the tottering run with his comrade on his back, once more the expectation of bullets smashing into him every second of the way. But his luck held, and he made it to the hut a second time. To his enormous disappointment both his bren-gunners were dead.

By anybody's standards Rambahadur had done enough, but he did not stop there. Next, he returned across the same ground, through the same hail of machine-gun bullets to retrieve the bren gun. This time several other riflemen joined him. Rambahadur picked up the bren to lead a last, furious rush on the enemy position that had killed his friends, firing long bursts from the hip as he did so. In the close-quarter combat that ensued Rambahadur personally killed four Indonesians. The machine guns were silenced. He had continuously exposed himself to protracted, close-range fire for twenty minutes and come through without a scratch. Little wonder Maunsell considered it a miracle. Typically, Rambahadur explained his survival with great modesty: 'The bullets whizzed past over my head. Fortunately the bullets always tend to travel higher if not correctly aimed, and it is not always easy to aim correctly in real action at moving human targets. A man with small stature like me has, therefore, some advantage.'[8] Perhaps his presentiment after his dream was justified, thinking back on it Rambahadur certainly thought so.

There was still a lot of fighting to do. Rambahadur participated in it when Maunsell switched 7 Platoon from the left over to the right, to out-flank the stiff resistance in front of Bhagat's platoon. There was no stop-ping the Gurkhas now, and within the hour the position was theirs. A series of counter-attacks then began from the direction of Babang. 9 Platoon on the Koruh ridge was reinforced by the Recce Platoon under Lieutenant (QGO) Bhuwansing Limbu, and they, together with the three GPMGs, had a field day blazing away at the advancing enemy. Corporal Krishnabahadur Rai fired a 150-round belt in one burst, and the mortars lobbed bombs as fast as they could be dropped down the tubes.

The Indonesians then regrouped to the north and NE of Tepoi, which effectively screened them from the Gurkha fire base on the Koruh ridge. This counter-attack was better co-ordinated, with at least seventy enemy troops trying to climb up the precipitous northern ridge. Maunsell called for artillery support and Fox quickly got the guns into action. The first rounds were short; one piece of shrapnel smashed into a tree trunk a few feet above Maunsell's head. He radioed the adjustment and from then on the shells were on target, breaking up the attack.

Maunsell decided it was time to go. Although he had not got a prisoner his action had killed at least twenty-four Indonesians, probably many more. A decisive defeat had been inflicted in their own territory at a cost of three Gurkhas dead and two wounded, one of whom was in a critical condition and would need carrying out. Maunsell sent 8 Platoon off first, carrying the stretcher case and the dead. The entire platoon took turns at humping these awkward burdens, teams changing every ten minutes. The remainder of the company held the hill to allow time for the wounded to get back to the RV. During this time the enemy kept up their fire, with the mortars in Koruh and Risau joining in. Both the summit of the hill and the withdrawal route were hit. The FOO, with consummate skill, switched the fire of the three guns on to all these targets, eventually silencing them. The Gurkhas left about 90 minutes after the first shot was fired and successfully withdrew back across the border. The seriously injured soldier was saved.

Rambahadur seems to belong to those stoical soldiers who believe that fate has decided when they will die and that there is little they can do about it. They contend that they will go when 'their number is up' and that's that

– a fatalistic view that undoubtedly fortifies some warriors. Years after the battle on Tepoi his comment on his astonishing good fortune in escaping unhurt was 'I was under the shower of bullets, but not a single bullet had my name written on it. I feel sometimes that I am going to outlive all my contemporaries by many years. I may even outlive my own children! God forbid it.' By his own admission anger was the first emotion that motivated him that afternoon. Rage at seeing his two friends struck down had the effect, at least momentarily, of driving out any fear for his own safety. This was quickly supplanted by a grim determination to save his comrades. He was able to forget his fear, forget the seemingly impossible odds and forget any possible military duties that he should perhaps have tried to do. His friends were down, nothing else mattered except to get them out, and he recklessly risked his own life to do so. The story of hundreds of VC winners are similar, but no less outstanding for that. Self-sacrifice is perhaps the greatest of man's virtues, and self-sacrifice unto death the supreme example of it. In Rambahadur's case this was not all. Having accomplished his rescue he returned to the battle, relentlessly resolved to destroy the enemy who had killed his men. Having survived so far, he continued to act with complete contempt for anything the enemy might do. He exposed himself again to collect the bren gun, and then, with the very weapon that been used by his comrades, proceeded to attack the machine guns and trenches from which they had been hit. He succeeded in leading this assault and in personally accounting for four of his adversaries. This part of his action was a display of deadly determination to fight professionally and coolly to even the score.

Rambahadur's performance ensured the defeat of the enemy on the left flank of the hill. He was responsible for killing five or six soldiers, and his actions were instrumental in accounting for the three machine guns that formed the core of the defence of that area. His gallantry had inspired all who saw it, particularly among 7 Platoon who were able to be switched to the right to clear the final trenches in front of 8 Platoon.

Two months later the 2/10 GR returned to their Singapore base at the completion of an unsurpassed operational tour. As getting approval for awards is a lengthy process, and highly confidential, Rambahadur had no inkling as to what was in store. His return home was, for him, far more devastating than anything the Indonesians could have done. It was five months since his wife had given birth to his second son, and she complained to Rambahadur of stomach pains. She was admitted to the British Military Hospital on 2 February, 1966. Within four days she died. Rambahadur has recorded his feeling. 'I was with her when she died. I had never thought she would die that way, talking to me to the very last minute. Her voice trailed. She could say no more. She looked at me and made an effort to give me a smile . . . She breathed hard and her head rolled on one side. That was the end. She was dead . . . It was the darkest day of my life.' When a doctor asked Rambahadur to sign an authorisation for a post-mortem he 'shouted like a madman', wanting to know why they had not operated to make her well, and what was the use of cutting her up now. He raged at them in Gurkhali, which they did not understand.[9]

Rambahadur's life was empty. He reported that he wished to leave the Army, to take his sons home to Nepal and put them into their mother's parents' care. The authorities were vague. While Rambahadur was going through this traumatic period the wheels were moving to get him his VC. Initially, Maunsell, thinking that as it was a Claret operation in an undeclared war no VC could be awarded, wrote out a citation for the DCM. This was soon changed, although it had to be carefully worded so as to give no hint as to the true location of the action.

In April the battalion received word that the Army Commander, Lieutenant-General Sir Alan Jolly, was to address the 2/10 at a formal parade on the evening of the 22nd. The battalion was formed up in hollow square, with the Pipes and Drums, facing a saluting dais. Colonel Myers was commanding the parade. In the front rank was Rambahadur, who, although he knew he was to receive some sort of award thought it would be a MID. A large crowd of spectators had gathered to watch. The Army Commander duly arrived, Myers called the parade to attention, then ordered the General Salute before marching forward to report to Jolly, who approached the microphone. He came straight to the point.

> 'Lance Corporal Rambahadur Limbu: Her Majesty, Queen Elizabeth the Second has graciously approved the award of the Victoria Cross to you for valour against the enemy on 21 November 1965 . . . You are the thirteenth Gurkha to receive it . . . The story of your bravery will soon be known all over the world . . . Nepal will be proud of you as we of the British Army are proud of you . . . It is the Queen's wish to invest you with the Cross at her Palace in London.'[10]

Rambahadur, who had been called forward to stand in front of the General, remained rigid, with an almost unblinking stare, determined not to show any emotion, although those who watched him closely noted a slight flicker of a smile cross his face.[11]

Rambahadur's visit to Britain started on 31 May and lasted for five memorable weeks. Accompanied by Maunsell, who acted as guide and interpreter, he was taken on a grand tour of London, Scotland, where they stayed in Edinburgh Castle, and on a series of official and semi-official functions that might have daunted a lesser man. The London Stock Exchange stopped working to cheer him on his visit there − a unique first. The climax was the

Investiture on 12 July. He described it thus: 'Then came 12 July, 1967 – a most important and memorable day in my life. Not because I was given the medal that day, but because I had the most wonderful opportunity of seeing Her Majesty The Queen with my own eyes. I could hardly stand to attention properly with excitement. I just could not believe the dazzling beauty of Buckingham Palace. Everything I saw there was beyond my belief. I wondered if I was not dreaming. The moment of my life came when Her Majesty came right in front of me and spoke to me. Although our Colonel Wylie was there to translate for me, Her Majesty was directly looking at me, and spoke to me with her very soft voice. As I was nervous or perhaps too excited, I cannot recall the words exchanged between Her Majesty and myself.'[12]

The Queen noticed he had brought his five-year-old son, Bhakte, and expressed a wish to see him. Afterwards he was taken to see her in a private room, but was too overwhelmed to be on his best behaviour. Rambahadur described what happened: 'Later I was told, to my utter dismay, that Bhakte was reluctant to greet Her Majesty The Queen. Not only that, but this stupid boy also produced a roll of caps in front of Her Majesty, and played with it, thereby causing Her Majesty to make the comment, "I hope he has not brought the gun as well!" '

For seventeen years, after Speakman's retirement in 1968, Rambahadur was the only serving holder of the VC in the British Army. During that time he had his medals stolen and replaced, and worked his way up through the ranks, ending his career as a captain (QGO). The Queen was to decorate him again, making him a Member of the Victorian Order (MVO), after he had completed a year as one of her Queen's Gurkha Orderly Officers. Within the Brigade of Gurkhas he was affectionately known as 'VC Sahib'. On 25 March, 1985, Rambahadur's battalion paraded at Church Crookham to say their final farewell to their hero. After 27 years Rambahadur was retiring. Scores of congratulatory messages had been received from humble unknown admirers, as well as the most eminent. The Queen responded to a farewell message from Rambahadur saying: 'I too am sad that you are leaving the Gurkhas. I send my thanks for your years of distinguished and gallant service, and my warm good wishes for your future.'

'VC Sahib' left the barracks in traditional style, garlanded and standing up in an open Landrover pulled by more than thirty officers and men of the 10th GR. At the gates a quarter-guard presented arms and Rambahadur dismounted to inspect them. Then, to the strains of Auld Lang Syne and a fanfare of trumpets, this most remarkable of men passed through to the other side, for his flight home to Nepal.

One of the soldiers seeing him off was his eldest son, Bhakte, then a lance corporal, as his father had been 19 years before. At the time of writing

Bhakte is a platoon sergeant and his son, Chandraprakash, is a signaller with the Queen's Gurkha Signals.

Rambahadur did not remain a civilian for long. He was given a contract to serve in the Sultan of Brunei's Gurkha Reserve Unit, which is commanded by a retired British Gurkha officer, but is otherwise entirely composed of Gurkha ex-soldiers. Its chief function is the protection of the Sultan and various key points. Rambahadur, whose contract expires in 1992, is presently commanding B Company. When his time is up he intends to run an ex-servicemen's welfare fund in Nepal, and has already started to raise capital.

Major-General G.D. Johnson OBE MC, Colonel of the Regiment, summed up Rambahadur's service with these words: 'For twenty years "VC Sahib" served in the spotlight. He has walked with the greatest in the land, and been feted wherever he went, and endured the constant curiosity of the public. It would have turned the head of a lesser man, but throughout it all Rambahadur, aided by an immense natural dignity and simplicity of demeanour maintained a steady path . . . He has been a marvellous ambassador for his race and his nation, for our Regiment, and for the British Army.'[13]

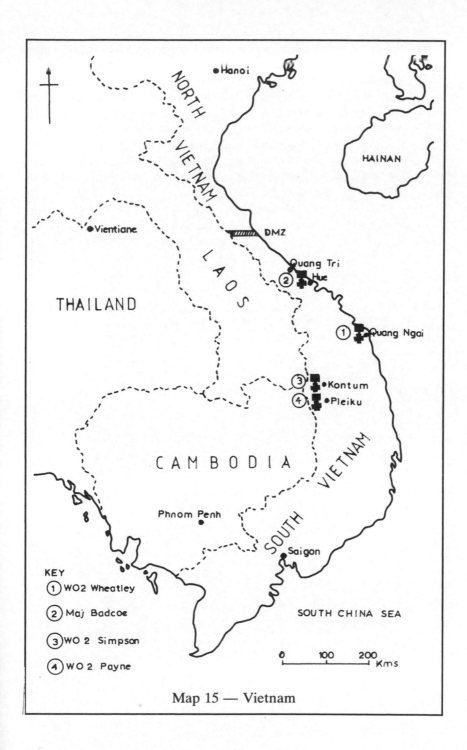

Map 15 — Vietnam

PART THREE

Vietnam

It is not often remembered that Australia had troops in Vietnam for well over ten years, almost as long as the Americans. The first group, of over thirty officers and NCO advisers, flew to Saigon on a Pan Am flight from Singapore on 3 August, 1962. Boarding in civilian clothes, they monopolized the toilets for much of the journey, as they took turns to change into uniform. On arrival they were escorted to the VIP lounge to be welcomed by the Australian Ambassador.

Years later, it was also Saigon that saw the end of the Australian commitment when Sergeant Bernie Boon from Queensland slowly and sombrely lowered his national flag from over the Free World Headquarters building. That was on 18 December, 1972. After that the only Australian troops in the country were those on duty as embassy guards. It was the end of Australia's longest war, although no war had ever been declared.

During the campaign Australia sent 47,000 men to Vietnam, 95 per cent of whom were soldiers, for one-year tours. All nine battalions of the RAR served there. Three of them completed two tours. Numerous individuals volunteered again and again, some serving for over three years. It was a war that saw conscription introduced, with national servicemen patrolling the villages, rice paddies and jungle alongside their regular comrades. In October, 1967, at the height of Australian involvement, there were nearly 8,000 servicemen in the country. In all 519 were killed in action and 2398 wounded.

As in the United States, it was not until the war was perceived as endless, unwinnable, and the media had brought the horrors of conflict on to television screens, that the anti-war protests gained momentum. These started early in 1968, after the Tet offensive had been defeated on the battlefield, but had been cleverly promoted as a psychological victory for the Viet Cong. The press continued to add fuel to the fire lit by the draft dodgers and anti-war students who marched through the cities carrying placards proclaiming: 'Hell no, we won't go'. A Melbourne newspaper carried the headline: 'Australian Battalion Wiped Out', when only five men had been killed. Some students went so far as to send money and cigarettes to the Viet Cong. The 50,000 demonstrators who blocked the Melbourne shopping centre in late 1970 were in marked contrast to the 300,000 Sydney-siders who had provided a tumultuous welcome home for 1 RAR in 1966. They had fought in a 'good' war, backed by 70 per cent of the population. Those returning later were, at best, ignored by a people who wanted to forget a war that was ending in defeat.

Not until 1987 were Australian Vietnam veterans able to march as a body again on Anzac Day parades. The similarity between the reception of American and Australian servicemen is striking. More than a decade was needed for public opinion, in both countries, to recognize that these men had done their duty with gallantry and distinction.

The four Australians who won the VC in Vietnam belonged to The Team, the name adopted by the successors of those first thirty men who had gone in 1962, sometimes nicknamed 'the last 100' or 'the expendables'. With their motto 'Persevere', they became a unique military unit. Officially designated the Australian Army Training Team Vietnam (AATTV), the Team was composed of officers and warrant officers, all volunteers, whose task, at the outset, was to assist in the training of local forces alongside the US Special Forces. Soon their role expanded, as did their strength, to include accompanying Army of the Republic of Vietnam (ARVN) units and Special Forces (SF) in the field as advisers. In many instances in combat they took command, as the stories that follow illustrate. Members were scattered in penny packets throughout the country, but predominantly in the north. They built up a reputation second to none. Their expertise in patrolling, small unit tactics and the techniques of jungle ambush gained great respect. They were to be found, with their US counterparts, deep in the mountainous jungle, in remote camps, well away from the main military bases. They worked with the ARVN, the Montagnard tribesmen, the Territorial Forces and local civilian community leaders.

The Team was the first unit into, and the last unit out of, Vietnam. This made it the longest serving unit in any theatre of war. Almost 1,000 men served in the Team, while its roll of honour lists 33 killed in action and 122

15. Major P. J. Badcoe. *(Australian War Memorial)*

16. Major Badoe's widow, Mrs Denise Badcoe, receiving her husband's VC from the Governor-General of Australia, Lord Casey. *(Australian Department of Foreign Affairs)*

17. Warrant Officer Class 2 R.S. Simpson. *(Australian War Memorial)*

18. Simpson receives his VC from Queen Elizabeth at Government House, Sydney. He was then within a day or so of finally retiring from the Army. *(Australian Department of Foreign Affairs)*

19. Warrant Officer Class 2 K. Payne VC. *(Australian Army)*

20. Payne receives his VC from Queen Elizabeth on board the Royal Yacht, *Britannia. (Australian Army)*

wounded. In addition to the four VCs, another 107 gallantry or distingui-shed service decorations were bestowed, excluding the 243 US and 376 Republic of Vietnam awards. In 1970 the US conferred on the Team its Army Meritorious Unit Commendation, and the following year Vietnam its Cross of Gallantry with Palm Unit Citation.

The stories of the four Australians that follow are unique in more ways than one. Not only were their actions exceptional in a fraternity where the outstanding is the norm, but they were, until recently, the last Australians who could receive the VC. This followed the Australian Government's decision in 1975 to replace the old British Empire honours with national ones. Now their highest bravery decoration became the Cross of Valour (CV), followed by the Star of Courage (SC), the Bravery Medal (BM) and the Commendation for Brave Conduct (CBC). These differ from the British system in that there is no stipulation that the CV can only be won in the presence of the enemy, so it, and the others, lost their battlefield only dis-tinction. The regulations state that the CV is awarded for 'acts of the most conspicuous courage in circumstances of extreme peril'.

For fourteen years the VC could not be won by an Australian service-man. However, pressure to reverse this decision eventually became irresist-ible. The new award could not match the VC's unrivalled prestige, its long history, and its battlefield-only criteria. To exclude Australians seemed to many unjust. Their views have prevailed. In 1989 Her Majesty The Queen agreed, following a submission from the Australian authorities, that the VC should be restored as Australia's highest decoration for courage in com-bat.

Of the four Australians only Warrant Officer Keith Payne is alive at the time of writing, 21 years after winning his VC.

CHAPTER 6

Tra Bong Valley, South Vietnam
13 November, 1965

WARRANT OFFICER 2 KEVIN ARTHUR WHEATLEY VC
Australian Army Training Team – Vietnam

'Greater love hath no man than this
That he lay down his life'.
The epitaph on Warrant Officer Wheatley's grave at Pine Grove
Memorial Park, Blacktown, New South Wales.

Warrant Officer 'Dasher' Wheatley and Warrant Officer 'Butch' Swanton were buddies. The buddy system was of immense importance to soldiers in Vietnam, particularly for American or Australian advisers who invariably went into action in pairs with indigenous troops, often of dubious reliability. It involved pairing with a comrade, the cementing of a friendship in a combat situation, the sharing of danger, food, accommodation and off-duty time. It was a relationship essential for the morale of both. Each knew that his buddy would stay with him to the end, even unto death. They would promise never to leave a battlefield without the other and would often entrust their comrade with burial arrangements in case one survived. It formed a bond that was seldom broken; if both lived through the war it could last a lifetime. This comradeship, created between soldiers who lived and fought together, frequently isolated from their fellow countrymen for months at a time, was a very personal thing. The knowledge that he could rely totally on his friend was a great comfort to an adviser in Vietnam. Ultimately he fought for his friend, not for his unit or South Vietnam, in order not to break faith. The buddy system was the root cause behind countless acts of courage.

The story of 'Dasher' Wheatley is unique among the post-war VCs in that it is the only one in which the recipient deliberately chose to die with his wounded friend when escape was possible. When all his efforts to save Swanton had failed, when the enemy were closing in, when he was urged by a South Vietnamese soldier to flee, Wheatley opted to stay, knowing full well that almost certain death was only moments away.

Wheatley was 28 years old when he gave his life in the jungle fringe of a rice paddy. In the comparatively short time of nine years as a soldier, Wheatley had done exceptionally well. Not many reached warrant officer rank as quickly. As a young lad he had worked as a milkman, machine operator and brick burner, before enlisting in June, 1956, at nineteen. Wheatley was a natural soldier. Although short and stocky, he was pugnacious, tough, well able to look after himself and an extremely determined fighter with the inborn ability to get others to follow him. He was very much a 'hands on' leader, thoroughly professional, with a hard exterior. But underneath the 'wild man of action', as his wife described him, was a 'rough diamond, very soft hearted [who] always thought of himself least'.

Wheatley had met Edna when he was a mild roundsman and she worked as a waitress in a Sydney milkbar. Although she was only 14 and he 17, they were married in July, 1954. Financial difficulties led him to join the Army, though his family had been closely connected with the military. His father had served in the Second World War and his elder brother had also enlisted but was tragically killed in a bren gun accident in 1952. Service in the 4th, 3rd, 2nd and 1st battalions of the RAR followed, including two years in Malaya, which gave him valuable jungle experience that he was later to use in Vietnam.

Never a man to avoid a scrap, or an aggressive game of rugby football, as his broken nose proved, Wheatley was, nevertheless, a family man with a great love for children. This affection came through again and again in Vietnam. He always had time for a joke, to hand out candy, to teach them questionable Aussie phrases, or to ensure they got treatment if sick. He taught the Vietnamese kids that 'Ned Kelly' was an Australian greeting, and got much pleasure from their friendly waves and shrill cries of 'Hi Ned Kelly' as he walked or drove through a village near his camp.

During his first few months in Vietnam, Wheatley served as an adviser with an ARVN battalion and quickly established his reputation for courage and his love for children. Once, when a Vietnamese woman with three children was forced to take cover in the roadside from heavy machine-gun fire, Wheatley risked his life to save the three-year-old girl who had suddenly run screaming on to the road. He ignored the bullets, leapt to his feet, rushed forward to grab the girl and, shielding her with his body, brought her back to safety. It was typical Dasher.

In October, 1965, Wheatley and Swanton, along with five other Australians, arrived at the Tra Bong camp to replace seven other Australians whose tours had ended. They formed the majority of the Special Forces A Team at the base, under the command of Captain Felix Fazekas, a Hungarian who had fought Russian tanks as a teenager, but who was now an

Australian. The team consisted of four American and seven Australian advisers. An A Team was, and is, an American concept. It consists of a group of 10-12 warrant officers or senior NCOs, each of whom has a particular military expertise or responsibility. There will be medical, radio, engineer, intelligence, demolition and heavy weapons specialists, under the detachment commander and his deputy. The team's task at Tra Bong was to advise and assist the garrison of Vietnamese and Montagnard troops in dominating the Tra Bong valley, with its rice fields and scattered hamlets (see p.160). Their mission was to obtain intelligence on Viet Cong activities and protect the people in the villages from enemy infiltration and control. This entailed extensive and continuous patrolling.

At the Tra Bong base were the Australia/US A Team, a Vietnamese Special Forces A Team under 2nd Lieutenant Quang, with a company of Vietnamese, and another of Montagnard tribesmen, both from the Civil Irregular Defence Group (CIDG). In November, 1965, the camp had been in existence for over a year, during which time the defences had been strengthened to include a central, underground, concrete bunker with above-ground observation. From here the advisers could hold out for several days if the camp was overwhelmed. Months of extensive patrolling into the hills, and up and down the valley, had confirmed the enemy presence in the area. It had also persuaded many of the local inhabitants to move closer to the base for protection − an encouraging sign.

Fazekas and his team faced difficulties typical of all Special Forces' bases in Vietnam (Map 16). Tra Bong was isolated, entirely dependent on a small airstrip for resupply or reinforcement. The strip was impossible to defend with the forces available and the narrow valley was enclosed to the north and south by 900-metre-high, jagged, jungle-covered mountains. The settlements clung to the single dirt road that followed the 10-mile valley floor, just south of the Tra Co/Tra Dong river. At its widest point the valley was only 1000 metres across, making troops moving by vehicle prime ambush targets. Perhaps the greatest problem was the invidious one of uncertainty as to the reliability of the local CIDG soldiers. Almost inevitably a few would be communist sympathizers, some would be neutral, waiting to see who would gain the upper hand, while others would only fight well in favourable circumstances. For the Australian and American advisers there was always the uneasy feeling that if serious opposition was encountered they would be on their own. Hence the importance of having a buddy, and the concrete bunker in the centre of the base. At this stage of the war the advisers could not command, could not order the local troops to follow a particular plan. They were restricted to advising, persuading, encouraging and demonstrating by personal example how to conduct operations. If these methods failed to prevent tactical errors they could not enforce their views;

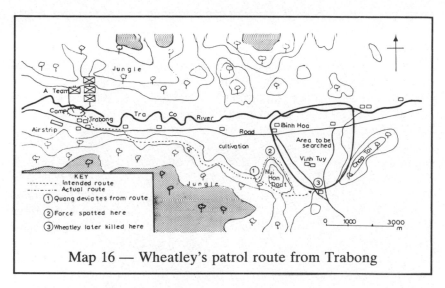

Map 16 — Wheatley's patrol route from Trabong

they could only threaten to refuse to accompany the local troops on a particularly foolhardy operation. Such a withholding of support was done with great reluctance, and only as a last resort, as it undermined the trust between advisers and advised that had to be built up gradually, and then sustained.

Captain Fazekas planned a two-day search-and-clear operation for 13 and 14 November. Some 10 kilometres down the valley to the east was a triangular area of rice paddies, hamlets and low hills that he felt certain harboured Viet Cong. Troops from Tra Bong had not previously ventured that far in strength, so it was considered necessary to take as strong a force as possible. A company, reinforced by elements of the combat reconnaissance platoon and the support weapons platoon, would make up the patrol. Actual command would rest with 2nd Lieutenant Quang, although Fazekas would accompany him. The other advisers going on the mission were Wheatley, Swanton and Staff Sergeant Theodore Sershen USSF.

Fazekas discussed the proposed plan with Quang, who agreed the timings and approach route (Map 16). It was imperative that the force arrived in the operational area undetected by villagers. This meant that movement along the road, or across the paddy fields, in daylight was impossible. The force would leave camp an hour before dawn on the 13th, then, before it was light, move off the road into the jungle fringes to the south.

By following the lower contours of the hills it should be possible to remain hidden from the workers in the fields and reach the search area by

119

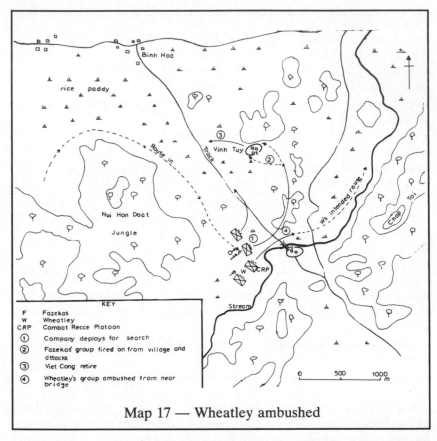

Map 17 — Wheatley ambushed

early afternoon. The objective was bounded in the north by the road, the eastern side by the Chap Toi and the western by the Nui Hon Doat mountains. Each side of the triangle measured about 3000 metres. Inside it were the hamlets, jungle-covered low hills and rice fields to be searched.

For five hours all went well, as the column wriggled its way quietly in single file through the jungle. At 10.00 am, as they reached the foot of the Nui Hon Doat mountain, a serious error was made. The company halted for a brief rest while the company commander, Quang, and Fazekas conferred on the next stage of the march. There was disagreement. Quang refused to accept the original intention to move up the nearby re-entrant, which would take them through deep jungle to the southern tip of their search area. He intended to keep following the contours around the northern edge of the mountain. This would lead them to the very edge of the cultivated areas and only a few hundred metres from habitation. It was unnecessarily risky. It was inviting discovery, but Quang was adamant.

120

Fazekas reluctantly agreed, as his only alternative was to abandon the mission, which at this early stage was unthinkable. Within half an hour Quang led the force too near the jungle edge and they were spotted by peasants working in the rice paddies. In an area where Viet Cong influence was strong this was tantamount to announcing the operation to the enemy. It gave them two hours warning. Sufficient time to disperse or concentrate to ambush the company.

By 1.00 pm the company was at the southern start point of their objective. The search was to be conducted by each of the three platoons fanning out in different directions. With only four advisers, and as they always worked in pairs if possible, one platoon could not have an adviser accompanying it. The left rib of the fan would be a platoon, without advisers, moving up the track towards Binh Hoa village (Map 17). In the centre Quang, Fazekas and Sershen would work with the second platoon, supported by a 60mm mortar and a .30 calibre machine gun, as it moved north towards Vinh Tuy. Wheatley and Swanton would operate with the third platoon, plus the combat recce platoon, as the right hand rib of the fan as it advanced eastwards along the line of the Suoi Tra Voi stream at the foot of the Chap Toi mountain. As the operation progressed the platoons would become more and more dispersed.

Within twenty minutes of moving off the second platoon, with Quang and Fazekas, had bumped the enemy in some huts to their front. After a brief fire fight the Viet Cong fled west and the platoon moved up to start burning the huts. Then Fazekas heard a few scattered shots in the direction of Wheatley's group. Over the radio Wheatley assured his officer that all was under control. Some sixty minutes later his anguished voice was heard yelling out: 'God, somebody help us, somebody do something.' In that period the battle on the right had slithered to the brink of disaster.

Wheatley had been expecting to return to Sydney in two months' time. In anticipation of this he had drafted eleven telegrams ready to send to the Civic pub, his favourite drinking spot in Sydney. The first read: 'Ten days to Dasher Day', and so on in a countdown to his expected arrival, when the proprietor would have been instructed in the final cable to: 'Roll out the barrel, the King is here'. Tragically, he was not destined to see the Civic again.

Wheatley and Swanton were moving east, across a rice paddy, with their CIDG platoon spread out over the 250-metre-wide open field (Map 18a). On their right was the Suoi Tra Voi stream, with a bridge that carried the Binh Hoa track north, and near the bridge a small group of thatched huts and trees. On their left was a low ridge covered with patches of jungle. Plodding slowly forward, the platoon was totally exposed as it crossed the track north of the bridge. At about 1.20 pm all heard bursts of firing to

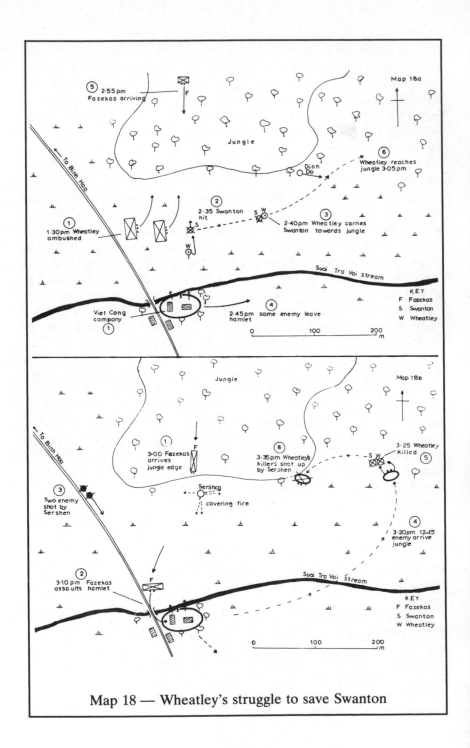

Map 18 — Wheatley's struggle to save Swanton

Map 18a

⑤ 2·55 pm
Fazekas arriving

Jungle

Dinh
Do

⑥ Wheatley reaches
jungle 3·05pm

② 2·35 Swanton
hit

S W

S

③ 2·40pm Wheatley carries
Swanton towards jungle

To Binh Hoa

① 1·30pm Wheatley
ambushed

W

Suoi Tra Voi stream

KEY
F Fazekas
S Swanton
W Wheatley

Viet Cong
company
①

④ 2·45pm some enemy leave
hamlet

0   100   200
m

Jungle

Map 18b

① 3·00 Fazekas
arrives
jungle edge

F

⑥ 3·35pm Wheatley's
killers shot up
by Sershen

S W

3·25 Wheatley
killed
⑤

To Binh Hoa

③ Two enemy
shot by
Sershen

Sershen

covering fire

④ 3·20pm 12-45
enemy arrive
jungle

② 3·10pm Fazekas
assaults hamlet

F

Suoi Tra Voi stream

KEY
F Fazekas
S Swanton
W Wheatley

0   100   200
m

their left (north), beyond the ridge as Fazekas and Quang's group made contact with the Viet Cong. Almost simultaneously some shots hit the platoon from their rear, wounding one soldier. Wheatley dived for cover along with the rest before seeking to locate the enemy, return fire and organize an assault. As he was doing this Fazekas came on the radio requesting a situation report, to which Wheatley responded that things seemed under control. A few minutes later very heavy machine-gun and automatic rifle fire hit the platoon from enemy positioned in the hamlet by the bridge. They had been caught in the open by a more heavily armed force.

Wheatley realized that the platoon could not cope without assistance; many troops were not shooting back, several had been wounded, and the volume of fire sweeping the paddy told Wheatley they could have walked into a company ambush. He got back to Fazekas to urge him to come to his support. Now began a one-sided fire fight with most of the platoon's shooting being done by Wheatley and Swanton. The bulk of the CIDG troops were more intent on getting away to the north, by crawling, or in short dashes, making for the jungle edge 200 metres away. As time passed Wheatley became more and more desperate. His force had dwindled in numbers through casualties and flight, the enemy fire had not diminished and it was now thirty minutes since he had asked for help, but none had arrived. He watched as Swanton struggled to carry a wounded Vietnamese towards cover when suddenly he collapsed in the mud. Swanton's gallantry had cost him a bullet in the stomach. Wheatley jumped up, crouched low and doubled across to his fallen buddy to flop down beside him, yelling for a medic as he turned his comrade over to see the extent of his wound.

Luckily Private Vo Trong Chan, a medical orderly, was still nearby and came to dress Swanton's wound. Wheatley continued to fire at the enemy in between frantically trying to get through on the radio for an airstrike and a helicopter casualty evacuation mission for his friend. Eventually he made contact with Sershen. By now few, if any, of the platoon were still in action as the bulk had broken for cover. This left Wheatley and Swanton virtually on their own, still in the open, still under intense fire, and with Swanton semi-conscious and unable to move. Vo Trong Chan later stated: 'I told the other Australian (WO Wheatley) that the wounded Australian was nearly dead. The VC firing was very heavy and I asked the Australian (WO Wheatley) to run . . . and leave the dying Australian. He refused, and started to half drag, half carry, the wounded Australian from the open rice paddy.'[1]

It was now around 2.40 pm. Wheatley fully appreciated the deadly peril he was in, as his last radio plea had made plain. That he should leave his friend was unthinkable, so, ditching his heavy radio, he slowly began to drag the inert body through the rice towards the jungle fringe 200 metres to the north-east. It was an endless, gruelling journey, during which he presented a perfect target to his attackers, some of whom were leaving the village, possibly, he thought, in an attempt to cut him off. Although Swanton was, in all probability unconscious, although Wheatley had been told he was dying, there was still a slight chance he might live if he reached cover, if reinforce ments arrived, if a helicopter took him out and if the enemy failed to find him first. Miraculously Wheatley was not hit during those terrible 10-15 minutes out in the open. Just before the jungle was reached Private Dinh Do broke cover to assist Wheatley stagger the last few metres.

Where was the rest of the company? Where was the airstrike? Where was Fazekas? Wheatley had been heavily engaged with superior forces for well over an hour, yet he was still on his own. Why? Wheatley must surely have asked himself these questions again and again. By the time he had reached a thicket of bushes some 50 metres inside the jungle it was after 3.00 pm, probably nearly 3.15. As he laid Swanton down he could hear intense firing from the area of the bridge and hamlet, and from the jungle 200 metres to his west. It could mean that the rest of the company were at last near at hand. He could also hear shouts and crashing in the under-growth, much nearer − some Viet Cong were closing in fast.

Dinh Do was the last person, apart from the enemy, to see Wheatley alive. He subsequently described his last moments with the Australian thus: 'I helped him (WO Wheatley) in the last stages and asked him to run with us. He refused to leave his friend, and he pulled the safety pins from the two grenades he had. I started to run when the VC were about ten metres away. Then I heard two grenades explode and several bursts of fire.'[2] Wheatley was entirely alone, apart from the motionless body of his comrade, when he made his final decision. He could have escaped as Dinh Do did. He had done all that was possible to save his friend, his rifle ammunition was gone, Swanton was in all probability dead (Wheatley may have known this for certain), and the enemy were only a few metres away. There was no military objective at stake, nobody would condemn him for leaving now, nobody would witness any last sacrifice. But Wheatley would never leave a buddy. Taking a grenade in each hand, with the pins out, he sat beside Swanton's body to await the inevitable. When it came, with the Viet Cong bursting through the bushes, Wheatley threw his grenades before calmly awaiting the close-range bursts of rifle fire that struck him and Swanton in the head. His was not only an act of great devotion to a dying comrade but it was an outstanding example of an heroic triumph over the terror of death in lonely and fearful circumstances.

Quite possibly Fazekas, with at least the central platoon, could have got back to retrieve the situation had it not been for further difficulties with

Quang. Although young and inexperienced, Quang was stubborn — averse to taking advice. Perhaps he resented Fazekas' presence, perhaps his adviser's suggestions as to what to do reflected on his lack of competence. Merely to comply with the Australian's plan, or to change his own, could mean loss of face. Whatever the reason, at about 1.40 pm, when Wheatley first asked for support, Quang refused to budge. For the second time that day, and not for the last, Quang declined to follow the obvious tactical course. How many times down the years, in battles great and small, have commanders rued their failure to march to the sound of the guns?

The central group was 1000 metres north of the rice paddy in which Wheatley and Swanton were pinned. Quang, Fazekas and Sershen had crossed the ridge to their immediate south, and the platoon was taking up defensive positions near the huts of Vinh Tuy when Wheatley's first appeal for help came through. Fazekas urged Quang to gather together his force and return at once to the scene of what he considered likely to be the main action. Quang objected, and a fierce argument ensued. Time passed as Fazekas tried to galvanize Quang into action. Finally, after some forty minutes of inactivity, Fazekas resolved to take Sershen and go back to Wheatley without Quang or his men. Short of doing nothing it was his only option. As the two set off, a few of the CIDG troops came with them. Seeing the advisers pulling out stirred the remainder and they began, reluctantly, to straggle along some way behind them.

Even travelling fast it would take at least half an hour before the two advisers reached the jungle fringe north of the rice fields. They started out around 2.30 pm and had been going for fifteen minutes when Sershen, carrying the radio, heard that Swanton was down, followed by Wheatley's agitated demand for an airstrike and helicopter. Fazekas arranged both through Tra Bong. Ten minutes later came Wheatley's last frantic cry for help. When they heard this Fazekas and Sershen were only 200 metres from the rice paddy, while Wheatley was just starting to drag his friend towards cover.

As Fazekas, Sershen and about fifteen soldiers, who had kept up, burst out of the jungle they were fired on from the huts by the bridge (Map 18b). Taking cover, Fazekas called up the machine gun and mortar but neither arrived, so he engaged the enemy by the bridge with rifle fire. Several Viet Cong were seen to fall and others to run off eastwards. Neither he nor any of his small group could see Wheatley who was at that time struggling to carry Swanton the last few metres into the jungle 200 metres east of Fazekas's position. Fazekas, leaving Sershen to give covering fire, dashed forward with the handful of soldiers across the rice field, over the bridge and into the huts. A short, sharp fight ensued.

Grenades were thrown before the remaining enemy fled east, leaving their dead and several weapons behind. It was nearly 3.15 pm.

Sershen, lying on the edge of the paddy, had been busy keeping up the covering fire. He killed two enemy who foolishly came down the Binh Hoa track. Next, he spotted a group of fifteen Viet Cong approaching from the east, near the jungle edge and less than 100 metres away. He watched as the enemy reached the paddy field, bunching up behind their leader as they peered across towards Fazekas who was now reorganizing his men to return to Sershen. Sershen opened up his automatic rifle into the easy target. He poured two magazines into the group, seeing seven or eight fall as the others scattered. He could not know that he had just decimated the band that a few minutes before had killed Wheatley.

Fazekas had no idea of the whereabouts of Wheatley or Swanton. The medical evacuation helicopter arrived and took out two wounded CIDG soldiers. Fazekas told the pilot to look out for Wheatley as he took off, as it was possible he had made some sort of LZ in the area. Next, fighter bombers roared in and were directed to strafe the area of the bridge. It was then time to seach for the missing advisers. Now, for the third time, Quang was unco-operative. He announced that he was taking his men out, up the Binh Hoa track, as they had had enough for one day. No amount of persuasion could move him. Fazekas radioed Tra Bong for another company of the standby reaction company at Da Nang to be flown in. It arrived at 6.00 pm, accompanied by the American Special Forces CO at Da Nang. By the time these troops had been briefed and deployed into ambush positions it was 10.30 pm − too late to look for the missing advisers.

Early the following morning the search began. Guided by Dinh Do, Fazekas was taken to the spot where they lay, side by side in a slight hollow, in thick undergrowth.

Wheatley had given his life for his friend. He gave it although he could have escaped. His loyalty to his buddy gave him the courage to overcome the fear of death − and we know he was frightened by his last despairing radio message − and it gave him the strength to face it alone.

Sadly, if things had gone as intended, Wheatley would probably never have been called upon to make his sacrifice. Like all battles this one was full of 'ifs'. If Quang had followed the intended route out the company might not have been seen and the enemy warned in time to set up positions around the bridge. If Quang had followed advice and returned immediately to support Wheatley, his troops would certainly have arrived in time to retrieve the situation. And finally, if Fazekas had not become embroiled in attacking the hamlet by the bridge immediately after his arrival, he might have discovered Wheatley before he was killed. Ironically it is possible that it was some of the Viet Cong who fled eastwards from the village during

Fazekas' attack who discovered and shot Wheatley and Swanton. Fate can be cruel. It was a graphic example of the difficulties under which advisors served.

Wheatley had previously served with the 1st Battalion of the 1st Regiment of the 1st Infantry Division of the ARVN. He had built up a reputation as an outstanding soldier and as a cheerful, friendly man. During his service with this battalion he won the Vietnamese Order of Military Merit leading a bayonet charge. The commander of the 1st Regiment took an unprecedented step when he heard of Wheatley's and Swanton's deaths. He paraded his men for a special commemorative service on 18 November — a unique tribute that reflected the esteem that his former South Vietnamese comrades felt for Dasher.

Two days later, in Saigon, Wheatley and Swanton, who had died together, were buried together after a moving memorial service. Gathered to pay their respects were twenty members of the Team from all over the country including Brigadier Jackson, commander of the Australian Force in Vietnam, with numerous high-ranking Australian, American and Vietnamese officers. Two honour guards were provided from I RAR and a Vietnamese unit. 1 RAR bandsmen played the Last Post and Reveille. Four beautiful wreaths of fresh flowers from the Australian Minister for the Army and Government, the Vietnamese Government, the United States Special Forces and the Team were placed one by one on the flag-draped coffins. Sergeant James Sharp USMC, who had been a special buddy of Wheatley's during his earlier days in Vietnam, helped place the Team's wreath on his coffin, while tears rolled down his cheeks. Chaplain Hoffman, an Australian, conducted the service and the pallbearers were fellow warrant officers from the Team.

There were two controversies arising from Wheatley's death — his burial in Vietnam and the later award of his posthumous VC.

When Wheatley's wife, Edna, was officially notified of her husband's death she was told that, in accordance with normal policy, if she wanted him to be buried in Sydney she would have to arrange transport of the body, and pay the costs — some £250-300. This caused an immediate outcry in the press. The *Sydney Sun* highlighted the issue just five days after he was killed. It produced an immediate response from the public. A group of nine Sydney businessmen set up a committee which quickly collected sufficient funds. Mrs Wheatley was immensely grateful, as she had been determined to have the burial in his home town despite the financial sacrifice it would have entailed. Within a few days Wheatley's body, in a simple aluminium casket, was flown home for a second burial with full military

127

honours on 26 November, at the Lawn Cemetery, Pine Grove Memorial Park, near Blacktown. Wheatley's case was one of two that persuaded the Federal Government to reverse its policy on not bringing servicemen's bodies home for burial at public expense. From January, 1966, they would be brought back if their relatives so requested. The government also agreed to reimburse those families who had already paid privately.

All these events happened within a short time of Wheatley's death, long before he was awarded the VC. It was to be exactly 13 months later that this was finally gazetted. The South Vietnamese government bestowed on him the knighthood of the National Order of the Republic of Vietnam, plus the Cross of Gallantry with Palm, but the Australian government seemed to be doing nothing to recognize his gallantry.

It was not that the military failed to make the recommendation. Statements were taken from Fazekas, Vo Trong Chan and Dinh Do within two days of the action. Lieutenant-Colonel Preece, the commanding officer of the Team, and Brigadier Jackson, Commander Australian Forces, wrote up the citation and forwarded it to the Defence Department in Canberra in December, 1965. Then followed a year's delay — why? Although never officially acknowledged, there is good reason to suppose that the hold-up was a political one, in London. The Australian authorities did not have national awards at that time, so for all decorations they depended on the British government approving them, before recommending to the Queen that she grant them. Some in Australia felt strongly that several acts of gallantry in Korea had merited the VC but, despite numerous DCMs, none had been given. There was the beginnings of a growing opinion that Australia should no longer be tied to the British imperial system.

Wheatley's recommendation was a test case. If he got nothing, and as he died in action, a posthumous VC was the only real option, Australia would probably have instituted its own awards immediately, instead of waiting another ten years. In London there was delay. Britain had refused requests from the US to send troops to Vietnam (the Gurkhas had been suggested), so it was not like Korea, where Commonwealth troops fought alongside each other in the same formation. Australia had committed her troops to a foreign war allied with the US Wheatley was an adviser to a South Vietnamese unit, serving with American Special Forces. Such was the argument of those in the UK opposed to awarding the VC. It did not bear too much scrutiny, as the Royal Warrant clearly made Commonwealth servicemen eligible, no matter where they were fighting. The fact that some politicians disapproved of the war, or that Britain was not a participant, was really quite irrelevant — but sufficient to cause a protracted argument. Ultimately the Queen approved Wheatley's Cross, 'on the advice of Her Majesty's Australian Ministers', and the three subsequent Australian VCs were gazetted far more speedily.

For Edna Wheatley and her four children it was a moment of profound pride when the Prime Minister, Harold Holt, announced the award. She said: 'I'm very thrilled and I've been crying and upset, but this will make the boys in Vietnam know that they are not being forgotten. People just don't know what's going on there.'[3] Harold Wilson, the British Labour Prime Minister, cabled: 'His heroism and unflinching devotion to a wounded comrade should be a source of inspiration and pride to all Australians.' On 1 April, 1967, the Governor-General, Lord Casey, held an Investiture at which he handed the Cross to George, Wheatley's twelve-year-old son, as his mother and sisters looked on. Lord Casey said 'The Victoria Cross is the highest decoration that can be won. You must also be proud of the cir cumstances of your father's tremendous feat.' George later said he would like one day to be a cadet at Duntroon Military College. Although this did not happen, George is now deeply honoured to wear his father's medals at veterans' parades.

Wheatley is remembered in other ways. A national appeal to sportsmen in Australia raised sufficient funds for the construction of the Kevin Wheatley Memorial Stadium at Vung Tau in South Vietnam. It was built by Australian Army engineers. The Soldier's Club at the Jungle Training Centre at Canungra has been named the Kevin Wheatley Club, in line with Army practice of naming such clubs after VC winners. At Fort Bragg in the US his photograph and citation hang in the Hall of Heroes at the J. F. Kennedy Center, while his name is commemorated in the New South Wales Garden of Remembrance at Rookwood war cemetery. In 1967 a Wheatley trophy was inaugurated for an annual competition between the Australian Services Rugby Union and the Sydney Rugby Football Union. Of all the memorials this would probably have pleased him most.

As recently as 1986 former Staff Sergeant Sershen, who had probably gunned down Wheatley's killers, visited Australia for an emotional meeting with Edna. He described Dasher as: 'A good friend, and the bravest man I ever met'.[4]

CHAPTER 7

Thua Thien Province, South Vietnam
23 February, 7 March and 7 April, 1967

MAJOR PETER JOHN BADCOE VC
Australian Army Training Team — Vietnam.

'He lived and died a soldier'
The epitaph above Major Badcoe's grave at Terendak Camp
cemetery, Malaysia.

At the end of eight months' service in Vietnam the 'Galloping Major', as Peter Badcoe was aptly nicknamed, had earned the Victoria Cross, two American Silver Stars, the Purple Heart, the U.S. Air Medal, the National Order of the Republic of Vietnam (Knight), three Crosses of Gallantry (with Palm, Gold Star, and Silver Star), the Armed Forces Honour Medal 1st Class, and the Vietnamese Wound medal. An American colonel had prophesied: 'Within two weeks he'll have won every medal in the war or be dead'. Badcoe took a bit longer, but did both. If ever a man could be relied upon to turn the tide of battle in his favour by single-handed, fearless, dynamic leadership, it was Badcoe.

Not that he looked the part. Short, slightly plump, with a roundish face, receding hair and wearing heavy-rimmed glasses, he looked more like a Canberra civil servant than the ultimate soldier he was. Although his eyesight was poor, wearing glasses did not fit with his image of the ideal infantryman. When he went for an eyesight test he would brief the soldiers ahead of him to memorize the chart, which he would learn before his check. He never drank or smoked. Away from the battlefield he was a quiet, almost introverted, family man with lots of friends, but few really close ones. But underneath that deceptive exterior was a man with a passion for soldiering that had been with him since boyhood. Badcoe lived for the Army. As his wife, Denise, put it: 'I could never imagine Peter doing anything else than soldiering'.[1]

A Vietnam veteran recalled: 'I don't think he knew the meaning of fear. If the Viet Cong opened fire on him, he simply sat down and sized up the situation for five seconds or so, then got stuck into them.'[2] Another remembered meeting him for the first time on operations: 'When I first saw him he was sitting on his camp bed in black cotton pyjamas — the uniform of the Viet Cong he had been out less than five hours previously to kill. "I find them lighter and considerably less conspicuous at night," he said. "The Viet Cong travel light — lean and mean — and we hope to do the same".'[3] His hobby was weapons, small arms of all kinds, which he took great pride in being able to handle with skill. As a boy his father had made him a toy machine gun which he treasured. He took great trouble to teach his wife and three daughters to shoot, even quizzing them on the *Small Arms of the World* manual, that became almost compulsory reading. When teased by his wife that he really ought to have a son he would reply: 'Why would I want sons? There is nothing my girls can't do that boys could do better.'[4]

An Australian NCO was once somewhat startled on being introduced to the 'Galloping Major'. 'An old, bright-red beret sat jauntily on his head. His drab jungle greens were almost hidden under the most amazing collection of weapons I have ever seen on one man. A Swedish sub-machine gun, his favourite, hung over one shoulder. It was balanced on the other side by a snub-nosed grenade launcher. On his belt an Australian pistol hung heavily, and in one hand he hefted an American machine gun.'[5]

Strangely, Badcoe did not have an infantry background. He was primarily an artillery officer. Commissioned in December, 1952, he went initially to the 14th National Service Training Battalion for a few months, before joining 1 Field Regiment RAA. Then back to the National Service Training Battalion in mid-1955, followed by a return to 1 Field Regiment, which included duty in Malaya in 1961-62. Finally, a further period of almost two years with 1 Field Regiment before he succeeded, in August, 1965, in transferring from the gunners to the infantry. During his thirteen years in the artillery, Badcoe had made it plain that firing large guns at an enemy you could not see was not his way of fighting a war. Whenever possible he applied for infantry or specialist courses, that would get him away from the gun lines or his staff officer's chair. He qualified as a parachutist in 1952, attended a special operations course in 1955, underwent jungle warfare training in 1961, again more jungle tactics at a senior level in 1964, ending up in 1965-1966 as an instructor at the Infantry School. Then he volunteered for the Team in Vietnam.

Although he missed the Malayan Emergency and his arrival in Vietnam in August, 1966, was the start of the only active service posting in his career, Badcoe had had a quick look at what it was like five years earlier. In late 1962, when he was a captain with the 103rd Field Battery at Terendak Camp in Malaya, the US authorities invited Australian officers to visit Vietnam for two-week periods as observers. Badcoe's turn came in November. His appetite for action was whetted during those few days in the field. For five days he was attached to a Vietnamese infantry battalion which was involved in several contacts, plus one major battle. Additionally Badcoe managed to fit in a helicopter trip to a Montagnard unit up in the highlands, during a brief rest period. Not content with this, when his return flight was delayed, he wangled an attachment to an ARVN reconnaissance company on an operation in the Mekong Delta. This entailed him leaping into battle from a hovering helicopter. It was noted that Badcoe had crammed more than the usual combat activity into his observer trip. His report was enthusiastic on the value of getting the feel of a guerrilla war.

Badcoe's father had not wanted his son to join the Army. On leaving high school he had joined the South Australian Public Service as a clerk, but was soon desperately bored and pestered his father for permission to enlist. Eventually this was given, so he joined the 16th National Service Battalion early in 1952. By July he had gained a place at the Officer Cadet School, Portsea, and five months later he was commissioned, a month before his nineteenth birthday.

In 1955, while Badcoe was a subaltern with 1 Field Regiment, the organizers of the local township's Mayor's Ball invited the Regiment to send a batch of young officers as escorts for some of the council's eligible ladies. The girls and their military chaperons were paired off by height. This blind date resulted in Peter Badcoe meeting Denise. Within a year they were married.

Badcoe's long-standing wish to return to Vietnam was granted in August, 1966. Together with his friend, Major Ross Buchan, he was posted to the Team. As a field officer (major) Badcoe's job was as an adviser on the staff of the Nam Hoa Sub-Section headquarters — Nam Hoa being a District of Thua Thien Province. The military administration paralleled the civilian system in Vietnam. Four Army Corps were established in the four civil Regions, the 44 Provinces were each a military Sector, while the 272 civil Districts became military Sub-Sectors. At each military headquarters a senior Vietnamese officer was in charge, with an American adviser working alongside him. Within a Province were several units of Regional Forces (RF), usually of company strength, which were standby units, at five minutes' notice, ready to be deployed as required. At District level there were the so-called Popular Forces (PF), of platoon strength, controlled by the district chief. These local forces were often referred to collectively as RF/PF troops, or 'Ruff Puffs'. Both types were regular soldiers on slightly lower pay than the normal ARVN units, as their service was restricted to their home area close to family and friends.

Badcoe took great pride in his boys — many were only seventeen-year-olds — and despite their liking for pastel scarves, flowers on their shirts, or multi-coloured straw hats, he made his units effective. As he put it:

132

'When I yell "assault forward" they actually advance, and don't simply go to ground'. Like many enthusiastic trainers he had little time for paperwork. His American superiors quickly gave him a clerk, after his first official report 'included every Australian military abbreviation and idiom I could think of'.

Within a week of arrival Badcoe was in action. From the start he seemed to go out of his way to build up a reputation for fearlessness, for exposing himself heedlessly to enemy fire, and for always being in front of the leading troops. By the time he was killed, nearly eight months later, his presence on the battlefield was worth a company of reinforcements. Whenever troops in his district wavered, Badcoe arrived to restore the situation. This is precisely what he did on that first occasion.

Badcoe joined a company of the RF that was deployed within a short distance of his sub-sector headquarters on a clearing operation. The company advanced towards a line of trees from which sporadic fire was being received. As the distance closed the fire intensified to include automatic fire from a well-constructed bunker. The RF troops took cover while Badcoe moved to the front. He located the bunker and began firing at it with his rifle, followed by a grenade launcher, but without visible effect. The Vietnamese company commander suggested that Badcoe call up an airstrike, but he scoffed at the idea of the Air Force being necessary to silence four or five men in a bunker. Instead, he went to the rear to collect two jerricans of petrol. Advancing again, he dashed forward with his heavy load in each hand, dodging from cover to cover. He made a conspicuous target at which the Viet Cong in the bunker concentrated their aim. Incredibly, he was able to get around their flank unscathed, on to their blind side. Calmly, Badcoe clambered on to the bunker to pour the contents of each can over it, before withdrawing a short distance to lob a phosphorus grenade. A huge whoosh of flame, screams of terror from inside, and then silence. The company advanced — the Badcoe legend had begun.

In December, 1966, Badcoe was moved to the Thua Thien Sector (Provincial) headquarters to become the operations adviser (Map 19). This was a staff position, with planning, co-ordination and liaison duties. As such there was no real requirement for him to go out on every operation and involve himself personally in combat. Staff advisers could make their own decisons on whether or not to go into the field. It was while in this position that Badcoe performed the three remarkable feats that won him the Cross.

On the afternoon of 23 February, 1967, an RF/PF force was taking part in a Sector operation in the flat, open, rice paddies of the coastal plain of Phu Thu district, SE of Hue (Map 20a). It was extremely hot, with good

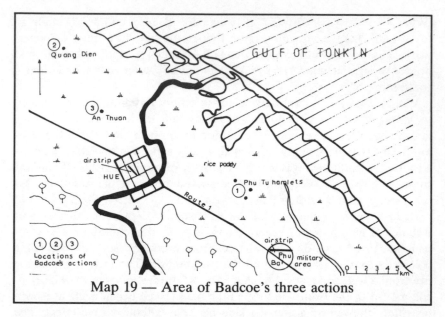

Map 19 — Area of Badcoe's three actions

visibility, as a PF platoon on the flank of the main RF company cautiously advanced over the fields. Without warning the enemy opened fire from 200 metres to the front. One of the leading PF soldiers fell wounded as a machine gun raked the ground with long bursts. Captain Clement and Sergeant 1st Class George Thomas were the two advisers with the platoon. Clement set off at once to try to assist the wounded soldier, but was hit and killed some 150 metres from the platoon's position. Thomas immediately tried to bring him in, but also fell wounded. On his radio Thomas contacted Badcoe.

Instead of co-ordinating from his headquarters Badcoe had joined the RF company involved, alternating between assisting the company commander and the leading platoon, as he checked direction, corrected formation faults, or kept track of the company's position on the map. He had heard the firing off to the flank where the PF platoon was some 600 metres away. As soon as he got Thomas's call for help Badcoe left his companion, Captain James Custar USMC, with the company and set off on his own towards the PF platoon. It was a long way. All the time as Badcoe jogged across the rice he was under aimed fire from the Viet Cong, but he made no attempt to take cover.

On arrival he instantly took charge of the platoon that had withdrawn slightly and gone to ground, with Thomas lying wounded a short distance in front and Clement further out some 150 metres away. Badcoe, by dint of his leadership and example, rallied the troops to advance. Placing him-

134

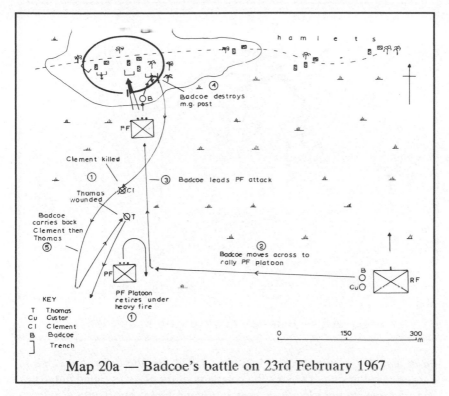

Map 20a — Badcoe's battle on 23rd February 1967

self in the lead, firing his weapon, yelling encouragement, he headed straight towards the machine-gun post. The Viet Cong gunner saw him coming and aimed directly at him, but Badcoe was unstoppable. Swerving, dodging, ducking, he worked his way up to the machine gun and shot the crew with his rifle. This superb example brought the PF platoon forward in a successful assault on an enemy that outnumbered them by at least three to one.

Badcoe returned to carry back Clement's body before going out again, still under fire, to rescue Thomas, who he brought in for medical attention. As Thomas himself said: 'Had it not been for his unhesitant actions and personal courage, I might not have survived the continuous hail of enemy fire'.[6] For this action Badcoe received his first American Silver Star, although like his second, and the VC, it was a posthumous award, given five months after his death.

On 7 March, less than two weeks later, Badcoe again saved a situation that had all the makings of a defeat. This time the district headquarters of Quang Dien, 25 kilometres NW of Hue, came under attack from an estimated two battalions of Viet Cong (Map 20b). Within half an hour of a

135

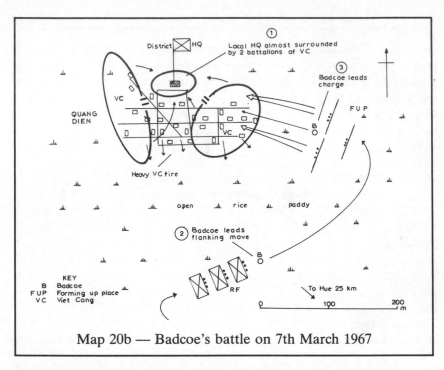

Map 20b — Badcoe's battle on 7th March 1967

dawn assault the district chief had been killed and the defence seemed in danger of collapsing. The standby company of the RF was called out. They had to travel in vehicles from Hue to Quang Dien, but it was a journey fraught with risks. One company was rushing to attack a force several times it own strength, while the urgency meant there was no alternative to roaring along the road on the shortest possible route. This was a classic ambush situation, one which the enemy had used on countless occasions, attacking a post with the object of catching the relieving force in an ambush en route.

Accepting that they had no real option but to hope that it was not a trap, the company, with its advisers, set off at speed. In the adviser's jeep were a US Lieutenant-Colonel, Badcoe, with his assistant, a US captain, and the driver. Indicative of the haste with which they drove was the fact that their vehicle careered off the road, crashing into a ditch, killing the captain and shaking up the others. Typically, Badcoe was only delayed long enough to hitch a ride with the Vietnamese company commander.

On arrival the village was found to be occupied, with the district headquarters buildings under close attack from three sides, but still holding out. Badcoe assessed the position and conferred with the company commander. He favoured an attack on to the enemy's flank, supported by the fire from the defenders, although this would necessitate a long approach over open

136

ground to a suitable forming-up position (FUP). The platoons were organized for the move, while the district defenders were appraised of what was to happen over the radio. With Badcoe out in front, the company crossed the ground under continuous fire as the enemy soon realized what was happening. Once in the FUP the troops were shaken out into extended line, the assault formation. Badcoe positioned himself in the centre, stood up, waved his arm to indicate the advance and the soldiers got to their feet to begin the attack. As the assault progressed Badcoe stayed ahead, now firing, now shouting, now talking on his radio, as the distance to the enemy shortened. It was a typical old-fashioned infantry assault under intense fire, which ended with a furious charge into the Viet Cong positions. The enemy withdrew, and the district headquarters was saved — an example of how a small force, vigorously led, can achieve surprising results against strong opposition.

In April, Badcoe was due for a short spell of leave, which he intended to spend in Okinawa with his friend Ross Buchan. He was due to depart on 8 April, and had written to his wife early on the 7th explaining that he was to go to Da Nang later that day in order to fly out from there with Buchan the next day. Tragically, by 3.30 pm that day, the 7th, Badcoe was dead. The letter was later delivered to Denise and she subsequently explained: 'I don't think he knew when he wrote the letter that he was taking part in an exercise [operation] that afternoon . . . The letter was a very personal one. Usually he told me of the exercises [operations] he had been involved in, and whether he was due to take part in any action. He wrote to me as if I was another soldier . . . I felt like part of the Army. But in this last letter he hardly mentioned the war at all.'[7]

Badcoe's final exploit involved him entirely by accident. There was even less need than usual for his personal participation. His friend Buchan had been visiting him in Hue for several days, and the two of them had been in the field together. Early on 7 April, the day on which he planned to travel to Da Nang for his flight to Okinawa the following day, Badcoe returned to his headquarters to be told that as an adviser had reported sick he must stand in as duty officer. This meant he could not go to Da Nang, so it was arranged that Badcoe would join Buchan there early on the 8th. Buchan flew out from Hue, with Badcoe seeing him off, little realizing that when he reached corps headquarters he would be shattered by the news of his friend's death.

Badcoe returned from the airfield to the operations room at the Sector headquarters to take over as duty officer. This involved checking on the operations of units in the field, receiving reports of progress, or intelligence on the enemy, maintaining the operational log, keeping the situation map up to date and co-ordinating requests for assistance or air strikes. The duty officer was in charge of the operations room on a roster basis for a period of hours, and was not permitted to leave without authority, having secured a replacement. Although Badcoe had not anticipated being put on the roster that day, it should have been no more than an inconvenience, a few hours spent listening to radio messages and supervising routine tasks — a slight delay in his leave plans.

On going through the reports Badcoe discovered that all was not going well with an operation eight kilometres from where he was sitting. A force of about two companies of Viet Cong had fortified themselves in the village of An Thuan, NW of Hue. A strong detachment had been despatched to flush them out, but had got into difficulties. The 1st ARVN Division had deployed their reaction company, on this occasion the elite Hac Bao (Black Panther) Company, together with a squadron of armoured personnel carriers and an RF company. Notwithstanding a spirited attack, the heavy and accurate fire from the village had thrown them back. Part of the problem was that, despite the size of the force, it had no accompanying advisers, which meant that the ARVN could not call up US air support. Badcoe learned that one of the usual advisers had gone sick, and his partner had not gone in to the field as the normal practice was for advisers to work in pairs. Fate was playing a hand. A duty officer sick had put Badcoe in the operations room, another man sick had meant no advisers with a unit in trouble.

To Badcoe there was only one response. He would go and sort it out. The fact that it was not really his job to go, the fact that he was due on leave in a matter of hours, and the fact that he was confined to the headquarters as duty officer in no way deterred him. He made immediate arrangements to find an officer to relieve him in the operations room and summoned his assistant and radio operator, Sergeant Alberto Alvarado US Army. The two armed themselves, jumped in a jeep and within a matter of minutes were approaching the battlefield (Map 20c).

The Viet Cong had entrenched themselves in and around the village. Although outnumbered by the ARVN, and lacking in armour, they nevertheless had the advantage of cover, good fields of fire across the rice fields, plus several recoilless rifles, mortars and machine guns. When Badcoe found the Vietnamese commander he was in the process of organizing a second assault. This time the APCs would lead, followed up by the Hac Bao Company. Fire support was provided by the RF company, and artillery and aircraft could be used as required. Badcoe and Alvarado climbed into one of the leading APCs for the attack. With engines screaming, rattling tracks, and the crackle of machine-gun and rifle fire, the squadron

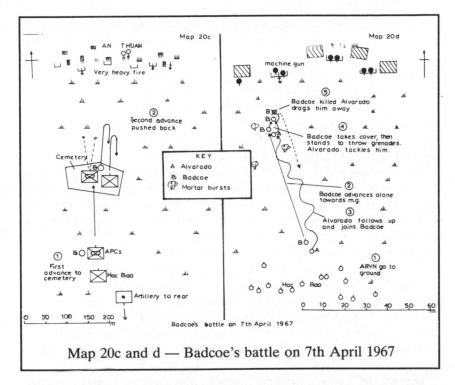

Map 20c and d — Badcoe's battle on 7th April 1967

advanced into the open. They had reached a cemetery, some 250 metres from the enemy, when the weight of fire from recoilless rifles, heavy machine guns, and mortars forced a halt. The APCs sought out positions from which to return fire, while the infantry began to move up through them to continue the advance. Once out from the shelter of the cemetery the troops quickly took cover from a deluge of bullets and mortar fragments. The Viet Cong position seemed impregnable.

Badcoe and Alvarado had dismounted in the cemetery to continue forward with the infantry. As they struggled to advance, the soldiers instinctively half-crouching, hunched up as though walking into driving rain, casualties climbed. Badcoe was up with the leading sections, yelling advice, waving them on, heedless of the danger. As the company started to take cover, indeed to slip back to the sanctuary of the cemetery, Badcoe's upright figure was conspicuous as he moved among the soldiers trying to rally them to continue. His efforts were not enough, and there was now a period of stalemate as both sides exchanged fire, while the attackers decided the next move. Despite the APCs and superior numbers of high quality troops, the dry, open paddy fields, with no cover except knee-high rice, gave the defenders a clear advantage.

Although an artillery officer by training, Badcoe had not insisted on softening up the position with guns or aircraft prior to the assault, merely joining an advance that had been planned prior to his arrival. The first two attempts to close with the Viet Cong had failed due to lack of sufficient heavy fire hitting them to distract their attention as the assault moved across the open ground. No attempt had been made to provide smoke to screen the attack from aimed fire. Now the guns were called into action to drop their shells into the village for several minutes. As the barrage lifted, Badcoe took the lead again, with Alvarado close behind.

The Hac Bao soldiers tried once more. Unfortunately the weight of fire that swept the field had not diminished despite the artillery preparation. As the infantry moved forward it seemed to be hitting them in the flank as well as from the front. The plan was again flawed by the guns ceasing fire before the assault got properly under way, no smoke being provided, and poor co-ordination between the cavalry APCs, who were immune to small arms and mortar fragments, and the infantry. Badcoe was not the commander. He could, and did, advise, but he could not force a tactical change in the plan. He chose, by personal example, to make the plan work regardless of the difficulties. He realized that somehow the attackers must cross the open field and close the distance to get sufficient infantry and APCs into the enemy position, so that the fight could be on equal terms in and around the village.

The ARVN troops responded initially. Badcoe kept going, seemingly indestructible, slowly drawing the attackers after him by sheer personality and determination (Map 20d). At this moment he was once more the leading soldier of an infantry assault. As another adviser later commented: 'Major Badcoe was always first into the fray. He never stayed in the centre of his unit to command, but got out in front and led them into battle.'[8] But even his outstanding leadership could not get the infantry to do the impossible. After 150 metres or so the attackers flopped down into the rice, hugged the ground, lay still, or started to wriggle back. Badcoe took cover momentarily to assess the situation. He had no intention of withdrawing again; rather he sought out the nearest enemy position that was holding up the assault. He spotted it — a machine gun 100 metres away. Badcoe started to run towards it, disdaining to duck or crouch, sometimes firing, sometimes turning to wave on his men and the carriers, until he saw a slight fold in the ground which offered meagre cover. Here he paused to decide how best to make his final charge.

Alvarado had followed his officer forward. Later he described what happened:

> 'Major Badcoe didn't waste time trying to tell them to advance
> again. He hopped down and started off alone, straight at a bat-

talion of Viet Cong. I jumped off the carrier and went after him. Even then he made me proud. While I ran low in the grass he paced out ahead with that silly red Aussie beret bobbing up and down, waving back at the carriers and trying to urge them forward. The mortar bombs were falling all around him like rain, but they might have been Sunday showers for all the notice he was taking.

'We were getting close to the Viet Cong now, real close. The major just charged ahead, firing at them. A few seconds later we were down in the long grass, and a Viet Cong machine gun was only about 27 metres in front, trying to get us.

'Major Badcoe stood up and started throwing grenades at them, so I brought him down with a tackle and they missed. He hopped up again to throw more grenades, but this time they were waiting. They got him in the head and he fell. Then I got zapped in the leg. I grabbed the major and started dragging him back towards the carriers. It took me a while to realize he was dead'.[9]

The Galloping Major had been stopped at last. Eventually Alvarado reached comparative safety. Only then did he call up an air strike which, combined with further artillery fire and proper co-operation between the APCs and infantry, enabled the ARVN's third attempt to storm the village to succeed.

The Team had lost its most outstanding officer. A deceptively mild, affable man out of action, but a tiger in battle, Badcoe may well have been one of those rare soldiers who really do not know fear. Certainly to those who saw him in combat he seemed truly fearless. He went out of his way to find a fight and, having found it, went to the front. Time after time his leadership, his coolness, his example inspired shaken troops to rally, to advance and to overcome. That he survived for eight months was miraculous. When he met his death it was undoubtedly the way he would have chosen to go — quickly, cleanly, at the head of his troops, only a few metres from an enemy position. As his wife said: 'He was a soldier through and through'.

Unlike Wheatley, and although the Australian authorities would now fly the bodies of servicemen home, Badcoe was buried in Malaysia, in Terendak Camp, where he had served with his artillery battery five years earlier. It was a moving military funeral, with the bearer party, escort and firing party pro vided by the 4th Battalion RAR who were stationed there. Oddly, there was no memorial service in Australia.

Almost a month before the gazettal of his VC the US President directed that Badcoe should receive a posthumous Silver Star, and a First Oak Leaf Cluster, which signified a second award. This was, and still is, an unprecedented award. Not only were these decorations being made to a foreigner, but he was receiving two Silver Stars on the same day, for different actions, both posthumously. This award is made for gallantry in action against an opposing armed force. Badcoe was given the first for his actions on 23 February, when he retrieved Captain Clement's body and rescued medical specialist Sergeant Thomas. His Oak Leaf Cluster was for his final battle on 7 April at An Thuan.

It was the sum total of these three exceptional displays of courage during the last six weeks of his life that secured him the VC. For such repeated gallantry there was only one possible reward. After it was gazetted on 13 October, 1967, Denise Badcoe proudly explained that her husband had been a professional soldier to his fingertips. 'If ever there was a breed of person who wins the Victoria Cross, it was his. The life in the Army was the only work he knew. He volunteered to go to Vietnam. He felt it was his duty. He felt he had a job to do.'[10] Strangely, the news of his award was not mentioned in any of the New York or Washington papers, nor on either the radio or television. Also, of the four Australians who gained the VC in Vietnam, Badcoe is the only one whose citation and photograph do not hang in the Hall of Heroes at Fort Bragg.

Denise and her three daughters later went to Government House for the Investiture. For the second time within a few months Lord Casey was presenting a posthumous VC to a proud but grieving family.

Later, Denise Badcoe presented her husband's medals to the Australian War Memorial for display. Other memorials include the naming of a hall at Portsea Officer Cadet School, Badcoe Hall; an Australian and New Zealand soldiers' club in Vietnam was opened as the Peter Badcoe Club; and a park is named after him in Adelaide, together with streets in Canberra and Sydney.

Badcoe will be remembered as one of Australia's greatest fighting soldiers, but certainly he would be equally happy to be recalled by the words of his seven-year-old daughter, Kim, who on being told her father had won the VC exclaimed: 'He was a great daddy. I will remember him forever'.

CHAPTER 8

Ben Het, Kontum Province, South Vietnam
6 and 11 May, 1969

WARRANT OFFICER 2
RAYENE STEWART SIMPSON VC, DCM,
Australian Army Training Team – Vietnam.

'I almost fell over. I just don't believe it.
It's incredible'.
Warrant Officer Simpson in August, 1969, after being told by the
Australian Task Force Commander in Vietnam that he had been
awarded the VC.

When Ray Simpson, or Simmo, as he was known to his mates, died in
Japan, of pneumonia, brought on by cancer of the lymph glands, on 18
October, 1978, Australia lost one of its finest soldiers. He was only 52 years
old, but he had packed more adventure and infantry combat into his life
than most would have thought possible. He was the only Australian soldier
to receive medals for every war or campaign in which Australia has participated from the Second World War onwards. Simpson fought the Japanese
in New Guinea, the North Koreans and Chinese in Korea, the Chinese
Communists in Malaya and the North Vietnamese in Vietnam. He was
among the first thirty members of the Team into Vietnam in August, 1962.
After three separate tours, totalling some four years' service, when he left
the country for good in 1970 he had won both the DCM and the VC. He
had spent longer in Vietnam than any other member of the Team.

Simpson had three enduring loves in his life – his wife, Australia and
soldiering. The word 'soldiering' is used advisedly instead of the Army, as
Simpson had several brushes with the military authorities, for he was a man
used to speaking his mind. During his 21 years in the Army he was discharged at his own request no less than three times. His most serious difficulty arose after he had been awarded the DCM, while he was back in Sydney convalescing from a leg wound, doing a desk job with a Commando
Reserve unit. As he himself put it in a letter to a friend: 'I was invited to
Government House Sydney in 1965 to receive it [the DCM] but owing to

143

the fact that I was disgruntled with the Army because they wouldn't allow me to return to Vietnam, I refused to attend the investiture and suggested they post it. Which they did.'

It was a combination of his passion for proper soldiering in Vietnam and his wish to be with his Japanese wife in Tokyo as often as possible that led to his taking his second discharge in May, 1966. His wife, Shoko, had returned to Japan in late 1964 to visit her elderly mother, who unfortunately had a heart attack during her daughter's visit. This necessitated her remaining in Tokyo to care for her, with the resultant long separation from Simpson in Australia. To Simpson, soldiering in Australia was not only tedious but it meant he could seldom afford the fare to see his wife. Vietnam, however, offered the type of soldiering he wanted, was much closer to Japan, and his leave trips were paid for by the military. When the Army decreed that he was not fit for Vietnam service any more, (his right leg was now slightly shorter than his left due to his wound), he was furious.

It was during this period that there was talk of Simpson being court-martialled, but one of his unit's (1 Commando) officers intervened to prevent it, at the cost of his own career being curtailed, and later terminated. Simpson left in disgust. He tried being a salesman for a while, but that did not work so he paid his way back to Saigon, and got himself accepted into the Team again.[1] When he got off the aircraft, in civilian clothes, it created a bit of a stir with officialdom as it was soon discovered that he was no longer in the Army. 'Never mind,' said Simpson. 'Just draw me a weapon and some greens and I'll get cracking.' When questioned as to how he had got back to Vietnam without authorization, he replied: 'Aw, it's not hard when you've got mates.' It was all highly embarrassing for the Australian authorities; even more so when he went on to win the VC — but it was typical Simmo.

Simpson was born in February, 1926. He had a brother and four sisters, but spent much of his childhood in an orphanage. In March, 1944, aged 18, he joined the Army and served in New Guinea. Discharged in early 1947 he spent the next four years drifting from job to job. He tried train conductor, builders' labourer, sugar cane cutter, and sailor until, at 25, he re-enlisted. Within a short time he was in Korea with 3 RAR, staying with them there until January, 1954, during which period he was promoted temporary sergeant. In Korea Simpson joined what one British officer described as 'the finest fighting infantry battalion I have ever seen'. The Australians were in the 28th Commonwealth Brigade and took part in the bitter battles over the Imjin in October, 1951. Simpson, in 3 RAR, was involved in the tough fighting on and around Hill 317, during the latter part of which Speakman, with the KOSB, gained his VC.

It was while on leave from Korea in Japan that he met Shoko, a young

Japanese woman who was working at the U.S. leave centre in Tokyo. Although it was only seven years since Simpson had been fighting the Japanese, although Shoko had been married before and had a daughter, and although he was only on a month's leave, he fell in love. They were married in 1952 at a Japanese Shinto ceremony at the end of his leave. It was the start of 27 years of happiness for them both. Simpson and Shoko had started a marriage that many would have said was doomed to fail. Added to the religious, cultural, and language difficulties was the undercurrent of anti-Japanese feeling among many Australians, whose recent memories of the war clouded their views on individuals, however innocent. Then there was the inevitable separation inherent in Simpson's career as a soldier. It says much for the character of them both that none of these problems, nor the fact that they could not have children of their own, marred their marriage.

From Korea he went to Malaya with 2 RAR from 1955-1957. Then followed five happy years with the 1st Special Air Service Company at Perth. By the time he volunteered for Vietnam in 1962 Simpson was a highly experienced infantryman. Outwardly tough, forceful in his speech as well as his actions, Sergeant Simpson was fully trained in the techniques of special operations and jungle warfare. His selection to be among the first Australians to go to Vietnam is a reflection on how highly he was regarded.

His first tour of twelve months was comparatively uneventful, in that he completed it without being wounded or winning any gallantry decorations. These came within two months of the start of his second tour. Restless for action after a year back with the SAS, Simpson returned to Vietnam in July, 1964. He was posted to an advisory group with U.S. and Vietnamese Special Forces in the mountainous jungles of the NW, near the village of Ta Ko. It was here that he played a major role in the setting up of a South Vietnamese patrol base, designed to monitor and control border infiltration. Simpson's task was to advise the local forces on training and operational matters. This meant that he accompanied the platoons on many of their patrols from the Ta Ko base.

On 16 September, 1964, Simpson, who was now a temporary Warrant Officer Class 2, joined a patrol under the command of a Vietnamese Special Forces officer. On this occasion the platoon was caught in an ambush in which the Vietnamese commander was shot and Simpson was hit by rifle fire in his right leg. His wound was serious and he found it difficult to remain on his feet. Despite this he rallied the platoon, formed a defensive perimeter, contacted his base by radio for reinforcements and by personal example and leadership held off repeated attacks by the Viet Cong. Eventually, with ammunition running low, and with Simpson faint from loss of blood and exhaustion, the relief force he had summoned arrived. Even then, not until he was satisfied that the position was secure and the injured troops of his platoon were being cared for did he permit himself to be evacuated by helicopter to the 6th Field Hospital at Nha Trang.

This action gained Simpson a well deserved DCM. But it cost him six months' hospitalization in Japan, the curtailment of his second Vietnam tour and a posting back to Australia. The shortening of his right leg was the cause of his disgruntlement with the Army and, finally, his taking his second discharge.

In May, 1969, Simpson was almost two years into his third Vietnam tour. His exploits, his DCM, and his successful snub of the authorities by paying his own way back to re-enlist had made him a legend within the Australian and Special Forces community. By the time he went on the operations during which he won the VC Simpson had already extended his tour twice, partly in order to get the 30-day extension leave in Japan, and partly because he was doing the job he loved so well.

There was another side to Simpson's character apart from his professional one. His soldiers saw the hard exterior, the tough, hard-drinking, hard-living image of an Australian infantryman. Simpson was proud of his Australianism, of his professionalism, and of the great respect these qualities engendered. But he was also a family man with a great tenderness, a profound belief in his principles, a man whose loyalty and devotion to his wife, his Queen and his country were forever showing through the hard-boiled exterior. Unlike many of his comrades, Simpson was very articulate, not in the least frightened of rank, well able forcefully to put forward his opinions to both his peers and his superiors. He read widely, his particular interest being military history, especially the exploits of unconventional soldiers. The German special operations specialist Otto Skorzeny was a favourite.

On 6 May, 1969, Simpson's company, the 232nd of the 3rd MFB, was moving cautiously through torrential rain in the rugged terrain west of Ben Het, barely 2 kilometres from the Cambodian border. Movement was slow due to the poor visibility, steep slopes and jungle, interspersed with dense bamboo thickets. Progress was made worse by innumerable old bomb craters and weapon pits. The only consolation was that the pouring rain deadened the noise of the troops when they inadvertently slipped, stumbled, or rattled the bamboo. The battalion was on the usual rather vague mission of searching and clearing an area known to contain Viet Cong infiltration routes. The task was to locate likely trails and ambush them. The CO of the 3rd MFB, Captain Green USSF, had three companies. The 231st was under Warrant Officer 2 B. Walsh, assisted by Warrant Officer 2 A.M.

21. At a 1987 Veteran's Welcome Home Parade in Sydney. Left to right —
George Wheatley (son), Kim Badcoe (daughter), Helen O'Hagan (niece
of Warrant Officer Simpson, VC), and Warrant Officer Payne, VC. Mrs
O'Hagan wore Simpson's miniature medals as the weight of the full-size
ones was too much for her dress. *(Captain Brian Swift)*.

22. The gully up which Colonel Jones charged to gain his posthumous VC.
The soldier on the left is standing by the trench Jones was attacking, the
one in the centre shows his route, while the man on the right marks the
trench from which he was shot. *(The Parachute Regiment)*

23. Lieutenant-Colonel H. Jones. *(The Parachute Regiment)*

24. Below: Mrs Sara Jones with her two sons, Rupert (left) and David (right), shortly after the Investiture. *(Mrs. S. Jones)*

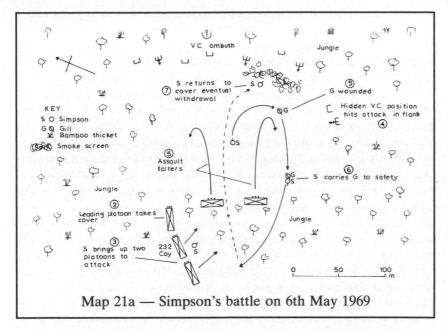

Map 21a — Simpson's battle on 6th May 1969

Kelly, both Australians. Simpson, with the 232nd, had Warrant Officer 2 M.S. Gill and Specialist Sergeant P. Holmberg USSF, as two of his three platoon commanders. The 233rd had no Australian advisers, and at this time was operating some distance away from the other two.

At around 2.30 pm, as the Montagnards approached a clearing, Simpson's company was leading, with Walsh's in reserve (see Map 21a). Just as the front platoon reached the clearing they were caught by heavy bursts of fire from the opposite side, where the enemy were lying in wait in well-concealed positions. Diving for cover, the Montagnards tried to follow their immediate action drills of locating the enemy and returning fire. While this was happening Simpson, with the rest of the company in hand, moved forward to read the battle.

His answer was a quick counter-attack with his two reserve platoons. Yelling instructions, he stood up to lead the assault. The advance started with the troops darting forward through the trees and undergrowth with Simpson, who was at the forefront urging his men on, becoming an unmistakable target that attracted intense fire. Unfortunately they were attacking regular NVA soldiers, well versed in the techniques of jungle ambush, who had set up a flank position with orders to hold their fire until the battle developed. These opened up just as Simpson's men were nearing the main enemy position. Caught by surprise again, the assault faltered as Gill, one of the platoon com-

147

manders, fell seriously wounded. The Montagnards started to pull back.

Simpson's instant response was to save Gill. Ignoring the renewed outburst of fire, he dashed across to his comrade and carried him back to cover, before returning to try to salvage the battle. He frantically sought to get his men moving by shouting in the Montagnard dialect, interspersed with suitable Australian curses whose meaning was unmistakable. His efforts were unavailing. There is nothing so nice as a fold in the ground, a rock, a tree, anything to hug, when bullets are cracking around you. To get soldiers to stand up again once they have taken cover from heavy fire requires not only exceptional leadership but highly trained troops and considerable covering fire. On this occasion Simpson provided the leadership, but the other two factors were lacking. The result was that the Montagnards either continued to withdraw or declined to move. For a while Simpson refused to accept that his attack had stalled irretrievably. He crawled forward on his own to within ten metres of the enemy bunkers where an old bomb crater gave him the opportunity to hurl grenades at the Viet Cong. But this was not enough, so Simpson reluctantly gave the order to withdraw, after gathering a group of five Montagnards to give covering fire. He himself stayed behind with them, tossing phosphorus grenades into the trees to build up a thick cloud of smoke behind which his men left the hill.

As dusk approached, Simpson's priority task was to secure an LZ to let in a casualty evacuation helicopter. He attempted to organize this about 250 metres north of the area of contact. His initial efforts were fruitless as the helicopter was driven off by hostile fire, while his soldiers refused to form a perimeter, preferring to lie along the trail ignoring all efforts to shift them. Simpson did not mince his words in his official report when he stated: 'The performance of the company was a damned disgrace, both during the contact and subsequently at the LZ.' After dark little could be done to get the wounded away. Gill died of his injuries during the night and it was not until the next morning that the company was able to link up with the remainder of the battalion, establish an LZ and get a helicopter to lift out the casualties.

There then followed three days of rest and reorganization as the battalion remained in position to receive an air resupply before trying to contact the enemy again. By 10 May the 3rd MFB was considered ready for another try. Within a short distance the leading troops once more went to ground as soon as they were fired on. Again they would not attack. Airstrikes proved ineffective − the attempt to advance had failed.

11 May saw the second major action that clinched Simpson's VC. It was to be witnessed personally by the Team's CO, Lieutenant-Colonel R.D.F. Lloyd, who arrived by helicopter at midday to see for himself the conditions under which his advisers were operating. He was accompanied by

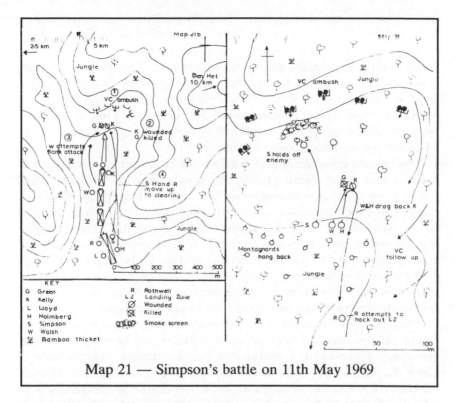

Map 21 — Simpson's battle on 11th May 1969

Captain P. Rothwell, a staff officer at the Special Forces' headquarters at Nha Trang, who had a week to serve before his tour finished.

After softening up the enemy position with artillery fire, the battalion advanced to find the bunkers and weapon pits deserted. Again the Viet Cong demonstrated their ability to ambush and surprise their opponents, and then slip away before the inevitable pounding with shells or bombs.

The battalion probed gingerly forward up the slopes of a steep hill (Map 21b). The commander, Green, felt that the only way to ensure his men went where he intended was to position himself at the head of the column. Behind him was the leading section of Walsh's 231 Company, with Kelly among them. Simpson's company, accompanied by Lloyd and Rothwell, followed the 231st. As they laboriously pushed their way up the slope through dense undergrowth there were signs of enemy activity all around. Early in the afternoon the sequence of events of 6 May was repeated. Heavy bursts of firing hit the leading soldiers as they approached a clearing through thinning trees and the Montagnards took cover. But this time it was Kelly who fell wounded

149

and Green who ran to help him. There the similarity ended, as Green's gallant effort was cut short by a fusillade of shots which killed him outright.

Kelly was still conscious and reported the situation over the radio to Walsh, saying that he thought a left flank approach might be successful. Walsh began to lead the next platoon in that direction, but the Montagnards hung back, refusing to close on the scene of the firing. Undaunted at this, by now, common reaction, Walsh pushed on alone. Meanwhile Simpson, Holmberg and Rothwell had moved forward, although they too could not induce their troops to advance.

Now began a three-man war, the object of which was to rescue Kelly and other wounded men, while at the same time holding off the enemy, thus allowing the Montagnards to pull back to regroup (Map 21c). Kelly was lying in an exposed position close to Green's body. The actions that followed, which saved Kelly, and during which the two Australians and one American participant remained unscathed, would have been rejected by the most gungho of U.S. war film directors. Walsh, Holmberg and Simpson took on the Viet Cong. While Simpson crawled forward to the left to within a few metres of the enemy, to put himself between them and Kelly, the other two squirmed their way up to their wounded comrade.

While Simpson, exposed to close-range fire, grenaded and fired at the enemy, Kelly, who had been hit again, was dragged back by Walsh and Holmberg. Holmberg had also moved over to examine Green's body to check he was dead, while Walsh had crawled up to retrieve Green's rucksack. These moves were visible to the Viet Cong who sprayed the area with machine-gune fire, ripping apart the tree beside which Simpson crouched. The majority of the Montagnards had disappeared, while the few nearby refused to assist in making a stretcher for Kelly. Walsh and Holmberg improvised one themselves and managed to carry him clear of the firing. The enemy had been deterred from advancing to overwhelm the remnants of the company by the solo efforts of Simpson, whose firepower permitted the wounded to be evacuated to the rear, where Rothwell was trying single-handedly to hack out a clearing for a helicopter. Again the Montagnards were unwilling to assist. When a helicopter approached, ground fire forced it away without any casualty pick up. It was Rothwell who then used his rifle and grenades to clear the Viet Cong from the nearby jungle, while the wounded were carried yet further back. With a handful of soldiers Rothwell continued to hold the enemy at bay until the rescue party had got clear.

During the battle Lloyd had remained on the radio, repeatedly calling for artillery or air support and a helicopter for casualty evacuation, only to be told that other targets had priority. Eventually, after dark and a long delay, a second helicopter arrived and, with the skilful use of landing lights, was able to hover over the trees to take on board the wounded. After a nervous night a helicopter lift was organized to fly out the battered remains of the 3rd MFB.

Lloyd was livid. He flew to see the U.S. commander of the 5th Special Forces Group to explain forcefully that he would be recommending the removal of Team members from Special Forces unless significant improvements were made. He had witnessed the low morale and poor training of the Montagnards, the lack of intelligence on the enemy in the area, the inadequate artillery support and the futility of throwing half-trained troops against a skilful, numerically superior enemy. In Lloyd's view it was a reckless waste of life.

Unfortunately no improvements were possible before the next operation, two weeks later, which was to bring about a similar situation in the same area, with the same result – another VC.

Along with brother advisers, Simpson was summoned to a special conference in Saigon on 21 August by the Australian Task Force Commander, Major-General R. Hay. Totally unaware of what was to happen, Simpson was called to the general two minutes before the meeting started. He was stunned when Hay told him he had been awarded the VC. At that moment he became Australia's most highly decorated serving soldier, whose awards would later include the US Silver and Bronze Stars. As he told correspondents: 'I almost fell over. I just don't believe it. It's incredible'. That night the Savoy, the Australian Warrant Officers' and Sergeants' Club, was the scene of a well-deserved celebration. Australian beer cans popped all night, but among the toasts drunk were several to the other two VC winners, Wheatley and Badcoe, Team members whose gallantry had cost them their lives. Peter Holmberg, the American medical sergeant, was at the party, and Simpson with his arm around Holmberg's shoulder explained: 'He was with me on those actions they gave me the VC for. He's a beauty'.

The next day Simpson flew to a new job in the Mekong Delta. His posting was to a small group of advisers training villagers in local defence. As Lloyd said: 'Ray's new posting is for a definite reason. He has had four pretty hectic years here so far. A time out of the regular fighting line will do him good. The posting was decided well before the Victoria Cross award was approved.'[2]

Simpson then had another four years to serve before completing a 22-year engagement, but within nine months he had taken his third, and final, discharge.

Her Majesty the Queen was to hold an Investiture at Government House in Canberra on 1 May 1970, at which Simpson was to receive his Cross.

151

Three days later he was out of uniform for good. It was a decision he took well before the Investiture. He loved soldiering, but he loved his wife more, and felt that as he could no longer serve in Vietnam, and as Shoko must remain in Japan caring for her invalid mother, he had no option but to leave the Army and join her.

Simpson, never a man for show or ceremonial, was later to tell a friend that he only came back to Australia to receive his VC from the Queen because his wife wanted to come — otherwise they could have posted it to him.[3] He was certainly determined that Shoko should share the honour he had won. At the time it was announced, Simpson, on being asked how he would like it presented replied: 'As long as they give it to me with the cheese and kisses there right beside me.' This had to be translated. 'You know, the Mrs. I want her to be there. She has been through a lot.'[4]

Whether he really meant it about mailing the VC will never be known, but for a soldier who seldom saw a parade ground Simpson was immaculate that morning at Government House. Wearing a well-tailored service dress uniform, with cloth belt, double row of medal ribbons surmounted by the VC ribbon, and the 1 Commando collar badges with their dagger and 'Strike Swiftly' motto, (he had worn this badge in his beret throughout his long third tour in Vietnam rather than the Team badge), Simpson stepped smartly up to the dais in front of his Sovereign. Her Majesty bent forward to pin the coveted award on his chest. She asked him whether he had served in the same unit as Warrant Officer Payne, to whom the Queen had presented the Cross less than three weeks earlier. Strangely, Payne, who won his award two weeks later than Simpson, received it about two weeks earlier, (see Chapter 9). The Queen also asked how long he had spent with the Special Forces in Vietnam. Afterwards Simpson joined Shoko, in her striking, traditional, Japanese dress, for the champagne reception. Not that Simpson had much time for champagne and somebody quickly slipped him his favourite Australian brew.

Three days later Simpson signed his discharge papers yet again, before departing with Shoko for Japan. It was the start of eight years together, the longest period without separation in their marriage. Simpson was fortunate to get a job as an Administrative Assistant at the Australian Embassy in Tokyo. He intended to stay on until Shoko was free of her responsibilities for her mother; after that a home in Australia was his wish. Like many long-service soldiers Simpson could never really be satisfied with civilian life, but he made the best of it. He enjoyed the family life, although the tiny units, or apartments, that so many Japanese called home were not to his liking. His affection for kids, typical of so many Team members, was obvious. He and Shoko were delighted when his step-daughter had a son, and came to stay with them for a month. The boy was born on 6 June,

1972, so Simpson immediately called him 'D-Day'. He summed up his situation in a letter to his niece in which he wrote: 'My job is fair enough. The pay is quite reasonable and the work is easy, but for me very boring. I was not cut out to be a "desk jockey". The outdoors for this bloke.'

It came as a great shock to Australians, particularly his old Army mates, when Simpson's death at the age of 52 was announced on 18 October, 1978. The immediate cause was double pneumonia, but what was not well known was that for 18 months Simpson had struggled very courageously, and very privately, with malignant cancer of the lymph glands.

Simpson's funeral took place in Tokyo two days later. There was considerable misunderstanding. Army headquarters in Canberra did not appear to know that the Australian Embassy in Tokyo had decided that, as Simpson had died there, he should be buried there, particularly as his wife was Japanese. Early on the day before the funeral the Army authorities were telling his family in Australia that Simpson's body, and his wife, could be flown home for a full military funeral at public expense. It was a great disappointment to his Australian relatives when they were told by Army headquarters later that night that the funeral would be in Tokyo the next day, especially as they had no chance of attending.

Appropriately the church at which the Requiem Mass was held was the St Ignatius Church, Sophia University, named after the warrior saint who died an heroic martyr's death grappling wild beasts in the Roman arena. According to Father Artillo, who conducted the service, one of Simpson's given names was Ignatius. Over 150 people attended, mainly Japanese friends, and staff from the Australian Embassy. The Australian Army and Navy and the British Army were represented. The chief mourners were Shoko and her family. The Australian Government sent their Ambassador, Mr John Menadue, who gave the eulogy. Afterwards, Simpson's body was cremated, with half of his ashes being buried at the Yokohama War Cemetery, the remainder being retained by Shoko.[5]

Other memorial services were held in Australia. The first was organized by his old Returned Servicemen's Club in Paddington, of which Simpson had been a patron. It was held on 29 October and was attended by his Australian relatives, together with many of his old Army mates. Strenuous efforts to obtain an official guard of honour and band failed, although a bugler was sent.

The second one, in Canberra at the Duntroon Chapel, was on 31 October. This service was well attended by senior military representatives, plus former Team members. Warrant Officer Kelly, whose life Simpson had saved nine years before, was present by accident, as he had only heard about the service two days previously when somebody happened to ask him if he was going.

Almost immediately following his death the three-year wrangle with officialdom began over a pension for Shoko. Because she was only a naturalised Australian, living overseas, and who had not resided long enough in Australia, social service benefits were not available. Because, at the time, there was nothing to relate his death to his military service, no war widow's pension was payable either. So said the authorities. But for the ailing widow of Australia's most decorated post-war soldier to be living in penury in the world's most expensive city was a disgrace. So said everybody else, including the media.

It took more than a year before intense pressure from relatives, newspapers and ex-service organizations finally forced the government into granting Shoko an Act of Grace pension of Australian $50 per week. This was only A$7.50 less than a war widow's pension, but, although better than nothing, was seen as a penny-pinching amount, extracted from an uncaring and ungrateful government. It was insufficient to keep Mrs Simpson from poverty in Tokyo, particularly as she still had to care for her mother, and was herself suffering from arthritis and deafness. In early 1980, in an effort to be helpful, the Australian Embassy offered Shoko a job at the embassy as a cleaner. Again, this was heralded as a degrading and menial task for a sick woman, and yet another example of the authorities' insensitivity.

The final outcry over Shoko's treatment came in April, 1980, when the Australian War Memorial (AWM) purchased Simpson's medals from his wife for A$15,500. Her financial position was so desperate that she was obliged to agree to the sale, albeit reluctantly. From the point of view of the AWM they saw the purchase as a genuine way of helping the widow, as this would be the first group of medals they had bought — they normally only accepted gifts for display in the museum. However, the price they offered was obviously well below the amount that might be raised at a medal auction. They had originally offered only $12,000, but had been forced to increase the price after much adverse comment. Even then the purchase was regarded with scepticism by the press, who saw it as officialdom taking advantage of a war hero's widow to get the medals on the cheap.

One of America's least sensible uses of technology in the Vietnam war was the large-scale use of defoliants on the jungle of the Demilitarized Zone and elsewhere. Over a period of eight years, 1962-1970, hundreds of aircraft flew thousands of missions, spraying nearly 50 million litres of this highly toxic liquid. It certainly killed the vegetation, huge stretches of jungle being denuded of leaves, but it also killed people. Frequent exposure, in areas where this chemical had been used, was later proved to account for cancer and deformities in children. The problem was that Agent Orange, as it was called, contained dioxin, one of the deadliest poisons known to man. It contaminated everything it touched. The Viet Cong, civilians, children, the ARVN and their allied troops were all vulnerable in areas in which it had been used. Eventually its use was halted as a result of appeals from the South Vietnamese government. After the war the chemical company in the U.S. that had manufactured it faced claims for billions of dollars in compensation by hundreds of servicemen who had suffered from exposure to it.

In May, 1981, Shoko Simpson was given a war widow's pension. It was accepted by the government that her husband's death could have been war-related. Pneumonia killed him, cancer caused the pneumonia, and Agent Orange could have started the cancer. There was no doubt Simpson had been exposed to it several times during his long tours in Vietnam, and therefore his death could have been caused by his military service. It was the Repatriation Review Tribunal (RRT) that finally made this judgement, after previous medical advice had resulted in the Repatriation Commission rejecting his death as service-related. The burden of proof in these cases is on the RRT to establish beyond reasonable doubt that the injury or disease was not war-caused. In Simpson's case the possibility that Agent Orange triggered the cancer could not be disproved, so Shoko's appeal was granted.

A senior officer under whom Simpson served in Vietnam, and Korea, and in the SAS, said of him: 'He was the most outstanding soldier among an elite bunch of men. He is a rough and tough sort of bloke, who knows more about soldiering than anybody I know. He's pretty much a loner, a man who knows what he's doing. He embodies all the characteristics that Australians like to think make up the Australian character.'[6] His medals, although not his American ones, are on display, alongside his portrait, at the AWM, and his photograph and citation are held at the Hall of Heroes in the J.F. Kennedy Center at Fort Bragg, U.S.A.

Tough he certainly was. At 43 he was old to be an infantryman leading soldiers less than half his age in some of the most rugged terrain in the world. Strength and stamina of body as well as mind were essential. That he was able to withstand the physical and mental stress and go on month after month, indeed year after year, continually in action, is exceptional. That he also had the courage to win both the DCM and VC is not likely to be equalled.

The words of the Australian Ambassador at Simpson's funeral sum up the man: 'He will be remembered by many generations of Australians as one of the bravest of the land; but to those who knew him at close hand two things will always remain in our memories. One was his Australianism, something he displayed with pride and without humility. He was the Aussie in all of us. The other was his utter loyalty to his Sovereign and to his wife. He served his Queen with an abiding passion, and stood by his wife with an abounding love.'

CHAPTER 9

Ben Het, Kontum Province, South Vietnam
24 May, 1969

WARRANT OFFICER 2 KEITH PAYNE VC
Australian Army Training Team – Vietnam.

*'I went into the action with 272 bullets and eight hand
grenades and came out with the VC'*
Warrant Officer Payne in a flippant mood, after returning home
from Vietnam.

It was hot at Brisbane airport on 19 April, 1975, as the Ansett jet from
Mackay taxied to the front of the terminal, but the 41-year-old man in the
two-tone casual shirt and slacks seemed cool as he descended to meet a
host of relatives, wellwishers and press gathered on the tarmac. Keith Payne
was one of Australia's greatest living heroes, a holder of the VC, who had
left the Australian Army only a month before after 24 years of outstanding
service. Now, he was having a 40-minute stopover on the way to war again,
but this time in Oman. He had signed a three-year contract to serve the
Sultan of Oman in his fight against the Communist rebels in Dhofar in the
rank of captain.

For a moment Payne almost lost his 'cool' as a pressman suggested he
had become a mercenary. His audience saw his fists clench and his veins
bulge, as he choked back his fury. Then, with an effort, he explained: 'A
mercenary is a man who would fight without principle for monetary gain.
I don't have to go to Oman for monetary reasons. I could be sitting on the
beach at Bucasia. But the Australian Government won't allow Australian
soldiers to fight the Communists. So, as a soldier, I'm going to fight them
the best way I can.'[1] Payne was merely continuing to do in a private capacity
what he had done so well since joining the Army in 1951 when he was seventeen. He had fought the Communists in Korea, in Malaya, in Borneo and
in Vietnam. For him it had become almost a personal crusade. 'I am
tremendously worried about the future of Australia,' he told his listeners
that day at Brisbane.

Payne is a man of strong personal convictions, a man of principle, an extremely patriotic Australian and a dedicated soldier. Nevertheless, after six months in Oman he returned on home leave, never to go back. He broke his contract because 'I was fearful that the next time I wouldn't perform. When you're a commanding officer, you are judge and jury and men's lives depend on you. It's not the firefight you're afraid of, but the fear of making a mistake and costing lives.'[2] Perhaps this frank admission was the realization that the illness that was to become so serious as to require psychiatric treatment was starting to affect his performance as a soldier.

During the late seventies Payne developed the symptoms of extreme stress. Probably having its origins in the rice-fields and jungles of Vietnam, it crept up on him slowly, so it was several years before he acknowledged his sickness. He then referred to his unreasoning outbursts of temper and ferocious arguments as his 'brainoes', saying: 'There's lots of blokes like me suffering this stress thing. It's your nerves, like metal fatigue.'[3] Unfortunately it eventually led to his having to give up his salesman's job to go into semi-retirement on his war service disability pension.

Payne has now got these problems well under control and is able to take part-time employment, travel, and enjoy his well-earned, more relaxing civilian life style. Of the four Australian Vietnam VCs Payne is the solitary survivor, the 96th Australian to be awarded the Cross. His place in history is assured, not only for his unsurpassed gallantry, but by the fact that he is likely to be the last Australian to win the VC for some time to come.

Compared to the other three Australians Payne was a comparative late-comer to the Team, as he did not arrive in Vietnam until January, 1969. A veteran, with plenty of active service experience, he was a family man, with five sons, and a natural leader. His appointment was as company commander of the 212th Company of the 1st MFB based at Pleiku. He had arrived at a difficult time in the development of these local Montagnard units.

One of the most intractable problems facing the ARVN and its advisers was how to prevent the wild, inaccessible, central highlands, with their countless jungle trails, from being used for the infiltration of troops and supplies from Cambodia, Laos and North Vietnam. It was the home of the Montagnard tribesmen − nomadic, aboriginal people with an historic anti-pathy, almost hatred, towards the Vietnamese. These people wanted auton-omy and objected vehemently, sometimes violently, to any interference in their lives. The South Vietnamese government had increased the animosity by seizure of tribal land for settlement by Vietnamese. From the military point of view it was vital to secure the active cooperation of the Montag-nards against the Viet Cong, but doing so was fraught with difficulties. The training of small units of tribesmen had begun in 1962, and then expanded rapidly. In 1964 there was a Montagnard revolt by several units, unable any longer to tolerate the behaviour of their Vietnamese commanders who, they alleged, treated them cruelly and stole their pay.

The Montagnards were mercenaries fighting for money. They could fight well if properly trained and led — but not by Vietnamese officers. This difficulty was never overcome. Nevertheless, as long as an American or Australian was in charge, they could perform adequately. Payne's arrival coincided with the push for Vietnamization. In September, 1968, orders had been received setting out how Vietnamese officers would take over full command throughout the Mike (Montagnard) Forces. Initially there would be joint command, starting at battalion level, but intended to extend quickly to all levels. Advisers were instructed to ensure that the Vietnamese flag was suitably honoured at all camps; political indoctrination classes in support of the South Vietnamese government were to be stepped up; and bounty money, paid for captured enemy weapons, was to be handed over by Vietnamese officers. The effect on Montagnard morale was predictable. Both U.S. and Australian advisers protested. They were expected to relinquish command to inexperienced, often incompetent, junior officers, yet still accompany units on operations, knowing that racial antagonism existed between leaders and led. In such a situation the advisers' lives were more at risk than ever.

Additionally, by early 1969, Mike Force units were increasingly being committed to tasks beyond their capacity, as U.S. troops were gradually withdrawn from combat. At best lightly armed, numerically weak, often undertrained, Mike Force battalions were now required to seek out and engage regular Viet Cong regiments. Such had been the case with Warrant Officer Simpson earlier in May, and it was repeated with Payne two weeks later.

Within eight days of taking command of his company Payne was in action. On this occasion he established his reputation as a forceful, competent and courageous leader, to the extent that he won the US Silver Star on his first mission. With a fellow Australian, Warrant Officer Kevin Latham, as his second-in-command, the company was being helicoptered into an operational area in the mountainous region south of Kontum when it was caught in an ambush just as the troops were landing. Ignoring the hail of fire directed at his company and the helicopters, Payne rallied his men, counter-attacked and fought his way out of the trap. The company's mission to locate the enemy had been achieved before most of his men had touched the ground. Three more days of heavy fighting followed, with Payne at the forefront, leaving his Montagnard soldiers in no doubt that they had got an exceptional commander.

In March Payne led the 212th Company up into the jungle, near the area of the Ben Het Special Forces camp, searching for Viet Cong who had overrun a nearby post. Although no contact was made, a huge logistic support facility, with tons of ammunition, was discovered.

The next month Payne was involved in another battalion operation which continued until 12 May. This time his reward was the American Distinguished Service Cross, a very rare decoration for a soldier of his rank, even though he was commanding a company. It came after Payne's leadership had held together his half-trained troops through several weeks of bitter battles, including being ambushed twice. The operation, to relieve a beleaguered border camp at Bu Gia Map, had started with another opposed helicopter landing, this time into bamboo thickets laced with sharpened stakes (panjies). Despite repeated air strikes, it took two days of close-quarter combat before respite was gained. Forty-eight hours later, as Payne's company was crossing a river, the second ambush was sprung. Payne, out in front, was stunned by a machine-gun bullet that grazed his head, so Latham charged forward firing an M-60 from his hip to silence the Viet Cong position. By Anzac Day the company were within 2½ kilometres of the camp, but were forced to halt their advance and take up a defensive position. Then began a series of enemy attacks which lasted for two weeks. During this period Payne's company hung on to a shrinking perimeter despite critical shortages of water and ammunition. Warrant Officer Barry Tolley brought in reinforcements and supplies which bolstered the defences. With their help, and heavy airstrikes, the remnants of 212 Company held on until the Viet Cong eventually broke off their assaults.

Six days later, on 18 May, Payne's battalion was deployed again. This time it was the start of the action in which he was to win his third gallantry award since his arrival — the VC.

By mid-May the special Forces camp at Ben Het was under siege from at least two NVA Regiments — the 24th in the north and the 27th in the east (Map 22). The camp and village sat astride route 512, under 15 kilometres from the tangle of trails and hills that covered the tri-border area where Laos, Cambodian and Vietnam meet. The road ran east to Dak To, another Special Forces camp 20 kilometres away, and thence south to the central highlands, Kontum and Pleiku. Already the 27th NVA Regiment had infiltrated between Ben Het and Dak To in an effort to isolate the garrison. If the enemy could capture Ben Het they would have complete control over this critical region, being able to pour in men and supplies with minimal opposition on the ground. Intelligence sources were certain that a third regiment, the 66th NVA, was also in the area, marching to join the others in a final squeeze to take Ben Het. Payne's battalion, the 1st MFB, was

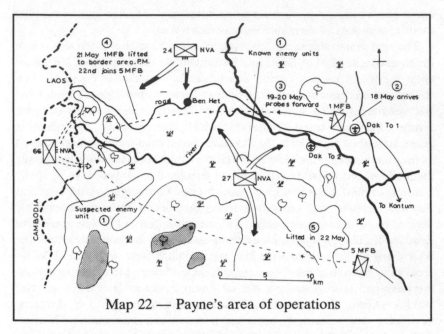

Map 22 — Payne's area of operations

given the task of finding the 66th NVA Regiment, engaging it and pinning it down until reinforcements could be helicoptered in to destroy it.

1st MFB had been engaged in rigorous operations for several weeks, suffering numerous casualties, and had had no opportunity to recuperate from the stress and fatigue of action. The battalion had lost its usual commanding officer (a USSF captain) on leave, so command was assumed by the executive officer, Lieutenant James. With him at his command post was Lieutenant Forbes, the US artillery liaison officer. The three weak companies were each under an adviser. Warrant Officer Barry Tolley had 211, Warrant Officer Keith Payne commanded 212, while 213 was under Sergeant 'Monty' Montez, USSF.

Not only had Payne's company been decimated by the recent fighting but there was a poor turnout for this operation. The Montagnards fought for money; they would report for duty if they needed more, but were inclined to stay away if their pockets were full or if the impending mission looked particularly hazardous. When Payne mustered his men he found he had only 52 — at full strength there should have been over 100, and without at least 75 he could not function as a company with three platoons. He went to his fellow Team comrade, Warrant Officer Jock Stewart, who ran the Training Company, to scrounge some recruits. He got 37 volunteers who had just twelve days' training. With a company of 89 ill-disciplined, poorly trained men, many of whom their platoon leaders did not even recognize, let alone know, Payne had to be content. He now had three platoons of less than 30 men each – one under Warrant Officer Latham, the second under Sergeant Jack Clement USSF, who also carried the radio, and the third commanded by Sergeant Gerard Dellwo USSF, the medical specialist.

The battalion was in poor shape for its task of locating and holding an NVA regiment which would outnumber it three to one, as well as being composed of experienced, regular troops. The Montagnards' main advantages of air mobility and the facility to call upon heavy airstrikes through their advisers were greatly diminished when the target was in dense jungle. But the main problem would be the lack of training and discipline.

The operation started on 18 May, with 1st MFB flying into Dak To preparatory to advancing towards Ben Het. Although coming under some shellfire, there was no infantry contact so the battalion was helicoptered to a ridgeline 9 kilometres SW of Ben Het, less than 5 kilometres from Cambodia, which seemed a likely infiltration route. On the 22nd the 5th MFB was lifted in, from another command, to a different ridge 4 kilometres to the south of Payne's battalion. At 4.00 pm that day the 1st MFB joined it, and both units took up defensive positions on the crest of the ridge. They were some 800 metres up, with the steep sided re-entrants and valleys choked with primary and secondary jungle, bamboo thickets and fern. On the ridgelines visibility was better and movement easier as the vegetation thinned, with some clearings and areas that had been blasted by B-52 bombers. The crests were fairly wide, with room for trenches and, for jungle country, reasonable fields of fire, but the sides plunged sharply hundreds of metres into the valleys.

Both battalions were ordered to start probing along the ridge on the 23rd. That morning aircraft strafed the ground nearby, hitting the jungle in areas thought likely to conceal the enemy. The Americans call it 'reconnaissance by fire' or sometimes, more bluntly, 'prophylactic fire'. It is seldom of much use in these circumstances. Tolley's company started out first, to run straight into strong hostile fire which quickly pushed the unenthusiastic Montagnards back. Montez was ordered to try. This was a somewhat unimaginative reinforcement of failure as his company merely moved through Tolley's to advance over the same ground, against the same position. Within 25 metres they suffered the same fate – casualties and another retreat. Nevertheless, the force had achieved part of its mission. By accident rather than design, they had been landed on the same ridgeline as the 66th NVA Regiment they were seeking.

That night new orders from Pleiku required that 1st MFB, supported by the 5th, should push the NVA off the ridge. There was no mention of holding them while reinforcements arrived. In effect, because of the narrowness

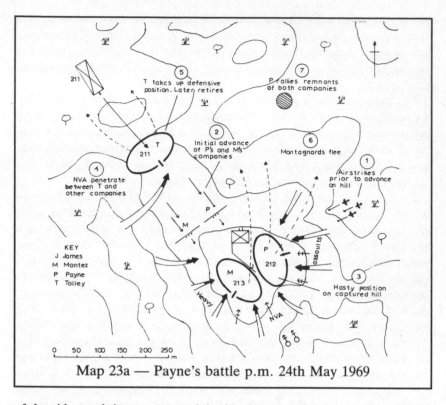

Map 23a — Payne's battle p.m. 24th May 1969

of the ridge and the steepness of the jungle-covered slopes, it meant there was little option but for the entire force to advance on a frontage of two platoons, following a thorough pounding of the enemy from the air — in other words a frontal attack by an inferior force against a superior one. The entire morning of 24 May was devoted to airstrikes. Flight after flight came screaming in low over the ridges in the sunlight, rocketing and bombing the bright green canopy below. The Montagnards were suitably impressed. At 2.30 pm 1st MFB began to push southwards along the 200-metre-wide crest of the ridge, with Payne's company on the left and Montez on the right (Map 23a). Both could only deploy one platoon across their front, with the other two in single file behind. Progress was hindered, not by the enemy, but rather by the confusion of shattered trees and craters. Tolley's company, moving up behind in reserve, was delayed by the need to search for enemy dead or abandoned weapons, so the gap between his men and the leading companies widened.

Of the enemy there was no sign until a position was spotted on a hilltop 700 metres from the battalion's starting point. Another airstrike was summoned, after which Payne and Montez occupied the hill without difficulty.

162

The battalion's commander, James, who was now up on the hill, decided to hold it and instructed his two company commanders accordingly. Tolley was still some way back along the ridge. There was little evidence of the opposition, apart from scattered trenches, on the otherwise quite bare hilltop, which measured some 300 by 120 metres.

For twenty minutes the Montagnards worked to prepare their positions, then the trap was sprung. Far from being destroyed or demoralized by the aerial attack, the NVA had merely pulled back off the hill into the denser jungle to organize their counter-stroke. It came suddenly, with mortars, rockets and machine guns pouring fire into the Montagnards from the jungle fringes on three sides of the hilltop clearing. Behind the two leading companies an enemy force advanced into the gap between them and Tolley. Encirclement was complete. Tolley, unable to join the rest of the battalion, formed his own defensive locality on the ridge, some 200 metres from the other companies.

The Montagnards, without adequate cover, soon suffered heavy losses from sustained, accurate and close-range shooting. Payne was the first to react. Supported by Montez, he attempted to galvanize his company into attacking the machine-gun positions by fire and movement. Despite his personal disdain for danger, he was asking too much of his soldiers. Fifteen metres was the furthest they could advance. Montez could do no better.

With the enemy pressing closer on all sides, the situation was now critical. Payne devoted his efforts to keeping his company in place, as the possibility of panic and flight was very real. He started jogging round his men, seemingly oblivious to the bullets, mortar bombs and rockets that were pouring into the position. Now firing his rifle, now yelling encouragement or instructions, now hurling grenades, Payne kept up his one-man war for some minutes. At one moment his radio operator was close beside him while Payne was firing his rifle, the next a rocket-propelled grenade decapitated his operator and blew the rifle from his hands. Without a pause he seized an M60 machine gun to continue the fight.

With blood pouring down his face from a head-wound Payne's frenzied actions brought about a slight respite. The enemy's hesitation was only momentary. As the assault was reinforced, increasing pressure was put on both companies, including a seemingly endless stream of withering fire from at least four machine guns. Even for seasoned troops there was probably only one likely outcome. With the half-trained Montagnards it came that much sooner — they ran. It had all the makings of an unmitigated disaster. Payne himself was wounded, Montez was lying badly injured on the hilltop, while Latham, Forbes and James had all been hit, but not so seriously. Many wounded Montagnards were left where they fell, while the majority of the uninjured disappeared down the slope, off the hill and into the comparative safety of the jungle valley to the NE.

Payne was determined to stop the rot. Arranging covering fire, he dashed across the open ground into the jungle, shouting and screaming at his men to halt. He succeeded in rallying a mixed bag of soldiers from both companies in a position about 350 metres from the ridge. Many men were missing, including Montez who had been abandoned on the hill. Although James was still in overall command, it was Payne whose leadership kept the force together. His filthy, sweat-soaked figure, with bloodied face, toured the area organizing a makeshift defensive perimeter, arranging for treatment of the wounded and calling up support from two helicopter gunships that had fortuitously appeared overhead. Ignoring more wounds from mortar splinters to his hands and arms, Payne coolly coordinated the protective fire from the helicopters on to the enemy. At the same time he instructed them not to fire directly on to the hilltop or ridge to avoid hitting his own wounded or Tolley's company that was still up there, making its way slowly back the way it had come towards the 5th MFB.

It was almost dark when Payne made the decision that was later to merit the award of the VC. He explained to James that he intended to make his way back up on to the ridge and hill to find Montez and as many other wounded or missing as possible and get them out. This appeared to be a suicide mission. Although James did not dissuade Payne, he felt certain that it was the last he would see of this audacious Australian. The obstacles were daunting. How was he to penetrate the NVA positons in the dark without discovery when he had no idea of their actual location? How was he to find the wounded, particularly Montez, crawling around over a large area of jungle and undergrowth? How could he be certain that any movement was not the enemy, rather than his own men? Any mistake would be fatal. How would he avoid getting hopelessly lost or disorientated by the twists and turns he must make? Even if he discovered wounded comrades, how would he get them out − carry them, drag them, with all the added risk of making a noise? How long would it all take? Did he have the stamina after all his exertions and loss of blood? If he had tried to answer these problems he would never have gone. But he did go − alone. All the other advisers were wounded except for Dellwo, who, as the medic, was required to stay. Payne could not trust the training or judgement of any Montagnards. He rightly felt that taking others would merely serve to increase the likelihood of noise and discovery. As he could not speak their language their presence in these circumstances would be a liability.

Payne set out, with a radio and an armalite rifle, on one of the most amazing solo missions of the war (Map 23b). Helped by the bright moonlight and the thinning jungle along the crest, visibility was about six metres.

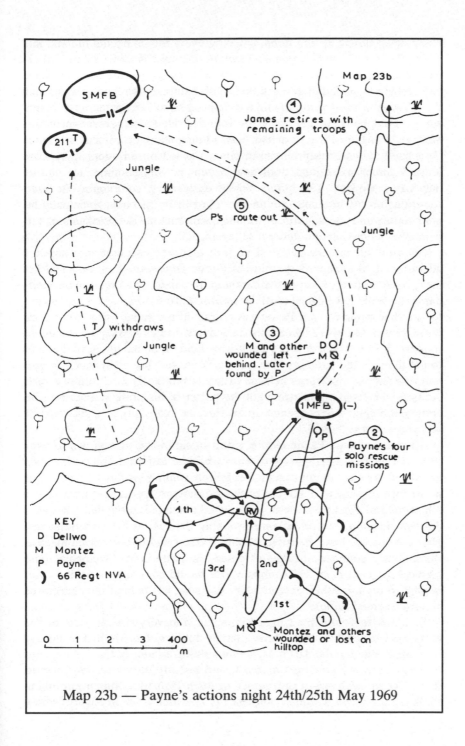

Map 23b — Payne's actions night 24th/25th May 1969

165

He crawled slowly up the slope, stopping every few moments to look and listen. He could hear movement, sometimes glimpse shadowy figures, obviously the enemy. At times there was the crack of a single shot as some unfortunate wounded man was killed. With extreme care Payne penetrated the NVA positions to gain the hilltop clearing he had defended a few hours earlier. Here he began his search for wounded. He found several, including Montez, to whom Payne's arrival was nothing short of miraculous. Then he started to lead the group back down the hill on an agonizingly slow journey, much more hazardous now he was no longer alone. He had to help carry Montez. The others helped each other, sometimes one man squirming on his stomach with another clinging to his back. Eventually he got Montez and the handful of Montagnards back to the remnants of the battalion. Payne immediately set off again.

This time he was trying to rescue, not his buddy Montez, not another adviser, but Montagnards he did not know. However, they were still his men, lying injured or lost in the darkness, so when, by all reasonable standards, he could have called it off, he returned. To succeed again was asking for another miracle — yet Payne was granted three more, for he went back three times. On these occasions he located more missing or wounded soldiers, guiding them down to a half-way point, as he did not have the time to get them to the battalion. Several times he was shot at by machine-gun and rifle fire, several times he sank exhausted to the ground. On one such occasion the fatigue and stress got the better of his professionalism — he crouched behind a log, opened up his shirt and carefully lit a cigarette. It was crazy, but it helped.

After three hours Payne led his group of survivors, now grown to over thirty, down to the temporary defensive base — to find it deserted. James had decided he could not stay on indefinitely waiting for Payne, who might never turn up, but to make use of the darkness to try and get back to the 5th battalion. He had no wish to be caught isolated in daylight. It was a difficult decision, but on balance probably the best in the circumstances. His next one was less defensible. Within 200 metres James resolved to leave the seriously wounded, including Montez, under the care of Dellwo and the medical sergeant from 213 Company. He would continue the withdrawal, hoping to organize their rescue later. To those left behind the chances of survival seemed remote.

To a less tenacious man than Payne the discovery that the rest of the battalion had left him would have shattered his resolve. He had seemingly been abandoned in the darkness, within a short distance of the enemy, with no extra men to carry the wounded, and nobody in any fit condition to fight. To Payne it was just another problem to solve. Still the thinking soldier, he noticed a trail of phosphorus leaf mould, overturned recently by passing soldiers, and opted to follow it. Within a short distance Dellwo and the small group of wounded Montagnards were found. They were delighted and amazed. Dellwo later commented: 'How he found us I'll never know . . . He said he followed our trail of phosphorus glowing in the dark . . . He insisted the NVA would find us as he did, if not soon, then in the morning. Also he wasn't convinced that help would be able to arrive. From past experience with Warrant Officer Payne I know he had about the coolest head when things seem to be the worst.'[4]

They now had at least 800 metres of thick jungle, steep slippery slopes, and enemy positions, to negotiate before they could reach the 5th MFB. Progress would be slow and noisy with a party of forty Montagnards, mostly wounded, together with the two medics and Montez, who had to be carried. In single file they struggled painfully through the darkness, forced to traverse the valleys rather than follow the easier ridges where the NVA might be expected. Payne still had sufficient strength to take turns at carrying the heavy Montez, check navigation and make whispered but fruitless appeals over his radio for a helicopter casualty evacuation. Montez was dying; only prompt evacuation could save him. At last a helicopter was made available, but as the group waited under a hole in the jungle canopy for the rig to be lowered, Montez died. His body was carefully wrapped in a groundsheet before being hidden for recovery later.

Pressing on, Payne radioed for a propeller-driven aircraft to fly low overhead to drown the noise they were making. Then, at last, he saw the sparks and heard the cough of mortars firing in the area held by the 5th battalion. At 3.10 am on the 25th Payne brought his party in. Although himself wounded early that afternoon, he had been in action non-stop for over twelve hours: his efforts had inspired all who saw him and he had personally rescued forty men, mostly wounded, from almost certain death. He had succeeded, in the face of seemingly unsurmountable difficulties, by a combination of physical strength, mental toughness, military professionalism, leadership — and luck. If ever there was an example of fortune favouring the brave it was Payne's achievement that night.

The battle had cost the 1st MFB over 50 per cent in killed or missing; Payne's company was down to thirty-one, many wounded. For them the war was over. For several weeks they were withdrawn from operations for rest, re-training and re-equipping. When the 1st MFB returned to action it was under an Australian commander.

In early September, 1969, Payne was summoned to a meeting at the Free World Building in Saigon to be stunned by the public announcement by Major-General Hay, the Australian Commander in Vietnam, that he had been awarded the VC. At first Payne could not believe it. His close friend 'Simmo', whose VC battle had been fought in the same area only two weeks before Payne's, was present to advise him to 'take it easy and get a few cans of beer into you'. Payne promptly obliged. Typical of many VC winners Payne did not consider his actions, either at the time or afterwards, as exceptional. He admitted he had been extremely frightened. Many years later he dismissed his actions with excessive modesty, saying: 'Oh well, I went out on my own and picked up a few blokes and hauled them in — somebody had to go out.'[5] On another occasion he said, 'You don't set out to win a Victoria Cross. And believe me, you certainly don't go back looking for another one.'[6]

Payne found the courage to overcome his fear, his instinct for survival, from his position of responsibility for others. As the leader he was looked up to, expected to do his duty. Like many other brave men, he found the fear of failure more frightening than concern for his own safety. Being in command, he was forced to think of others, not himself; his responsibilities kept him busy and kept his mind on other things. As he put it: 'I think it's the conscious responsibility you assume for other men's lives, the moral obligation you have towards your soldiers. Your instinct is to be a survivor, but your instinct also demands that your soldiers survive as well . . . You just do what you have to do. You do it without the luxury of thinking will I or won't I.'[7]

The memory of those hectic hours, and of combat elsewhere, remains with Payne. Although he believes passionately in the need to defend freedom, his country, and above all his mates, he freely admits the horror of war. Reflecting on that brotherhood of soldiers the world over, which no civilian quite understands, he explained: 'In war we are closer than blood brothers. There is nothing closer than those you have felt and smelt the full horror of war with . . . You have to feel it, smell the carnage, the death, the horror and the noise — my God the noise. Only the men who have been there can know it, it's that terrible, that horrible.'[8] It was perhaps to be expected that Payne singled out noise as being particularly horrific. Back in 1951 he had enlisted to escape being an apprentice cabinet maker because, 'I didn't like confined spaces, and I didn't like the noise'.

Shortly after the announcement, Payne was flown home for hospitalization for a duodenal ulcer that had been diagnosed, almost by chance, when he was having his wounds treated. He was angry and depressed by the anti-war feeling then prevalent in Australia. There were no more tumultuous welcome-home receptions such as 1 RAR had received a few years earlier. At best Vietnam veterans were ignored, at worst abused. Payne recalled that despite his VC he 'couldn't go anywhere in uniform, and my kids had to fight their way through school in Canberra, where the children of the public servants told them their old man was a murderer.'[9]

On his recovery Payne received a prestigious posting as an instructor at the Royal Military College, Duntroon. From there he went, on 13 April, 1970, to receive his Cross from the Queen on board the Royal Yacht *Britannia* in Brisbane harbour. Other honours include his being a freeman of Brisbane and the shire of Hinchinbrook, a Brisbane suburb park being named Keith Payne Park, and his photograph and citation being displayed in the Hall of Heroes at Fort Bragg, U.S.A.

After retiring from the Army in 1975 and shedding his Arab uniform in 1976, Payne settled down to a quiet but enjoyable life in Mackay. He appreciates the peace of that lovely coast, the palm trees, and the relaxing pleasure of fishing. He took a part-time job as Secretary of the Mackay Totally and Permanently Incapacitated Pensioners' Association, which still permits him time for travel.

His most momentous trip was in 1986. The US Special Forces Association held a national reunion in San Antonio, Texas, and the Australian airline, Qantas, agreed to fly Payne to America to attend. His reception, not only by his old Special Forces' buddies and officials, but by the American people, was overwhelming. He was driven from the airport to the city centre to lay a wreath at the door of the Alamo. He was welcomed personally by the Governor of Texas and San Antonio's Mayor, before marching through the streets with thousands of other veterans. But Payne did not just join the march, he was singled out for exceptional treatment. He was to lead the entire parade with the Texas Medal of Honor recipients. Wearing a Special Forces beret and badge, blazer, the Team tie, and with no less than fifteen medals glittering on his chest, Payne stepped out proudly through the cheering crowds. It was a profoundly moving experience. The parade was followed by a huge public reception. There, over 1500 people heard how he had won his Cross, how he had saved so many lives, including two Americans, and how he had struggled so long in his endeavour to save Montez. The crowd stood to cheer him to the echo.

Keith Payne is a man of integrity, a man with strongly held beliefs, an unshakeable patriotism, and is seldom frightened to speak his mind. Two subjects in particular can arouse his wrath. The first is the growing infiltration of the Japanese into Australia, through ownership of companies and increasing financial influence. He recently told a reporter: 'I am very angry and very upset at the trend. What's happening amounts to a wholesale sell-out of the country to Japan. It makes a mockery of all we have fought for and insults the memory of the men who died on the Burma railway.'[10]

The second matter involves medals. His own VC in particular, let alone the other fourteen, is priceless. His Cross is the last to be won by an Australian and, as such, would fetch in excess of A$100,000 – his complete set probably double that amount. To Payne the mention of selling his medals disgusts him, and he cannot understand how others have done so. His VC belongs to Australia, the Army and his family, so he has worded his will in such a way that it can never be sold. As recently as 1989 he told the *Queensland Sun*: 'I think it is downright sacrilegious for a person to take money from selling a war decoration.'

Payne's pride is not boastful. He avoids publicity if he can, his ultimate satisfaction is in belonging to the greatest family in the world – which is how he describes his fellow VC holders.

PART FOUR

The Falkland Islands

At around 11 pm on the 1st of April, 1982, ninety-two Argentinian marines of the Amphibious Commando Company under Lieutenant-Commander Sabarots landed from small inflatable rubber boats, two miles south of Stanley. They split into two parties, the largest making for Moody Brook barracks, some six miles away, where they hoped to catch the bulk of the Royal Marine (RM) garrison asleep. The other group of sixteen was heading for Government House. The invasion had started.

After six hours, during which they had seriously underestimated the difficulties of moving across country at night, the marines arrived to find the barracks empty. The eighty-two RMs, under Major Norman, were well aware of imminent invasion so were not spending the night in their beds. At Government House Lieutenant-Commander Giachino simply planned to walk into the building and demand the Governor's surrender. He attempted to do this with four men. As the house was packed with over forty fully alerted troops his temerity was rewarded with a hail of fire. Giachino was a victim of his own audacity – he fell badly wounded, with a severed artery in his thigh. He was to be the first Argentinian fatality of the attack. The assault had been launched at 6.30 am on the 2nd of April. Three hours later the Governor ordered the RMs to cease fire in view of the large-scale follow-up landings and the consequent futility of further resistance.

Before the eighties only a tiny fraction of Britains could place the Falk-

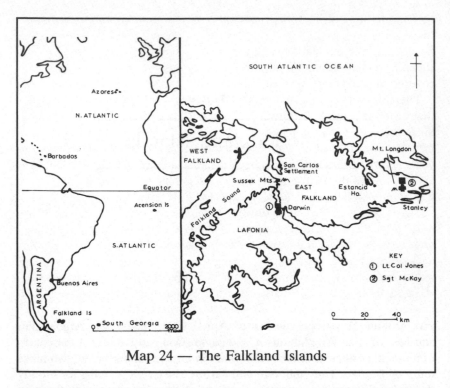

Map 24 — The Falkland Islands

land Islands on the map. Of these, fewer still knew anything about them, or that their inhabitants were as British as themselves. Prior to the war the population was 1,800 and falling. This remote colony was a mere 450 miles from Argentina, but some 8,000 from Britain. Captain John Davis had discovered them in 1592, although it was not until almost a hundred years later that they got their name. A Captain Strong sailed between the two main islands, made several landings and named the passage Falkland Sound, after Lord Falkland, the then Commissioner of the Admiralty. From this the group of 200 islands took its English name.

In the centuries that followed history largely passed them by. Only briefly, in late 1914, did they hit the headlines, when a squadron of Royal Navy warships sailed out of Stanley (then called Port William) to meet and defeat the Germans under Graf von Spee. Of the five German cruisers only one escaped sinking, while the British, with four dead, came through virtually unscathed. Regrettably, the RN was not to escape so lightly in 1982 when five ships were sunk, many damaged, and of the 252 servicemen killed, 197 died aboard vessels at sea.

The two principal islands, East and West Falklands, are divided by the narrow strait of Falkland Sound. It was East Falkland that saw the bulk of

172

the land fighting during May/June, 1982. That was where the main Argentinian garrison had dug itself in, particularly around Stanley, a village that housed half the population. The remaining islanders were scattered in tiny sheep-farming settlements all over the 'camp', or open grasslands that covered most of the rest of the islands.

The colony's revenue before the war came from sheep and stamps, in that order of priority. Afterwards the importance of the two was reversed. Since the end of the campaign the islands have received millions of pounds in aid for infrastructure and development that was undreamed of a few years ago. British territory had been invaded and the ousting of the attackers was to cost the British government and people dear in terms of money, if not quite so much as had been expected in terms of men.

The Falklands War will go down in British military history as one of her most improbable victories, almost a military miracle. The Argentinian attack caught Britain totally unprepared. Not only did she have to assemble a suitable task force within days, when no such eventuality had been contemplated, but the operations would take place 8,000 miles away. They would have to start with a large-scale amphibious landing. The British had not been involved in such a task since the Normandy landings nearly forty years before. What expertise existed was confined to a small group of RN and RM planners, neither of whom had the scale of amphibious equipment or craft necessary to undertake what had every possibility of being an opposed landing. Even the aircraft carrier, upon which the entire operation depended for air cover, was only available through good fortune – it had been sold to the Australians, but had not yet been delivered.

In the event it was a close-run thing, with, as always in war, luck playing a prominent part. Fortunately it only took 25 days of ground operations to force capitulation before the weather worsened; fortunately the Argentinian Air Force was flying at the limit of its range; fortunately the quality of the enemy conscripts was often poor and their leadership frequently at fault. That it was all over so quickly, and that out of 28,000 servicemen committed to battle, only 252 died, was in retrospect, astonishing.

As always in land conflict, terrain dictates the tactics. The Falklands countryside and climate resembles that of the Outer Hebrides – miles and miles of treeless, windswept, open, soggy peat, with no roads, and comparatively low hills, interspersed with occasional steep, rocky crags. In soldier's language it was 'bare-arsed' country, with the only cover from view or fire provided by the folds in the ground. In military terms this meant movement by day was a last resort. The defenders had the advantage. Of the six set-piece British battalion attacks, all took place at night.

The critical shortage of helicopters, particularly after so many went down with the *Atlantic Conveyor*, together with the almost total lack of vehicles, meant that the infantry were burdened with loads well in excess of 100 pounds. Ask any infantryman of his abiding memories of the conflict and most will single out the endless plodding over soft peat under crippling loads. The 'yomping', as the RMs called it, ('tabbing' to the Parachute Regiment) was frequently more of a strain than actual combat. It was made worse by the weather. Not that the climate is as extreme as is sometimes imagined, but the troops could seldom keep dry. The everlasting bitter wind, driving rain and soaking clothes rendered living in the open misery. Feet were the main problem. Being compelled to march and fight for day after day without being able to dry one's feet led to the unforgettable agonies of trench foot. This was to cause as much suffering as the enemy. In the end it was the sheer doggedness, determination and guts of the foot soldier that overcame both the elements and the enemy. This aspect of warfare has not changed much over the centuries.

The Parachute Regiment won both the VCs in the Falklands. Both were posthumous awards; both were gained by individuals charging, singlehandedly, an enemy position. Lieutenant-Colonel Jones, the Commanding Officer of 2 Para, won his in the opening battle of the campaign; Sergeant McKay of 3 Para won his just two days before the final surrender.

CHAPTER 10

Darwin Hill – Falkland Islands
28 May, 1982

LIEUTENANT-COLONEL HERBERT ('H') JONES VC OBE
The 2nd Battalion The Parachute Regiment

'I'll sue the lot'.
Lieutenant Colonel Jones, referring to Margaret Thatcher, John
Nott (Minister of Defence) and the BBC, on hearing of the
BBC's broadcast that 2 Para were poised to attack Goose Green.

It has been said that Colonel Jones won his VC doing the job of a subaltern or NCO, that he should never have risked his own life, or those of his command group, by deliberately involving himself in personal close-quarter combat. That he was not doing what was normally expected of a commanding officer in action at the moment he was killed is true. But the situation at that time was far from normal. It was Jones's conviction that the advance had bogged down, that daylight had brought a crisis to the battle, that there was every likelihood that the Argentinians would now get the upper hand, and that his presence and leadership at the front were essential if the attack was to continue. It was a matter of military judgement, made on the battlefield, by the man in command and ultimately accountable for the entire operation. Whether or not, in retrospect, it was a sound decision will no doubt be argued for many years to come, but whatever the answer it is no reflection on Jones's gallantry, or on his winning a VC, bestowed for outstanding courage in the presence of an enemy.

There are plenty of precedents in military history for what Jones did. One of the earliest is worth quoting. 'I recognized that this was a crisis, there were no reserves available. I had no shield with me but I snatched one from a soldier in the rear ranks and went forward to the front line . . . and shouted encouragement to the rest of the men . . . My arrival gave the troops fresh hope; their determination was restored because, with the commander-in-chief looking on, each man was eager to do his best whatever the risk to himself. As a result the enemy's attack was slowed down a little.' Over 2000 years ago Julius Caesar, a commanding general not a battalion commander, recognised a situation that demanded the risking of his own life to achieve an objective. Throughout history armies whose officers led from the front invariably triumphed. In tough fighting the casualty rate among senior officers is often indicative of the quality of the army, or formation, under them. Compare the high proportion of German generals who died in combat during the latter half of the Second World War, with that of the Americans of similar rank in Vietnam. Both were losing a major war, but the German leadership on the battlefield was the prime factor in creating probably the most effective fighting force seen in modern times. Whereas, with the Americans, the early seventies saw their army in Vietnam reduced to a rabble by drug abuse, desertion, combat refusals and 'fragging'.[1] In 1967 out of 781 Israelis of all ranks killed, no less than eight were brigadiers or higher. Jones was in good company.[2]

There can be little doubt that, at 2.00 am on 28 May, 1982, as the leading companies of 2 Para were squelching slowly forward through the rain lashed blackness towards their start line, Jones had got what he wanted. He was about to lead a parachute battalion into battle. Not only was it the first such battle of the Falklands campaign, but it was the first time a British battalion had launched a set-piece night attack since Korea, thirty years earlier. It was the pinnacle of Jones's career as a soldier. Since boyhood he had never wanted to do anything except soldiering; the Army always came first in his life. As he sloshed his way down the track from Camilla Creek House he barely noticed the cold wind or driving rain, his mind totally preoccupied with the task in hand. He was utterly determined that 2 Para would succeed. The climax of his career had arrived. All the years of training, all the pestering of the MOD to get his battalion to the Falklands, all the intensive preparations on the voyage out, had culminated in this advance into the unknown on a filthy black night 8000 miles from home.

Jones had been the CO for a year and had had his 42nd birthday exactly two weeks before. Although now a permanent Parachute Regiment officer, most of his career had been spent in the Devon and Dorset Regiment. An old Etonian, he was to be the 35th to win the VC. After five years with the Devon and Dorsets he was seconded to 3 Para as a captain for three years. The next fourteen years saw the normal sequence of regimental and staff appointments – adjutant of his battalion, junior staff officer at HQ UKLF, a student at the Camberley Staff College, company commander, brigade major in Northern Ireland (which earned him an MBE), instructor at the School of Infantry, then a senior staff post back at HQ UKLF where he was awarded the OBE for his part in planning operations for the Zimbabwe peace keeping force. Finally promotion to Lieutenant-Colonel and the command of 2 Para.

During his year as CO he had made his mark. He was an enthusiast, very much a black and white person, who became extremely frustrated and angry at delays. His wife, Sara, maintains that he would have been impossible to live with if he had not succeeded in getting to the Falklands. She illustrated his impatience by describing how, when the family were playing a board game, usually a wargame, 'he would move everyone else's counters to hurry things along'.[3] This inclination to intolerance came to the surface in situations where he witnessed something being done incorrectly or badly when he could seldom refrain from forceful intervention. He was, however, a remarkably fine soldier, with the knack of inspiring his men by his example and his ability to talk to them in a blunt but effective manner.

On training he was always to the fore, getting involved with everything that was happening. Sometimes this had its humorous side. His former padre, David Cooper, described one such occasion in Kenya when Jones was right up front with the leading section during a dawn attack exercise using live ammunition. There was a prominent hill just ahead and the CO pointed out an imaginary enemy bunker on it to the soldier carrying the 66mm anti-tank rocket launcher. Jones vigorously pressured the soldier to take it out, and quickly. The unfortunate man became flustered and the more he fumbled the more his CO yelled. At last the 66mm was fired, with the rocket sailing up, right over the hill. There was absolute silence for several moments; then the muffled roar of the explosion, followed by the Colonel's explosion − 'Christ, he's missed the fucking mountain!'.

Jones had been fortunate to take over a battalion that had a sound staff structure, with a highly trained and experienced cadre of NCOs. The previous CO, Colin Thompson, had laid the foundations upon which Jones was able to build. Despite the shock of the Warrenpoint ambush in Northern Ireland, 2 Para's morale recovered quickly, and Jones's enthusiasm for aggressive training, sport and shooting had ensured a battalion at its peak when it landed in the Falklands.[4] Within the year he had won the respect of everybody for his military skills, for his intense loyalty and for his determination to make 2 Para the best. Not that everybody liked him. His reluctance to compromise, his strong will and inability to suffer fools could sometimes lead to feelings of intense dislike by others, but they were a small minority. To most he was a first-class CO who had the complete confidence and respect of his men.

When Brigadier Julian Thompson, his brigade commander, told him that the cancelled raid on Darwin and Goose Green was on again, Jones was delighted. Political pressure demanded action. London no longer regarded the acute operational and logistic problems caused by the loss of three big Chinook and six Wessex helicopters on the *Atlantic Conveyor* as acceptable reasons for more delays. From a strictly military point of view it is doubtful whether a battalion attack was justified, but after the brigade had sat six days at Ajax Bay the planners, and the public at home, could no longer tolerate the seeming inaction. Jones was told that the Argentinians on the peninsula he must take were a mixed force of a weak battalion reinforced by some artillery, AA guns and engineers. If this was true then 2 Para were about to attack with a 1:1 ratio of infantrymen. Military manuals set down that attackers should outnumber defenders by 3:1 to give them a reasonable chance of success.

Relative strength was not the only problem that faced Jones. Just to push southwards down the long narrow peninsula was not to his liking — there was little scope for manoeuvre or flanking attacks. It was a purely frontal effort which went against all his tactical training and instincts. Unfortunately, he had no option. Suggestions that the assault be heliborne, with the battalion descending in darkness to the south of Goose Green, were vetoed due to lack of available helicopters and a shortage of pilots trained in the use of passive night vision equipment. An indirect approach from the sea was ruled out on advice that entanglement in the thick seaweed (kelp), navigational problems at night in Benton Lock, or striking submerged rocks around the peninsula would prevent upwards of 50 per cent of the landing craft reaching the shore.

As Jones saw it, the only way to succeed was by maximum use of the Paras' speed and aggressiveness in the dark. Surprise could not be achieved by day and the bare countryside meant that the troops would be completely exposed in daylight to observed small arms, mortar or artillery fire, and, above all, to air attack by Pucaras. A night advance was the only possibility. Move fast, hit hard, keep going were the prerequisites of success. Jones felt strongly that, if surprised, Argentinian resistance would crumble.

Then came the ever-present problems of time and space calculations. There were many imponderables, but two inescapable facts — that last light was at 4.15 pm and first light at 6.30 am. Over 14 hours of darkness to move from the assembly area at Camilla Creek House to the high ground overlooking Darwin and Goose Green — a distance of 8 kms to the former and 10 kms to the latter (see Map 25). In purely mathematical terms this meant that by advancing at around 700 metres per hour the unit would reach Goose Green at dawn. Ample time? Perhaps, if it were not for so many other factors, all tending to delay. Time was needed to secure the start line, position Support Company's Milans,[5] machine guns and mortars, to avoid or cross obstacles and minefields and to carry out a series of company or platoon actions against known or suspected intermediate enemy positions. After each such action time would be consumed reorganizing to resume the advance. Darkness itself doubled the difficulties of every move, slowing progress, complicating navigation and creating additional uncertainty. Jones's final plan envisaged the battle being fought in six successive pha-

25. Sergeant I.J. McKay.
(Imperial War Museum)

26. The rocky summit of Mount Longdon, looking east towards Stanley. It was near this spot that Sergeant McKay was killed winning his VC. *(The Falkland Islands Squadron, RE)*

27. The Sergeant McKay Memorial Trophy, awarded annually to the winners of 3 PARA's inter-platoon military skills competition. *(The Parachute Regiment)*.

ses, with companies leap-frogging down the peninsula. A Company would be the first into action, crossing its start line to assault a suspected position at Burntside House at 2.00 am. Major Farrar-Hockley, the company commander, would then have 4½ hours of darkness left to reach Darwin Hill overlooking the tiny settlement. Possible, but by no means certain.

There were some difficult decisions to make on what to take and what to leave behind. The problem was lack of transport for heavy weapons and ammunition, which meant humping everything a total distance of 15 kms during the night of 26/27 May, and then 8-10 kms down the peninsula on the 27/28. It was essential the Paras were not overburdened, so ammunition, two full waterbottles per man, plus 48 hours of rations, had priority. Radio sets were kept to a minimum: A Company decided not to take their 2″ mortars (HMS *Arrow* was to provide star shell illumination); many left their entrenching tools behind. Initially Jones declined to take any 81mm mortars either, because of the weight of the bombs, but was persuaded to take two, rather than rely entirely on the three 105mm supporting guns from 8 Commando Battery. Only three Milan firing-posts and seventeen missiles would be carried forward, together with six GPMGs.

The battalion was to attack with minimal ground fire support – two mortars and three guns. Without the presence of HMS *Arrow* with her 4.5 inch gun such a plan would have been unthinkable. By day the Harriers and helicopters with SS-11 missiles should be available, while the Argentinians could be expected to fly Pucara sorties from Goose Green airstrip or Stanley. A daylight battle, however, was the last thing Jones wanted. He intended to retain a tight personal grip of the battalion, keeping close behind the leading companies with his tactical headquarters to make certain he was in touch with events and to ensure momentum was maintained.

Known or suspected enemy positions, together with Jones's outline plan, are shown on Map 25. The battalion would leave Sussex Mountain at last light on 26 May for Camilla Creek House. There it would lie up during the next day, before the actual attack during the night of 27/28. 2 Para would advance with two companies up – A Company left and B Company right, with D Company in reserve following them down the centre of the peninsula. From what he knew of the enemy it seemed that the western side of the peninsula would provide most of the opposition, so the particularly aggressive B Company, under the experienced Major Crosland, took that flank. A Company's 2.00 am attack on Burntside House would start the battle, followed, on its completion, by B Company taking the 50-foot hill 1200 metres to the west. From then on the plan envisaged B and D Companies leap-frogging forward to the various low hills down the western side and in the centre of the peninsula, exploiting up to Goose Green, while A Company took Coronation Point and Darwin in the east. Hopefully, both

179

Darwin and Goose Green would be dominated before first light, so that the final advance into the settlements could be made in daylight to minimize civilian casualties. It was a tight timetable.

The weather was foul. A chill wind cut through combat jackets and driving rain added to the misery of the soldiers at Camilla Creek House. Jones took a calculated risk in allowing virtually the entire battalion to squeeze itself into the farmhouse, outbuildings, barns and sheds. He reasoned that the concealment, shelter and rest thus provided were well worth the possibility of serious casualties if caught by artillery fire. It was here that the first setback occurred. Around midday on the 27th 2 Para tuned in to the BBC World Service to hear that a 'parachute battalion is poised and ready to assault Darwin and Goose Green'. This was unbelievable. All the careful concealment of the move forward, all chances of surprise, had been blown. It enraged Jones to such an extent that he vowed he would sue everybody responsible for manslaughter. It was a gross error which meant that the battalion advanced convinced that their enemy had been alerted and probably reinforced.

Jones had given out his orders late in the afternoon, so it was dark when the company commanders grouped their officers and senior NCOs around them to explain the plan. It was rather rushed and hampered by a shortage of maps. The advance was to be silent, with no preparatory bombardment. All possible targets were registered and on call for the moment that contact was made.

C Company was away first, to check the route to, and secure, the start lines for A and B companies. It was closely followed by Support Company with the Naval Gun Fire Observer (NGFO) to control HMS *Arrow*'s shooting, the assault pioneers acting as ammunition carriers, as well as the Milans and GPMGs. They were to set up their fire support base on the high ground on the west bank of Camilla Creek, directly opposite B Company's first objective. The two 81mm mortars had a separate base plate position at the northern end of the peninsula.

A Company commander had allowed himself some three hours to get his men on to their start line − a convenient fence 500 metres east of Burntside House − but even this proved insufficient. Despite the C Company guides, the pitch blackness, numerous streams and fences, plus the need to change direction, combined to make A Company some 35 minutes late in launching its attack. Burntside House was shot up, the leading platoons closed on the objective but met with no effective resistance. Four shocked civilians survived the hail of fire that penetrated the farmhouse, but the enemy had fled leaving two bodies some distance from the house.

Next it was B Company's turn. They crossed their start line at 3.10 am and were soon fighting a series of section skirmishes with Argentinians entrenched on the low hill that was their objective. In the midst of this battle HMS *Arrow* ceased firing due to a turret fault. Although it was rectified later, HMS *Arrow* was forced to leave at 5.20 am in order to regain the shelter of the air defence umbrella at San Carlos. Thus, an hour before first light, 2 Para was to have her gun support cut by 75 per cent. In the meantime the Argentinians' guns had started to fire their DF tasks and shells began falling across the peninsula. Fortunately they frequently sank deep into the soft peat before exploding, which reduced their effectiveness considerably.

Jones was soon worried about the timetable. D Company became engaged in the centre of the peninsula, with positions bypassed by B Company in the darkness. More time was consumed clearing them, while A Company waited for these battles to be concluded before continuing on to Coronation Point where anything up to a company position was anticipated. At 5.15 am, with 1¼ hours of darkness left, 2 Para was a long way from its final objectives. On the right B Company had been engaged and was still 1000 metres north of Boca House, while D Company, 3500 metres from Goose Green, was still sorting itself out after its successful engagement in the centre. Only on the left was A Company within striking distance of its final destination – Darwin. It had not had to fight its way forward and so was well in hand when it arrived at Coronation Point shortly after 5.15 am. There was no fire-fight. The platoons moved up through the blackness to find the rising ground west of the Point deserted. A Company had arrived on their phase 3 objective unscathed.

Up to this point 2 Para had done remarkably well. In three hours of confused skirmishing with pockets of enemy there had been only four or five casualties, opposition had collapsed when attacked, and Darwin was only 1000 metres away. Although B and D Companies were still sorting themselves out and were not yet ready to push on, it was to be nearly an hour before A Company moved south again, an hour in which darkness started to evaporate, revealing the bare, grassy slopes of the low hills west of Darwin. Why the delay? Farrar-Hockley, A Company Commander, knew his task was to be in a position to move into Darwin at first light, but he remained at Coronation Point while vital minutes slipped away. His orders had been perfectly clear – to take Darwin in phase 6, but to move up to the high ground to the west of the Settlement during phase 5. Nevertheless phase 4, the move of B Company on the other side of the peninsula to the high ground overlooking Boca House, had not yet been attempted. For A Company to push on immediately would be a major change of plan, with the possibility of it getting well ahead of the rest of the battalion in the

181

dark, with the risk of heightened control difficulties for Jones. Farrar-Hockley wanted to press on. He sought permission to do so over the radio, but was ordered, by Jones, to stay put until the CO could join him and verify the situation. Meanwhile, as they waited, 3 Platoon, under 2nd Lieutenant Guy Wallis, was despatched down to the causeway linking Coronation Point to Darwin. His instructions were to cover the rest of the company for its final phase – the move into the Settlement after first light.

When the CO arrived and spoke with the company commander he urged an immediate advance, but it was by then approaching 6.30 am. Jones had been keeping a very tight hold of the reins. Frustrated by radio failures, he had given Major Neame, commanding D Company, a fearsome rocket earlier on when his Company had somehow got ahead of him in the blackness. He now insisted on seeing for himself. Up to dawn 2 Para was winning; after that the battle hung in the balance for nearly five hours.

As it started to grow light 2nd Lieutenant Mark Coe's 2 Platoon led A Company (less 3 Platoon at the causeway) forward along the western side of the inlet (Map 25). Advancing with his leading section in arrowhead formation, Coe was making for Darwin Hill. Immediately to his right was the 100-foot high east-west hill that straddled the peninsula, and on whose exposed southern slopes B Company would shortly be caught as they tried to move on Boca House. To his front, only 400 metres away, was the Darwin Hill ridge running westwards, its summit over 100 feet high and split by two re-entrants, or gullies. Across the top of the ridge was a long black line of gorse. The left-hand gully was the largest of the two and separated Darwin Hill proper from the rest of the feature. It was partially filled with clumps of thick, high gorse. Coe's orders were to advance up this re-entrant, then swing left on to Darwin Hill, thus overlooking the settlement. But it was not to be that easy. After a virtually unopposed advance, so far, A Company was approaching its rendezvous with reality – the main line of the Argentinians' defences.

Corporal Camp's leading section was near the entrance to the gorse gully when three figures appeared on the high ground to the right. At first neither side was sure who the others were. Shouts and waves were exchanged, then the firing started. Camp led his men forward into the gully to seek cover in the gorse and dead ground. Corporal Hardman, with the left rear section, followed, but the right rear section, under Corporal Adams, was caught out in the open and charged forward into the smaller right-hand gully. In doing so he was shot in the shoulder and his machine gunner was also wounded. Realizing he was isolated, close to strong opposition, he led his men back into the gorse gully. As 2 Platoon dashed for the gully the enemy machine guns and rifles, firing from trenches on the hills, caught both company headquarters and 1 Platoon, under Sergeant Barrett, in the

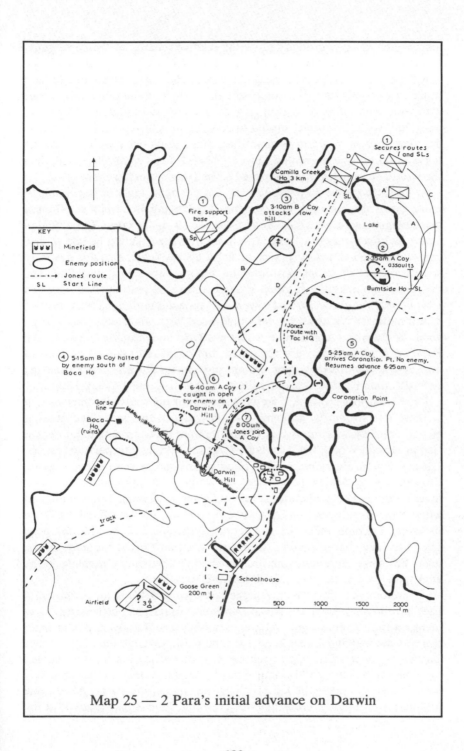

KEY

🐛🐛🐛	Minefield
⬭	Enemy position
·–·–→	Jones' route
SL	Start Line

① Fire support base

Sp

③ 3·10am B Coy attacks hill

Camilla Creek Ho. 3 km

B

SL

D

C

① Secures routes and SLs

A

C

Lake

A

② 2·35am A Coy assaults

Burntside Ho→SL

B

A

D

'Jones' route with Tac HQ

④ 5·15am B Coy halted by enemy south of Boca Ho

⑤ 5·25am A Coy arrives Coronatior Pt. No enemy. Resumes advance 6·25am

Coronation Point

⑥ 6·40am A Coy ( ) caught in open by enemy on Darwin Hill

Gorse line

Boca Ho (ruins)

A

? 3Pl

⑦ 8·00am Jones joins A Coy

Darwin Hill

track

Schoolhouse

Goose Green 200 m ↓

Airfield

? 3

0	500	1000	1500	2000
				m

Map 25 — 2 Para's initial advance on Darwin

long stretch of open ground before the relative security of the gorse gully. In getting forward two more men were wounded, and the attached Marine Royal Engineer, Corporal Melia, was killed. There now began the difficult business of trying to bring some sort of order into the situation. Under extremely heavy fire confusion reigned as individuals and sections intermingled, sought cover, attempted to advance or return fire. Smoke grenades were thrown, the gorse caught fire, more casualties occurred, and the noise and confusion prevented officers or NCOs from controlling more than the two or three men who happened to be lying closest to them.

At much the same time B Company, on the right, found it impossible to move down the forward slope of the ridge facing Boca House. Intense machine-gun and mortar fire drove them back over the crest. The battalion attack had been checked. Jones was faced with the situation he had so desperately wanted to avoid. It was daylight, his two leading companies were stalled in front of strong positions, the troops were taking casualties and dangerously vulnerable in open ground, the naval gunship had departed leaving only the three 105s who were low on ammunition, as were his two 81mm mortars. Whatever he did would need time, and Jones was worried about a possible Argentinian counter-attack and strafing runs by the Pucaras. The Harriers were requested, but could not take off because of mist at sea. Nevertheless, this did not prevent the Pucaras from attacking both battalion headquarters and the gun lines at Camilla Creek House.

Jones went forward to A Company again. For a man of his temperament in those circumstances, knowing that the crisis of the battle had arrived, any other action was impossible. With him went his tactical headquarters – Captain David Wood, the Adjutant; Sergeant Norman, his personal escort; Lance Corporal Beresford, another bodyguard; the mortar officer, Captain Worsley-Tonks; Major Tony Rice, the artillery battery commander, and several gunner radio operators. In total some 8-10 men. Jones had been with Farrar-Hockley at first light when A company moved off and had seen the company come under fire and get into difficulties. He had himself been forced to take shelter behind the steep bank that skirted the edge of the inlet. For some 20 minutes he had watched A Company struggling in the gorse gully before he made his decision to join them.

At around this time Neame suggested taking D Company, who were back in reserve, down to the western shoreline to start an outflanking movement on the extreme right. Although nobody could know it at the time, this was the very move that would win the battle several hours later. Jones was having none of it. 'Don't tell me how to run my battle,' he snapped over the radio. Then to his tactical headquarters, 'Come on, we can't stay here all day.' So saying he led off along the edge of the water. After some 300 metres of running, crouching and crawling, Jones's party arrived at the

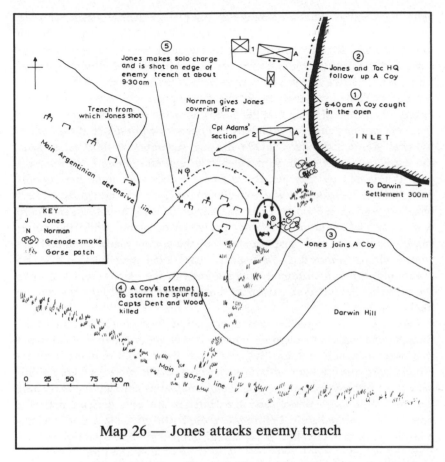

⑤ Jones makes solo charge and is shot on edge of enemy trench at about 9·30 am

Trench from which Jones shot

Norman gives Jones covering fire

Cpl Adams' section 2

② Jones and Tac HQ follow up A Coy

① 6·40 am A Coy caught in the open

INLET

To Darwin Settlement 300 m

③ Jones joins A Coy

Main Argentinian defensive line

④ A Coy's attempt to storm the spur fails. Capts Dent and Wood killed

Darwin Hill

Main gorse line

0   25   50   75   100 m

Map 26 — Jones attacks enemy trench

western corner of the inlet, with perhaps another 200 metres before they could reach A Company in the gorse gully. Fortunately there was a convenient patch of high gorse between them and the entrance to the gully. With the CO leading, the group doubled into the gorse, which gave good cover from view if not from fire. Forcing their way through, they found another 100-metre gap before the gully proper. To dash across under close-range fire would be foolish, so there was a slight pause while tactical headquarters was divided into two. Sergeant Norman threw the first phosphorus smoke grenade and they all ran forward quickly before the wind blew it away. Another smoke grenade, thrown by A Company's sergeant-major, got the second group over without mishap.

Now the CO's party was within 50-60 metres of the nearest enemy trenches (Map 26). Jones flopped down beside the company commander to ask the inevitable senior officer's question in the circumstances — 'What the hell is happening? What are you doing about it?'. Farrar-Hockley, who was later to get an MC for his efforts that day, was probably none too happy to have his CO literally leaning over his shoulder for the second time, but explained the confused situation as best he could. He had previously called for a Harrier strike but it had been rejected due to bad weather. Artillery fire was requested but also refused due to the proximity of the Paras to the enemy, the problem being that the 50-60 knot wind could marginally deflect the shells at that range. A Company had been trying to take out the nearby trenches. Some had fallen, but the fighting was bitter, at short range, with the Paras out in the open, running short of ammunition and, for the most part, dominated by trenches above them. Without adequate fire support from heavier weapons, it was exceedingly difficult for individual soldiers lying exposed in the open, or in the gorse, to bring fire to bear. There were only two platoons available, casualties occurred, while the noise, smoke, confusion, and close proximity of the enemy made command and control almost impossible. Individuals were doing their best, and would eventually, through sustained chipping away at the enemy trenches, force the surviving defenders to surrender, but at that time this did not seem the likely outcome.

Jones had to do a quick mental appreciation. Nobody can be sure of the thoughts that passed through his mind as he lay under fire in that gully, but they were probably not too different from these. 'A Company can't lie around here much longer without suffering grievous losses; we are chronically short of heavy weapon support, and small arms ammunition is running low; we can't use artillery, and the Harriers are out; decisive action is needed now, immediately, before the whole battle grinds to a halt. A Company is weak numerically. What would happen if the Argentinians suddenly launched a counter-attack? We just don't have the time to bring up reinforcements (C and D Companies), and have no way of knowing if their advance would succeed either. Also, there is still a long way to go to Goose Green, and I shall need these companies later. Deduction – I must take personal command, grip the situation, stimulate A Company into one last effort, using my own headquarters personnel if need be. Bold action now with a few men could well be more effective than 100 men in an hour's time. To try and withdraw A Company would invite heavy losses and would mean the probable end to the battle. 2 Para is going to succeed; I will not accept failure.'

Turning to Coe, who was lying nearby, Colonel Jones asked him if he could get some of his men up into the gorse line at the head of the gully in a left flanking move, taking the mortar officer with him. Coe thought he could, but it would be a bit 'hairy'. Farrar-Hockley had already tried this earlier without success and he advised strongly against it, so Coe and the mortar officer, who were on their way, were recalled. The mortar officer called for fire on to the top of the spur. Jones then told the company commander that he must organize an assault on to the summit. Farrar-Hockley cobbled together an assault party under cover of mortar smoke. The attackers consisted of some 15-20 men, including the company commander, the company second-in-command, Captain Chris Dent, and the adjutant, who joined in uninvited. The line surged up to the crest into the smoke, to be met by fierce machine-gun and rifle fire. At that moment the mortar smoke ran out while the strong wind dispersed the remaining screen. Within moments Captains Dent and Wood were shot dead, as was Corporal Hardman. The assault went to ground. With everybody now exposed, Farrar-Hockley had no option but to pull back again into dead ground.

Jones had witnessed this assault. Turning to Norman and the others in his group, he leapt to his feet shouting, 'Follow me', and ran to his right down the gully. Then he swung left around the base of the spur, making for the second, smaller, gully that seemingly outflanked the positions on the summit. Behind him came Norman, and then Beresford. Others nearby who saw him go were uncertain of what he intended, so did not follow. The Colonel was fit and was soon some 25 metres ahead of Norman. As Norman came round into the second gully he could see his CO ahead, beginning to turn up the slope to his left. Just then somebody yelled from behind: 'Watch out, there's enemy to your left'. Norman saw the trench, instinctively diving for cover, just as the Argentinians opened up. He frantically fired off a complete magazine — 20 rounds — as fast as he could pump the trigger, then fumbled to pull another from his back pouches, cursing at the delay. Glancing up he saw his CO change his magazine on his Sterling and start up the slope towards the enemy trench on the left of the gully. Norman then spotted another trench, near the top of the opposite slope, behind Jones. It was some 30-40 metres from the Colonel. Norman shouted a warning: 'Watch your fucking back', but Jones ignored it. Desperate to support him, Norman continued to fire at the position his CO was charging. Then, as Jones neared his objective, the machine gun in the trench to his rear on the other side of the gully opened fire. At first it missed, the bullets kicking up the ground behind him. A split second later Norman saw him fall, propelled forward to the lip of the trench by the force of the rounds striking him in the small of the back.

There were two enemy in the trench, one of whom was wounded, but the other stuck his head up to try to finish off Jones, who was lying semi-conscious and moaning a foot or two below the trench. Norman's renewed firing drove him back under cover. Next, the enemy soldier tried raising his rifle blindly for a moment, but could not get the angle, before abandoning the attempt as too dangerous.

Norman was only 25 metres from his Colonel, but there was nothing he could do other than to keep firing and hope that somehow others would sort out the situation. They did; but it took some 10-15 minutes, probably the longest quarter of an hour in Norman's life. A Company gradually gained the upper hand, principally due to the efforts of individuals like Corporal Abols, who came forward with a 66mm rocket launcher to blast the trench from which Jones had been shot. This quickly resulted in white flags being waved, followed by the speedy surrender of the remaining positions.

Norman went immediately to his CO, who was barely conscious, removed his webbing and turned him over. There was not much blood, probably indicating internal bleeding. Norman could see he was in deep shock and immediately used his own saline drip. Jones took the full litre very quickly, so was given a second, his own, while others who had gathered round attempted to keep him warm. Sergeant Hastings, from 2 Platoon, stressed that casualty evacuation by helicopter was vital and this was radioed back. Although the first request was refused, a second, couched in more forceful language, produced a positive response, although with tragic results. The Scout, piloted by Lieutenant Richard Nunn RM, with Sergeant Belcher as gunner, was pounced on by two Pucaras. Frantic evasive flying did not prevent the 20mm cannon shells from smashing the helicopter out of the sky. Nunn was killed outright. Belcher lived, but had his right leg amputated at mid-thigh.

Back in the gully Norman and his helpers struggled to improvise a stretcher from pieces of wood and a corrugated iron sheet from the trench, to move the Colonel to an LZ suitable for the helicopter. As they lifted him the ramshackle structure broke, Jones falling to the ground, although by this time he was unconscious. They carried the CO up to the top of the spur where Farrar-Hockley came to see him and reassured Norman that a helicopter was on its way. Jones, however, died within a few minutes of being brought up, some 40 minutes after being hit.

It had been the brief but stunning radio message at about 9.30 am, 'Sunray is down', that alerted the battalion second-in-command, Major Chris Keeble, back at the main headquarters, that he was now in charge. The story of how he took over, of how D Company successfully put in their right flanking attack along the western beach, and of how the following day the Argentinians capitulated, is not part of this book. Suffice it to say that 2 Para triumphed; some 1400 enemy, mostly air force personnel, surrendered to the 400 or so exhausted paratroopers. It was a magnificent victory, achieved in the face of immense difficulties and much stiffer opposition than expected. For all that there were moments when it was a 'close run thing'.

Jones's actions are not difficult to understand. Never the sort of soldier to give in, always putting the battalion's reputation and its objective first, he did what was typical of him as a man of courage and honour – he led by example from the front. The sudden decision personally to attack the enemy was, in his view, essential at that critical moment. He had seen the chaos in the gorse gully, he had seen the death of two officers and an NCO in the assault over the spur, and he believed that a quick right-flanking move round behind the enemy by a small group could well tip the balance. At that time, and in the prevailing cirumstances, there was little else he could have tried.

While his solo charge did not of itself inspire A Company at that particular moment, as so few were aware of what he was doing, Jones's leadership to the time he was hit had been the driving force that maintained the impetus, that sustained the collective will to keep going. A Company, with only two platoons and company headquarters, fought long and hard to inflict 18 dead and 39 wounded among the 92 Argentinians defending the ridge. The presence of their CO, under fire with them, was a major factor in their ultimate triumph. As Farrar-Hockley was later to say: 'His inspiration and example were to remain with us for the rest of the campaign'.

The battle for Darwin and Goose Green cost 2 Para 16 dead and 35 wounded. Those killed were buried two days afterwards at Ajax Bay, under the arrangements of 3 Commando Brigade. It had been Padre David Cooper's sad duty to collect and account for all the bodies, so he was not surprised when he was invited to attend what he was told was a memorial service for Colonel Jones and the others. With him went Major Keeble, the six company commanders, and RSM Simpson. On arrival at Ajax Bay, however, he was stunned to be told by the RM Senior Chaplain that he was conducting the burial service without any opportunity to prepare. He was not impressed with the organization or the long wait at the graveside before he was able to start. There was no bugler or firing party. It was a simple service, a group of 2 Para and others standing sadly round the large grave, headed by the Land Forces Commander, Major-General Jeremy Moore RM, as each of the 16 bodies in its plastic body bag, draped with a Union flag, was placed side by side in the grave. All present saluted as the RSM scattered a handful of earth over the dead.

On 25 October, 1982, Jones was one of 14 men reburied at Blue Beach Military Cemetery, overlooking the beach at Port San Carlos. He was staying in the land for whose freedom he had given his life. On one side lay seven soldiers, on the other seven Marines. The Defence Secretary, Mr John Nott, laid the first wreath. Each coffin was lowered into the grave by bearer parties of the REs and Royal Pioneer Corps, who had laid out the cemetery. Three volleys were fired, the Last Post and Reveille were sounded, the 23rd Psalm was sung. Out in the bay a wreath was cast from a naval launch onto the grey water, as a solitary piper stood on the shore playing a lament. The only relative present was Jones's brother, Commander Timothy Jones, whose ship happened to be in the Falklands at the time. He placed the family wreath.

The landing ship, *Sir Bedivere,* brought back 64 bodies for reburial at home; three others remained buried at other sites on the island, while the remainder had died at sea. Repatriation of the bodies was an unusual precedent as traditionally servicemen who die overseas have always been buried there. After much delay and hesitation next of kin were eventually given the choice.

In the case of Jones, his wife had all along assumed that those killed would be buried on the island, and Mrs Thatcher's later decision to give an option did not change her mind. The islanders erected a small cairn of white stones on the spot where he fell. It is frequently visited, sometimes as part of official battlefield tours arranged by the military authorities. Sara Jones has, along with many other relatives, visited the islands. On the first occasion she planted some Devonshire heather on her husband's grave.

It was not until 11 October, 1982, that Jones's award of the VC was officially announced, although several newspapers had their actions in releasing the news two days earlier 'deplored' by the Press Council. Sara Jones and her two sons, David and Rupert, were immensely proud. Her comments were: 'It's a marvellous honour . . . He knew what was needed and went into action without hesitation. It was typical of 'H' . . . He always led from the front. It was characteristic.' 'On receiving the news she opened a bottle of champagne and the family drank to him. 'He would have expected it of us.' On 4 November Mrs Jones and her sons went to Buckingham Palace for the second time to attend an Investiture, the first one being when he had received his OBE. Somewhat overawed, this time the three of them waited nervously on their own for 10-15 minutes before Her Majesty arrived to present the Cross, prior to the main Investiture.

In addition to the national or Regimental memorials and services in which Colonel Jones was remembered, along with his comrades, his name is recalled in a number of other ways. Sara unveiled a memorial at Eton College in April, 1983, his home village of Kingswear in South Devon held a memorial service and placed a plaque in his honour on a tree trunk on a coastal foothpath. A pub in Lowestoft is named 'The Colonel H', while Aldershot has an 'H Jones Crescent'. A painting by Terence Cuneo, depicting his charge, hangs in the School of Infantry Officers' Mess at Warminster, and his former Regiment, The Devon and Dorsets, have a portrait in their Mess. At the annual Bisley rifle meeting a new inter-county match was inaugurated in 1983 The firers compete for a 'Colonel H' statuette, with ten gold medals for winning team members. Mrs Jones presented the trophy in 1988.

Mrs Jones, now a magistrate, has moved from the family home in Devon to live near Salisbury, while her two sons have followed their father into the Devon and Dorset Regiment. At the time of writing (June, 1989) David is a Lieutenant commanding a platoon in Northern Ireland, while his younger brother Rupert is a 2nd Lieutenant reading history at Reading University under an Army Cadetship. He expects to join his Regiment in 1991. Colonel 'H' would have been just as proud of them as they are of him.

CHAPTER 11

Mount Longdon, Falkland Islands, 11/12 June, 1982

SERGEANT IAN JOHN McKAY VC
The 3rd Battalion, The Parachute Regiment.

'I'll see you in Stanley'
Sergeant McKay to Colour Sergeant Brian Faulkner DCM, four
hours before being killed.

At about 6.00 pm on Sunday, 30 January 1972, Support Company of 1
Para were ordered into action in Londonderry. An illegal march by around
3000 people had been infiltrated by a hooligan element bent on trouble.
As the crowd approached the security forces in the centre of the Catholic
Bogside area, serious stone-throwing began at the police. The Para battalion was in reserve and, being near the end of an 18-month tour of the Province, was the brigade commander's most experienced unit. That afternoon
he sent the paratroopers in, as an arresting force, to catch and detain ring-
leaders.

Within moments of Support Company troops debussing from their vehicles in Rossville Street they were fired on from the Rossville Flats, only a
short distance away. Private 'T', of the Mortar Platoon, heard a burst of
fire from a semi-automatic rifle only a few moments after dismounting. The
crowd were hurling bricks, stones and petrol and acid bombs. One of these
bombs burst nearby, splashing acid on his legs, and he thought he spotted
the thrower on the third floor of the flats. Private 'T' yelled to his sergeant, who gave him authority to fire. 'T' fired two quick shots but appeared
to have missed. 'T' was the letter used to conceal the identity of Private Ian
McKay at Lord Chief Justice Widgery's inquiry into the events of 'Bloody
Sunday', which saw 1 Para kill 13 men aged between 18 and 26 years. The
inquiry did not support the media in their portrayal of the affair as a mass-
acre of innocent civilians. There had not been a breakdown of fire discipline by the troops, they had been fired on first, and while some innocent
persons may have been hit, this was probably unavoidable given the confusion at the time. It was significant that although many women, children

and elderly people were in the crowd, only young men were killed. Nevertheless, the outcry was sufficient for the authorities to excuse McKay, and the others who had given evidence, from further service in Northern Ireland for reasons of safety.

McKay was then eighteen years old, but he was only seventeen when he had first been posted to Northern Ireland in early March, 1971. Not long after this, three young Scottish soldiers, who were all under eighteen, were killed in a single incident. This caused great public disquiet and from then on no seventeen year-olds were permitted to serve in Northern Ireland. For McKay this meant a transfer to England, a few weeks' leave to await his birthday, and then back to 1 Para, well in time for Bloody Sunday. In one of those odd military inconsistencies lads of seventeen were later permitted to fight and die in the Falklands, but not on internal security duties in the Province. Nobody was more aware of this than McKay as no less than three seventeen year-olds fought and died in his company on Mount Longdon. One was killed on his eighteenth birthday, while another, Private Jason Burt, was shot dead with McKay in the action that won him the VC.

McKay's father was not keen on his joining the Army. He would have preferred his son to develop his sporting talents, perhaps becoming a physical education teacher. McKay, however, had set his sights on the Parachute Regiment and insisted that if his father would not give his consent to enlist at seventeen, he would merely wait until his eighteenth birthday. Mr McKay relented. There was talk of the possibility of McKay trying to get to Sandhurst as he was physically strong, a well above average sportsman and had got several 'O' levels at Rotherham Grammar School. He rejected this suggestion as he was impatient to start his soldiering, did not relish further prolonged academic study and felt he would prefer to work his way up through the ranks.

He enlisted on 3 August, 1970, three months after his seventeenth birthday. Six months later he completed basic training and passed out, proudly wearing his maroon beret as a qualified paratrooper. Both his younger brothers suffered from cystic fibrosis, whereas Ian McKay was renowned for his physique and his ability at football and other ball games.[1] His only problem in this respect was his tendency to put on weight easily, as he enjoyed good food and, in the Army, his beer. In the Parachute Regiment McKay acknowledged that it was sometimes a struggle to maintain the peak standard of fitness required.

His CO in the Falklands has described McKay as bright, cheerful, enthusiastic, outgoing, interesting and utterly dedicated to his profession.[2] He also had a very determined streak in his make-up. Once he had made up his mind to do something he wanted to excel; he hated to lose. He had inherited some Yorkshire stubbornness which, in many situations but not all, was also to be counted an asset. During his twelve years prior to going to the Falklands McKay steadily worked his way up the promotion ladder, becoming an acting sergeant in November, 1979, and proved himself to be a first-rate instructor of recruits. Had he not been killed it is likely he would have been sent to Sandhurst as a senior NCO instructor of officer cadets – an appointment only for the best, and often a stepping stone to much higher rank.

McKay joined 3 Para shortly before it sailed for the Falklands, via Ascension Island, on the *Canberra* on 9 April. The weeks at sea were spent in keeping fit, weapon and medical training, attending briefings and sunbathing. McKay was the platoon sergeant of 4 Platoon under Lieutenant Andrew Bickerdike, in B Company. As a newcomer he spent much of his time getting to know the young soldiers under him.

D-day for the landings at Port San Carlos was 21 May. The weather was foul – stormy, low cloud and poor visibility which, although it made most of the paratroopers violently sick in their landing crafts, at least kept the Argentinian Air Force away. 3 Para was not to go into action in earnest for over three weeks, but those weeks tested the toughness of every member of the battalion. 3 Para and 45 Commando were the only units to march (or tab as the Paras called it) every step of the way from Port San Carlos to Stanley, carrying loads of up to 120 lbs. If a man sat down he needed assistance to get up. The total distance was over 50 miles, 40 of which were covered by 3 Para in two exhausting night marches on 27/28 May and 29/30 May. By day they lay up, tried to rest, conceal themselves and dry out. In none of these activities were they successful. The difficulty was not the distance, or even the weight of their bergens, so much as the miserable weather which multiplied their discomfort threefold.

In a letter home from Estancia House area, which was where 3 Para was deployed awaiting their attack on Mount Longdon, McKay voiced the opinions of everybody when he said: 'I have never know a more bleak, windswept, and wet place in my life. We spend our life with wet feet, trying to dry out and keep warm. The wind blows constantly but it is cooling rather than drying. You cannot walk 50 paces anywhere, even on the mountainsides, without walking in a bog. I thought the Brecon Beacons was bad, but this takes the biscuit.'[3]

3 Commando Brigade RM was far larger than a normal brigade as it had three RM commandos, two parachute battalions, a commando regiment RA, plus light tanks, engineers, signals, transport and medical squadrons, together with SAS troops and the RM Special Boat Squadron. The rivalry between those wearing the red and the green berets was intense. For the march across East Falklands the original orders were for 3 Para to follow 45 Commando to Douglas, but this did not suit the Paras. To tag along

behind the Marines was not thought a good idea and, as the ultimate aim at that stage was to get to Teal Inlet, it seemed foolish to march along two sides of a triangle instead of one. 3 Para sought and obtained permission to tab due east, thus overtaking 45 Commando. The Paras then stayed in front, much to their delight, all the way to Stanley.

By the night of 31 May/1 June 3 Para had reached the Mount Estancia – Mount Vernet area, and taken up defensive positions to await the final push to Stanley, which was clearly visible some ten miles away to the east. Only the western outskirts of the town were obscured from view by a rocky hill called Mount Longdon.

McKay saw Stanley, but sadly he was never to get there. Before the battle he wrote to his parents in Rotherham: 'Mind you things are much quieter now than for some time, and finding things to occupy our time is now a problem. Some clown has put one of our artillery batteries just behind our positions, and as the Argentinian guns try to range in on them they sometimes drop one in around our position . . . the papers we get . . . mention only Marines and Guards so if we aren't officially here we might as well come home . . . things should be over one way or another in a week . . . we will be home hopefully about two weeks afterwards.'[4]

Three days later McKay died winning the first VC ever awarded to a member of 3 Para, and the last of the eleven post-war ones – perhaps the last ever.

The struggle to secure Mount Longdon took ten hours of vicious infantry fighting in the dark, involving frequent hand-to-hand encounters with boot and bayonet among the rocks and bunkers. Its capture cost 3 Para 20 dead and over 40 wounded, making it the most bitter battle of the campaign. Like all the actions it was won in the end by the superior qualities of junior NCOs and soldiers, who frequently fought forward in small groups on their own initiative. It was a typical soldiers' battle where, once the attack was launched, senior commanders had little influence over its outcome, other than to try to commit their reserve at the right place and the right time. In the event it was largely B Company of 3 Para that fought it out with B Company of the Argentinian 7th Regiment. For much of the night the result hung in the balance.

Although the Argentinian company was composed of young conscripts it had a number of advantages. The ground favoured the defence. Mount Longdon is a narrow ridge, 1200 metres long, running roughly NW to SE. Its rocky summit towers 400 feet above the valleys on all sides, giving the defenders clear fields of fire of at least 2000 metres in every direction. All approaches are devoid of cover until the boulder-strewn upper slopes of the ridge are reached. Added to this, the Argentinian troops had had nearly two months to prepare themselves, to build bunkers, sangars and trenches. Minefields had been laid, particularly in the west and south. Major Carlos Salvadores, their commander on Mount Longdon, had time to duplicate his telephone line communications to all his sub-units and to register potential targets for his 81mm and 120mm mortars, as well as for the artillery in the Stanley area.

He had a total garrison of 278 men, composed of the three platoons of B Company, another of engineers, some logistics troops, his command post personnel, plus the marine crews for the six .50 calibre heavy machine guns (HMGs). But perhaps his greatest single asset was the RASIT radar set, with which he could scan the countryside at night to reveal any hostile troop movement within several thousand metres. It proved extremely effective in pinpointing Para patrols as they probed the defences during the nights prior to the attack. This radar, coupled with the lavish distribution of passive night vision equipment, gave the Argentinians a clear superiority over the Paras as far as seeing at night was concerned. Salvadores knew that Longdon was the lynchpin of the north-western outer defences to Stanley. He was determined to hold it.

3 Commando Brigade launched the first phase of the battle for Stanley, indeed the battle to win the war, on the night of 11/12 June. 3 Para would start by taking Longdon, then 45 Commando would tackle Two Sisters 2000 metres to the SW, and finally 42 Commando would seize Mount Harriet 2000 metres further south still. If all went well units were poised to exploit further east on to Wireless Ridge and Mount Tumbledown.

To Lieutenant-Colonel Hew Pike, 3 Para's CO, Longdon's capture posed several problems. There was the 5000-metre approach march across open ground to the start line, followed by another 1000 metres up the long exposed slopes of the mountain, probably through minefields. A night attack was the only option, but the narrowness of the objective meant that only one company at a time would have room to assault. Darkness, coupled with the jumble of boulders, would combine to cause confusion and control difficulties once the assault went in. Finally, intelligence estimates had put the enemy strength on Longdon as a battalion of 800 men. At the last moment a message arrived increasing the estimate by 50 per cent. If this was correct the attackers would be outnumbered by more than 2 to 1. Fortunately these figures were wildly inaccurate, although to the Para officers at the time the arithmetic was daunting.

Pike's plan was straightforward — the first step to success with any night attack (Map 27). The battalion would move, after dark, almost due east over the Murrell River to a start line (Free Kick) along the line of a stream running north-south 1000 metres west of Longdon. A Company would

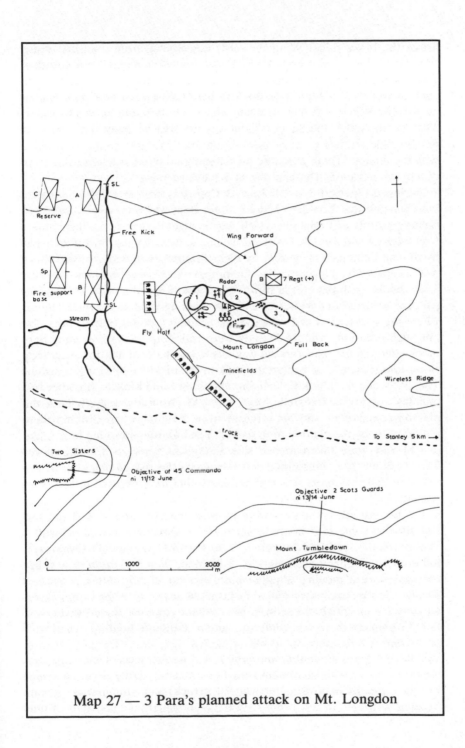

Map 27 — 3 Para's planned attack on Mt. Longdon

197

attack the lower ridge (Wing Forward) running NE from the main objective. From there it was hoped it could support B Company as it assaulted the western summit of Longdon (Fly Half). C Company would be held back in reserve, to exploit forward to take the eastern end (Full Back), or possibly Wireless Ridge, at a later stage. The advance was to be silent. That meant neither the Support Company fire base weapons, near the start line, nor the artillery or naval guns would open fire until contact was made with the enemy. There could be no softening up bombardment prior to or during the advance. The aim was to achieve surprise.

During the period 3 to 10 June B Company had established a patrol base beneath the shoulder of Mount Kent from which they could send out fighting patrols to Longdon, which they now knew was to be their objective. McKay was heavily involved in this activity. Living in wet trenches by day and conducting patrols by night drained everybody, physically as well as mentally. Opportunities for proper sleep were minimal, so Pike arranged for each platoon in turn to go down to spend a night in the comparative security and shelter of a sheep shearing shed at Estancia House, where the quartermaster had set up his echelon (administrative) area. On one such occasion, when 4 Platoon were rolled up in their sleeping bags in the shed, an air raid warning was received. The drill was for everybody to get into trenches, or behind the bank of the nearby inlet, for protection. The QM woke the platoon, including Bickerdike and McKay, but after five minutes nobody had stirred. Next, the QM physically dragged both the platoon commander and his sergeant from their bags and ordered them out. Eventually the platoon took shelter. The following morning Bickerdike and McKay were taken to one side and given a severe dressing down. They had felt that undisturbed rest was worth the risk of being hit by the raid, but had they been attacked nothing would have excused unnecessary casualties.

The two assault companies were to cross the start line at 8.01 pm and had allowed some four hours to get there. B Company moved off with 4 Platoon in the lead, led by guides from Patrol Company (D Company), followed by company headquarters, 5 Platoon, then 6 Platoon. The other companies were moving simultaneously but on slightly different routes. Slowly, silently, except for the odd whispered order, with the troops carrying only the essentials for action, the company columns moved eastwards. For B Company there was confusion, and a 30-minute hold up, when Support Company fire support teams cut across their line. Half of 5 Platoon and all of 6 Platoon were temporarily lost. The delay was frustrating, but typical of the type of unexpected snarl-ups that inevitably occur. Another was the difficulty in crossing the Murrell River, which also gave everybody freezing wet feet. In the event the seemingly generous allocation of four

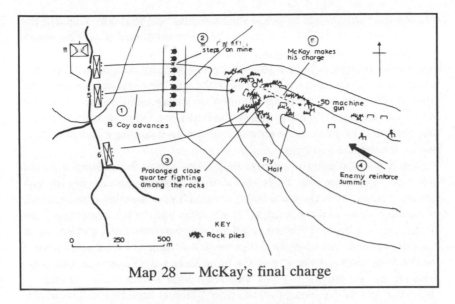

Map 28 — McKay's final charge

hours for an approach march of 5000 metres was not quite sufficient — B Company crossed the start-line fourteen minutes late.

Despite a solitary Argentinian star shell and the moon rising to the east of Longdon, 3 Para reached Free Kick without being discovered. What they could not know was that luck had played its part. On this night the Argentinians were not using their radar, which had been switched off for fear that the British would detect its emissions and shell it. Had it been used the companies on the start line would have been clearly visible, the enemy fully alerted, and the chances of the paratroopers being able to reach the enemy positions much reduced.

As it was, B Company shook themselves out into their assault formation without mishap (see Map 28). Their objective was Fly Half. On the right 6 Platoon was guided to the forward assault position (FAP) opposite the SW corner of Longdon; their attack would be to the south of the crest. In the centre was 5 Platoon, with the Patrol Company guide group under Sergeant Pettinger to their left. Left again was 4 Platoon with McKay. All were in closed-up extended line, 5 Platoon making for the western summit and 4 Platoon for the northern slopes of the feature. Company headquarters was close behind the assault platoons. It was around this time that McKay briefly saw Colour Sergeant Faulkner, the Regimental Aid Post (RAP) colour sergeant, staggering along with his load of rifle, GPMG, 300 rounds of ammunition, missiles and medical kit. They were good friends. 'See you in Stanley,' said McKay, grinning widely. Four hours later he was dead.

The advance started well for B Company. With bayonets fixed they

199

stepped over the stream to begin the long haul up the slope. This was the agonizing bit. Still there was no noise. The sections moved slowly but steadily across the bare ground nearer and nearer to the enemy, with the clear night silhouetting the jagged summit against the sky. Corporal Milne was leading the left forward section of 4 Platoon as they reached the half-way point of the advance when he stepped on a mine. The flash, bang and Milne's scream signalled the start of the battle for Mount Longdon at 9.00 pm. Forty-five minutes to advance 600 metres illustrates how cautiously and quietly the assault had begun.

Now it was the deadly business of fighting up on to, and through, the objective. The noise was horrendous. Both Argentinian and British supporting artillery, plus the naval guns, opened fire, combining with the rattle of machine guns, and the banging of grenades and rocket launchers. Each action was fought out between small groups of paratroopers and enemy in bunkers, at ranges of a few metres, among the clumps of rock that crowned the crest and slopes leading to it. Corporal Bailey, a 5 Platoon section commander, has described how his men used their 66mm rocket launchers: 'Whoever was in the best position to spot targets fired; the others passed spare rockets to them. It was a very good bunker weapon; there wasn't going to be a lot left of you if your bunker or sangar was hit by one of those.'[5]

The rocks channelled the fighting in between them. Both 4 and 5 Platoons became intermingled and bunched up. Casualties were heavy on both sides, control was difficult, and even company headquarters became involved in close-quarter combat. Both the Naval Gunfire Liaison Officer, Captain McCraken RA, and the CSM, Warrant Officer 2 Weeks, personally took out positions with 66mms and rifles, while Major Argue sought to bring some sort of order to the battle over the radio.

On the extreme right 6 Platoon had reached their objective, the summit and southern slope of Fly Half, by 9.30 pm after grenading a number of bunkers. But here the platoon ran into problems. They were shot up from the rear, from a bunker they had by-passed in the dark, then automatic fire hit them from the east along the ridge, causing four more fatal casualties. Attempts to aid these men failed, with a further eight being wounded. 6 Platoon was pinned. They sought and received permission to hold where they were and recover casualties.

On the northern slope of Longdon men in 4 and 5 Platoons were falling fast. As the leading paratroopers fought their way through the boulders to the top, the ridge opened out and sloped gradually eastwards, giving the Argentinians further along the ridge easy targets. As Bickerdike and 4 Platoon headquarters got to the summit, bursts of fire hit them from the east. The platoon signaller took a shot through his mouth but continued to operate his radio, and the platoon commander's thigh was smashed by a bullet. He yelled: 'Sergeant McKay, it's your platoon now'. McKay realized that it was a .50 HMG in particular that had halted the attack, so he grabbed a number of nearby soldiers from his own platoon and Corporal Bailey's section of 5 Platoon.

McKay was about to win his Cross. There was nobody ordering him forward, there was every reason for staying under cover in the rocks below the crest, but this was not his way. Bailey later described how, for a few moments, he and McKay lay side by side deciding what to do. It was a matter of getting across to the next cover, rocks about 30 metres away in which there were Argentinian positions, although their exact location was impossible to pinpoint. McKay decided that was the objective of his group – himself, Bailey, the 17-year-old Burt and two other privates. McKay arranged covering fire from three GPMG teams nearby. As their fire started McKay leapt up shouting: 'Let's go'. The five men dashed up towards the rocks. Immediately two fell dead, cut down by machine-gun fire, one of whom was young Burt. The other private got across into cover, as did the two NCOs. They grenaded the first position in the rocks and McKay and Bailey went on without stopping. It was then that Bailey felt a tremendous blow in his hip. It was like a sledgehammer. He went down instantly, having been shot by a rifle at a range of ten feet. McKay continued on his own, utterly committed to destroying the position that was devastating his platoon. Bailey later said: 'The last I saw of him, he was just going on, running towards the remaining positions in that group.'[6] Lying unable to move, Bailey heard shouts for the platoon sergeant, but there was no response. A few moments later Bailey was hit again in the neck and hand.

The exact circumstances of McKay's death will never be known. His body was later recovered within a few feet of an enemy bunker with several dead Argentinians nearby. He had killed some before being cut down by automatic fire. He had led a desperate charge into intense fire, he had inspired others to follow him to almost certain death, he had proved beyond any doubt his courage and his leadership. Hours later, after the battle, the task of removing the dead befell B Company Sergeant Major, Weeks, and others. Each had to be documented, searched for personal effects, which were removed, as were wedding rings and, leaving one dog tag (ID disc) on the body, had to be put in a large plastic body bag.[7] The business of getting a body into a flat plastic bag is not easy and is decidedly unpleasant. When it is your friend's body it is a traumatic and scarring experience. Weeks was in tears when he and A Company Sergeant Major carried McKay down the hill.

Although McKay had not personally destroyed the HMG, his bold action had silenced several other positions, which allowed the remnants of 4 and

5 Platoons to reach their crest and consolidate their hold. The company commander then sent Sergeant Fuller forward to take command of the battered 4 Platoon. But it was not until dawn that 3 Para could confirm the capture of Longdon. B Company had secured Fly Half and exploited some way to the east, but could not reach Full Back. Their casualties had been almost 33 per cent, so the company was permitted to pull back slightly to reorganize and allow the guns to bombard the crest. This was in preparation for A Company to take the eastern end (Full Back). This A Company was able to do after more stiff fighting. Their initial attack on to Wing Forward had not been satisfactory as they were dominated by the main Longdon feature, so the CO had withdrawn them to bring them back round to the west.

3 Para had equalled, if not excelled, their sister battalion at Darwin/ Goose Green in terms of securing their objective against heavy odds. The price was high, especially for B Company. The Argentinians had been tenacious opponents, killing 13 and wounding 27 of B Company and its attached personnel − these out of 118 all ranks that had crossed the start line. The cost to the Argentinians was between 150-200, of which at least 50 were dead.

It was a drab, grey, dawn on 16 November, 1982. At Marchwood Military Port a tiny group of civilians and military representatives stood quietly watching as the logistic landing ship *Sir Bedivere* docked. There was no bunting, no flags, no band, only a lone piper, Sergeant McKinnon of the 2nd Scots Guards. On board the ship were 64 bodies of soldiers killed in the Falklands. They were coming home to be buried again, at the request of their families. They included the body of Sergeant McKay. As the two containers, draped in Union Jacks, were swung ashore the slow, lilting, skirl of the pipes playing 'Flowers of the Forest', a traditional Scottish lament that dates back to the Battle of Flodden in 1513, highlighted the emotion of the grieving relatives. The containers went to the customs shed where individual coffins were transferred to black hearses for the journey to their final destinations all over Britain.

For McKay, and fifteen others, the drive took him to Aldershot, the garrison town he had known so well and the home of the Parachute Regiment. On 26 November McKay and his comrades, including young Burt who had fallen with him in his final charge, were laid to rest with full military honours.

After a bright morning, the weather turned cold and wet for the actual burial, as if to remind the mourners of the conditions in the islands in which they had died. Through the ages the burial of a warrior has always been a memorable occasion; a modern military funeral is equally impressive. It has a special sadness and poignancy. It is both beautiful and immensely moving to see soldiers giving their final salute to fallen friends. Some 800 relatives, plus both the 2nd and 3rd Battalions of the Parachute Regiment, together with many members of the public, had gathered that morning. After a buffet lunch, relatives were taken in coaches to the Royal Garrison Church for the service, conducted by Padre David Cooper, 2 Para. The Colonel Commandant read the lesson, while McKay's padre, Derek Heaver, gave the address.

At the cemetery the route for the coffins was lined by guards from both battalions with arms reversed. As the sixteen bearer parties moved slowly forward 3 Para band played. McKay was carried by NCOs who had known him well, among them Sergeant Fuller, who had taken over his platoon for the final stages of the battle, and Corporal Bailey, now recovered from his wounds, the last paratrooper to see him alive. On the coffin was the Union Jack, his paratrooper's maroon beret, his medals, including the VC, and his belt and bayonet. Each individual was buried by his respective battalion padre. Three volleys rang out for each; a piper from 15 Para (Scottish Volunteers) played a lament; buglers sounded the Last Post and Reveille.

It had been on 9 November that McKay's wife, Marica, her son by her first marriage, Donny, and McKay's daughter Melanie, together with Mr and Mrs McKay, went to Buckingham Palace for the Investiture. On the same day McKay's CO, Lieutenant Colonel Pike, was given his DSO. At about 10.00 am the Queen entered the Blue Room to greet the family group, who were waiting in line. Her Majesty spoke to Marica first and, after offering her condolences, expressed disappointment at not being able to find her nugget of metal from the Russian cannon from which the VC was made. She had wanted to bring it that morning to show the family.

Marica was later to present her husband's medals to the Parachute Regiment, who loaned them for a time for display in the Imperial War Museum.

Sergeant McKay is unlikely to be forgotten. Not only may he go down in history as the last winner of the VC, but a number of memorials have been established since his death. In June, 1988, Princess Margaret opened the McKay Memorial Cottages at Barnsley; his old school, Rotherham Grammar, have erected a plaque in his honour; portraits of him hang in Rotherham Town Hall and 3 Para Sergeants' Mess; another, of his winning the VC, is in 3 Para Officers' Mess; and a commemorative march, 'Ian McKay VC', is now often played by 3 Para band. But probably the memorial that would have pleased him most is the McKay Trophy. This is a silver statuette of a Para sergeant in Falklands battle order, with a rifle in one hand and a grenade in the other, moving into the assault. It is kept in the safe custody of 3 Para Sergeants' Mess, and is competed for annually.

McKay would have approved the toughness of the competition. It is an inter-platoon event, devised to test both section and individual battle skills, but particularly marching and shooting. It takes place over three days, and was first held in September, 1983, when the victors were 8 Platoon of C Company.

To end this chapter, and indeed the book, it is appropriate to read the words from a letter written by the mother of a young paratrooper who survived Mount Longdon, to Ian McKay's mother. It is dated 12 October, 1982, just after the announcement of the VC award.

'I personally had never met him although my son, Simon, who is 18 years old, was in his platoon during the campaign in the Falklands. Since my son's return to England at the beginning of July he has spoken often of Sergeant McKay, and of his deep admiration of your son's actions during that time. In fact had it not been for his bravery I doubt very much that my son would have been returned safely to me.

I know that in the short time that Ian was Simon's platoon sergeant he taught him everything about soldiering, and that he had the utmost respect for your son's dedication . . .

My son was privileged to have known him, and to have fought alongside him. He was an inspiration, not only to my son, but I am sure to many others in 3 Para to whom he will be remembered as a great hero in time of conflict.'

Postscript

And so in the strife of the battle of life
It's easy to fight when you're winning;
It's easy to slave, and to starve and be brave,
When the dawn of success is beginning.
But the man who can meet despair and defeat
With a cheer, there's the man of God's choosing;
The man who can fight to Heaven's own height
Is the man who can fight when he's losing.

From *Carry On!* by Robert W. Service.

Most, if not all, VCs have been won by men facing defeat, or in circumstances of seemingly unsurmountable adversity. The very nature of the award means that recipients must have tackled almost hopeless odds, with death the likely outcome of their deeds. It was their will that triumphed, their resolution to overcome, never to admit defeat. Their determination to achieve an objective was stronger than their fear, stronger than that most basic of human instincts − self-preservation.

At the start of this book I felt any postscript to be unnecessary, inappropriate even; that the deeds would speak for themselves, and that further comment would be superfluous. I certainly felt that it would be invidious to single out any act, or acts, as being more deserving of merit than the rest. Now, I am not so sure. Having spent these months researching, reading and studying the circumstances leading to the award of these eleven VCs, and interviewing and corresponding with witnesses or relatives, I wonder if all are absolutely equal.

Of course, many men have performed as gallantly and received nothing.

The element of luck is always present. The need to be noticed, the need for witnesses to survive, and the requirement for somebody in authority to make the recommendation, have been mentioned earlier. But, within this brotherhood of singularly brave men, is there an elite within the elite?

Of the eleven men in this book, those that strike me as perhaps belonging to a class of their own are the Australians. I emphasize that what I say is purely personal, but for me the deeds of these four stand out.

All were doing the job of a company commander in exceptionally difficult circumstances. They were not serving with their own regiment or battalion, not even with their own countrymen, except for a tiny handful of fellow advisers. They went into action with troops whose language they could not speak, often their soldiers were complete strangers to them. The quality of their men was always questionable, and with the Montagnards there was open racial hostility between the Vietnamese officers and the soldiers. The Australians had no real way of enforcing orders, they had to get results entirely by personal example. Not for them the benefit of unit loyalty, esprit-de-corps, sound discipline and weeks, if not months, of training together. The men they led were unknowns. It is surely more difficult to show extraordinary courage under these conditions. They were not being watched by the critical eyes of their peers, their own fellow Australians. In most cases if they had failed nobody was going to point the finger.

These four all won their Crosses for single-handed efforts. Badcoe was always out in front on his own, Payne went back repeatedly by himself through enemy lines, Simpson twice fought a one-man war to cover a withdrawal and the evacuation of casualties, and Wheatley died alone with his buddy. For them there was no immediate backup, no reliable troops were nearby — it was a solo effort.

Each Australian, with the exception of Wheatley, was given his award for multiple acts of gallantry. Badcoe had already saved a similar situation twice before he was killed rallying hesitant troops; Payne risked his life four times; Simpson performed two acts of courage within five days. Only in Wheatley's case was the VC given for a single act. He did, however, demonstrate a particularly rare form of self-sacrifice. Having been urged to save himself, he had been deserted by everybody except his senseless, possibly dead, comrade; yet in these lonely and terrifying circumstances he chose to die with his friend.

The final common factor with these men which, when added to those discussed above, gives them, I think, their uniqueness, is that alongside their other actions they saved, or attempted to save, the lives of others.

It is my belief that the stories of these eleven outstanding soldiers bear witness to the enduring truth of battles over the centuries, that it is not numbers that count, but the will to win.

NOTES

Introduction

1. *The Times,* 27 June, 1857.
2. *The Evolution of the Victoria Cross,* Midas Books, in association with the Ogilby Trusts, 1975.
3. Ibid.
4. The oldest living holder at the time of writing is Brigadier L.M. Campbell VC, DSO and Bar, TD, Officer of the Legion of Merit (US). He was born on the 22 July, 1902, and won his Cross in Tunisia in 1943, when commanding the 7th Argyll and Sutherland Highlanders.
5. *The Evolution of the Victoria Cross.*
6. Lucas was commissioned on the spot and later rose to Rear Admiral.
7. He is now General Sir Anthony Farrar-Hockley GBE, KCB, DSO, MC, M.Litt (Oxon).

Prologue

1. Strangely, Speakman wore six medal ribbons at his Investiture, three of which he was not, apparently, entitled to. Photographs show two Second World War ribbons and the General Service medal 1918-1964. He did not join the Army soon enough to qualify for the first two, and it was not until he served in Malaya, in 1953, that he became entitled to the third.

Chapter 1

1. Boswell rose to be a Lieutenant-General, and at the time of writing is the Governor of Guernsey.
2. Penman was wounded in the battle, and accidentally later by his own men. He was discharged from the Army and then took ordination.
3. The son of Field-Marshall Viscount Slim, now himself Colonel The Viscount Slim OBE.

Chapter 2

1. Mercer is now the Public Relations Secretary of the British Korean Veterans' Association.
2. Waters was posthumously awarded the George Cross for his courage in captivity, as described in the Introduction.
3. The Reverend Sam Davies, MBE, wrote a vivid account of life as a prisoner of the Chinese called *In Spite of Dungeons.* He now has a parish near Exeter. He still uses the paten, subsequently returned to him after being lost on the battlefield, when giving Sacraments to the sick.
4. General Ridgway was nicknamed 'Iron Tits', from his habit of hanging a grenade on each breast pocket.
5. Letter to the author from Mr Norman Tuggey.
6. *Daily Express, 7 July, 1954.*

Chapter 3

1. General Peng Te-huai was promoted to marshal in 1955, but fell from grace during the Cultural Revolution. He was sent to labour in the provinces, where he suffered severe beatings and maltreatment. He died in 1974.

2. Yang-Teh-Chi later commanded his country's forces during the short war with Vietnam. He then became chief of staff of the People's Liberation Army.

3. See *In Spite of Dungeons*.

Chapter 4

1. 3 RAR then contained another future VC winner, Private Ray Simpson, whose deeds are described in Chapter 8.

2. *The Borderers' Chronicle,* December, 1951.

3. *Sunday Express,* 17 November, 1968.

4. *Sunday Express,* 10 November, 1974.

5. Excluding Captain Rambahadur Limbu VC MVO, who presently resides in Brunei.

Chapter 5

1. *My Life Story* by Rambahadur Limbu VC, published by The Gurkha Welfare Trusts.

2. Ibid.

3. Ibid.

4. Ibid.

5. Ibid.

6. Ibid.

7. Ibid.

8. Ibid.

9. Ibid.

10. *Bugle and Kukri,* page 435.

11. Captain (later Major) C.E. Maunsell and Lieutenant Ranjit Rai were both awarded the Military Cross.

12. My Life Story.

13. In 1989 the British Government decided on the future of the Brigade of Gurkhas after Hong Kong returns to China in 1997. The Brigade is to continue as a part of the British Army, largely centred in the United Kingdom. There will be four infantry battalions instead of five, plus engineer, signals, and transport squadrons. The total strength will be about 4,000 instead of the present 8,000.

Chapter 6

1. *Sun Herald,* 15 December, 1966.

2. *The Chronicle,* Vol. 4 No. 1, 1986.

3. Statement of Private Vo Trong Chan, 15 November, 1965.

4. Statement of Private Dinh Do, 15 November, 1965.

Chapter 7

1. *Sydney Morning Herald,* 17 October, 1967.

2. *They Dared Mightily,* published by the Australian War Memorial, 1986.

3. Ibid.

4. Letter to the author from the former Mrs Denise Badcoe.

5. *They Dared Mightily.*

6. Statement of Sergeant George Thomas.

7. *Daily Mirror,* 17 October, 1967.

8. *They Dared Mightily.*

9. An article by P.J. Watson in *Parade,* June, 1972.

10. *Sydney Morning Herald,* 17 October, 1967.

Chapter 8

1. *The Sun*, 22 August, 1970.

2. *Daily Telegraph and Daily News*, 23 August, 1969.

3. Letter of one of Simpson's friends to the author.

4. *Daily Telegraph and Daily News*, 22 August, 1969.

5. It was 18 months before the ashes were returned to Simpson's Australian relatives after prolonged difficulties with the authorities. In the end Simpson's niece went to collect them from Shoko, only to find that the Australian Embassy had sent them back without telling the family, and after being specifically asked not to.

6. Lieutenant Colonel R.L. Burnard, in *They Dared Mightily*.

Chapter 9

1. To a reporter at Brisbane airport on 19 April, 1975.

2. *New Idea*, 14 March, 1987.

3. Ibid.

4. *They Dared Mightily*.

5. *New Idea*, 14 March, 1987.

6. Ibid.

7. *Good Weekend*, 1988.

8. Ibid.

9. *Australian Post*, 23 October, 1986.

10. *Good Weekend*, 1988.

Chapter 10

1. Fragging was the killing of officers or senior NCOs by their own men, often by the use of a fragmentation grenade.

2. Of the 675 German generals in their Army List 223, or 33 per cent, were killed in action. Some 500 U.S. generals were serving in 1971, and during the period 1961-1972 three were killed in action.

3. *The Times*, 11 October, 1982.

4. On 27 August, 1979, a convoy of three vehicles with men of 2 Para on board was blown up by a 500lb bomb at Warrenpoint. A second 1,000lb bomb was detonated soon afterwards, to catch reinforcements rushed to the incident. Eighteen soldiers, mostly Paras, were killed.

5. A Milan is a wire-guided anti-tank missile with a maximum range of 2,000 metres.

6. *The Times*, 11 October, 1982.

Chapter 11

1. Ironically, both his disabled brothers reached the age of 30, whereas Ian McKay died at 29. The McKay family has had more than its share of misfortune. The younger brother has had a heart and lung transplant, and Sergeant Mckay's father a quadruple heart by-pass operation.

2. Letter from Lieutenant Colonel Hew Pike, DSO, to Mrs Freda McKay.

3. Letter to Mr and Mrs McKay.

4. Ibid.

5. *Task Force*, page 333. Corporal Bailey, now a sergeant, was awarded the Military Medal for his conduct that night.

6. Ibid, page 334.

7. The practice of removing wedding rings was not always well received by wives, a number of whom would have preferred them to remain with their husbands when they were buried.

BIBLIOGRAPHY

Arthur, Max, *Above all Courage*, Sphere Books, 1985

Barclay, C.N., *The First Commonwealth Division*, Gale & Polden, 1954

Baynes, John, *Morale*, Cassell, 1967

Carew, Tim, *The Glorious Glosters*, Leo Cooper, 1970

Carew, Tim, *The ·Korean War*, Pan Books, 1967

Carr, Jean, *Another Story*, Hamish Hamilton, 1984

Crook, M.J., *The Evolution of the Victoria Cross*, Midas Books, 1975

Cunningham, Ashley, and Farrar, Peter, (Editors), *British Forces in the Korean War*, The British Korean Veterans' Association, 1988

Davidson, Phillip B., *Vietnam at War*, Sidgwick & Jackson, 1988

Davis, Reverend S.J., *In Spite of Dungeons*, Hodder & Stoughton, 1954

Farrar-Hockley, Anthony, *The Edge of the Sword*, Buchan & Enright, 1985

Fox, Robert, *Eyewitness Falklands*, Methuen, 1982

Frost, John, *2 Para Falklands*, Sphere, 1984

Hastings, Max, *The Korean War*, Pan Books, 1988

King, Peter, (Editor), *Australia's Vietnam*, Unwin Australia Pty. Ltd., 1983

Linklater, Eric, *Our Men in Korea*, HMSO, 1954

MacDonald, John F.M ., *The Borderers in Korea*.

Malcolm, G.I., *The Argylls in Korea*, Thomas Nelson & Sons, 1952

Marshall, S.L.A., *Infantry Operations & Weapons Usage in Korea*, Greenhill Books, Washington DC, 1988

McAlister, R.W.L., *Bugle and Kukri*

McNeill, Ian, *The Team*, Leo Cooper, 1984

Middlebrook, Martin, *The Fight for the Malvinas*, Viking, 1989

Middlebrook, Martin, *Task Force*, Penguin, 1987

Moran, Lord, *The Anatomy of Courage*, Avery Publishing Group Inc., New York, 1987

Republic of Korea, *History of the UN Forces in Korea*, Ministry of National Defence, Seoul, 1977

Sandro Tucci, *Gurkhas*. Hamish Hamilton, 1985

The Register of the Victoria Cross, This England, 1988

Thompson, Julian, *No Picnic*, Leo Cooper, 1985

Turner, John F., *VCs of the Army*, Harrap & Co. Ltd., 1962

INDEX

Abols, Corporal, 188
Abyssinia, 4
Adams, Corporal, 182
Adams, General, 2
Adelaide, 142
Aden, 87
Admiralty, The, 172
Afghanistan, 5, 25
Agent Orange, 154
Air Contact Team, 36
Aircraft
B-52 bombers, 161; Harriers, 179, 184, 186; Mustangs F-51, 23; attack A & SH, 23, 33-34; Pucaras, 178, 179, 184, 188
Ajax Bay, 178, 189
Alamo, 169
Albert, Prince, 2, 15
Aldershot, 202
Aldrich, Winthrop, 71
Alexandria, battle of, 54
Altrincham, 12, 74, 86
Alvarado, Sergeant Alberto, 138-140
American Rangers, 40
Americans in Vietnam, 114, 118, 176
Amphibious Commando Company, 171
Angier, Major Pat, 39, 43; actions on Castle Hill, 48-49; death of, 51; defensive plans of, 44-45; in World War 2, 39
An Thuan, 138
Anzac Day, 114, 159
Argentina, 172
Argentinian Air Force, 173, 194
Argentinians, at Darwin/Goose Green, 175, 178, 180, 182-184, 186-187; at Mount Longdon, 196, 200, 202; seizure of Falklands, 173
Argue, Major, 200
Arlington National Cemetery, 5

Armies
Army of Republic of Vietnam (ARVN), 114, 127, 132, 155, 157; British, 26; Chinese People's Volunteer, 59; 63rd Chinese, 46, 59-61; North Vietnamese Army (NVA), 161, 163; US 8th in Korea, 20, 26;
Army Council, 78
Arrow, HMS, 179-181
Ascension Island, 194
Atlantic, 3
Atlantic Conveyor, 173, 177
Australia, involvement in Vietnam 113-115, 128, 143-144
Australian Army Training Team Victnam (The Team), 118, 127, 131-132, 141, 143-144, 148, 151, 152, 157, 169; composition of, 114
Australian Embassy Tokyo, 152-154
Australian Government, 127, 141, 153, 156; institutes own honours and awards, 115
Australian Services Rugby Union, 129
Australian War Memorial, 142, 154-155

B-52 bombers, see Aircraft
Babang, 99-103, 106
Back Badge Day, 54-55
Badcoe, Major Peter, 4, 151, 206; character of, 130-131; action at An Thuan, 137-141; action at Phu Thu, 134-135; action at Quang Dien, 135-137; arrives Vietnam, 132; awarded VC, 135, 142; burial, 141; character 130-131; daughter Kim, 142; early career, 130-132; first combat, 133; first visit to Vietnam, 131; other decorations, 130, 135, 142

211

Badcoe, Mrs. Denise, 130, 132, 137, 142
Bailey, Corporal, 200, 201, 203
Barnsley, 203
Barrett, Sergeant, 182
Battalions
 1st Bn Argyll and Sutherland Highlanders (1A & SH), 40, 75; battle
 for Hill, 282, 23-36
 Belgian battalion, at Imjin, 56-59,
 62, 64
 1st (Cadet) Bn Cheshire Regt, 74
 42 Commando RM, 196
 45 Commando RM, 194-196
 Filipino battalion, at Imjin, 67
 1st Bn Gloucestershire Regt (The
 Glosters), 40, 43, 46, 48, 54, 57; 'A'
 Company of on Castle Hill, 38-39,
 41, 43-45, 47-51; C Company, 47-48;
 'D' Company of, 43, 45; final parade of, 71; at Imjin battle, 57-62,
 64-69
 1st/2nd Gurkha Rifles, 89
 2nd/10th Gurkha Rifles, 97-98,
 107-109; C Company of at Gunong
 Tepoi, 97, 99-106
 8th Gurkha Rifles, 91
 1st Bn King's Own Scottish Borderers (1KOSB), 11, 12, 16, 25, 75,
 85, 144; attacks Hill, 355, 77-78; 'B'
 Company on 'United', 79; defends
 Hill 317 feature, 78-81
 1st Bn King's Shropshire Light
 Infantry (1KSLI), 75
 1st Bn Middlesex Regt, 25, 27, 40;
 assists A & SH, 36; attacks Plum
 Pudding and Middlesex Hills, 27-30
 1st Mike Force Battalion (1 MFB),
 160-162, 167; 212th Company, 157
 3rd Mike Force Battalion (3 MFB),
 148, 151; 232nd Company, 146-151
 5th Mike Force Battalion (5 MFB),
 161, 164-167
 1st Bn Royal Northumberland Fusiliers (1RNF), 40, 57; at battle for
 Hills 317 and 355, 78; at Imjin battle, 56, 57-59, 62-64
 1st Bn The Parachute Regt
 (1PARA), 192
 2nd Bn The Parachute Regt
 (2PARA), attacks Darwin/Goose
 Green, 174, 176, 180-182, 188-189,
 203
 3rd Bn The Parachute Regt
 (3PARA), 4; attacks Mount Longdon, 174, 176, 194-196, 199, 202-203
 1st Bn Royal Australian Regt

(1RAR), 114, 127, 168
 2nd Bn Royal Australian Regt
 (2RAR), 145
 3rd Bn Royal Australian Regt
 (3RAR), 75, 78, 144
 4th Bn Royal Australian Regt
 (4RAR), 145
 1st Bn Royal Ulster Rifles (1RUR),
 40, 57; at Imjin battle, 56, 59, 63, 64
 2nd Bn Scots Guards, 202
Bau, 98
Belcher, Sergeant RM, 188
Belgium, 6
Bengal Civil Service, 5
Bengal Ecclesiastical Dept., 5
Bengal Veteran Establishment, 5
Ben Het, 146, 158, 159, 161
Benton Lock, 178
Beresford, Lance-Corporal, 184, 187
Bhagatbahadur, Lieutenant (QGO),
 104-106
Bhuwansing Limbu, Lieutenant (QGO),
 106
Bickerdike, Lieutenant Andrew, 194, 198,
 200
Bijuliparsad Rai, Rifleman, 98, 102, 105
Binh Hoa, 120-121, 126
Bisley, 191
Blacktown, 128
Blakang Mati, 98
Bloody Sunday, 192
Blue Beach Military Cemetery, 189
Boca House, 181-184
Bodmin, 53
Boer War, 6
Bomber Wing, 93rd, 36
Boon, Sergeant Bernie, 113
Borneo, 89-92, 156
Boswell, 2nd Lieutenant Sandy, 29, 30, 34
Brigades
 Heavy at Balaclava, 3
 Gurkha, 9, 91, 109
 27 Brigade, 24-25, 27
 29 Brigade, 56-57, 75; at Imjin batt-
 le, 58-61, 65
 28th Commonwealth, 75, 78, 144
 25th Canadian, 75
 3 Commando RM, 189, 194, 196
 8 Commando Battery, 178, 179
Brisbane, 156, 169
Brisland, Sergeant, 69
Britain, 172
Britannia, Royal Yacht, 169
British Broadcasting Corporation, 180
British casualties in Falklands War, 173
British Military Hospital, Singapore, 17

212

British North Borneo (later Sabah), 90
British Somaliland, 55
British troops to Vietnam, 128
Brodie, Brigadier Tom, 44, 57-59, 65, 67, 69
Brooks, 2nd Lieutenant, 80
Brown, Colonel, 69
Brunei, 87, 89, 90
Buchan, Major Ross, 132, 137
Buchanan, 2nd Lieutenant David, 30, 33
Buchanan, Private, 83
Buckingham Palace, 11, 37, 52, 85, 108,
    190, 203; State Rooms in, 11-16
Bu Gia Map, 159
Bukit Knuckle, 99
Burchett, Wilfred, 70
Burma, 3, 55, 91, 169
Burntside House, 179-180
Burt, Private Jason, 193, 201-202
Buscasia, 156
Buss, Drum Major, 68
Buxcey, Colour-Sergeant, 41, 63

Cabral, Lieutenant Henry, 47
Cambodia, 157, 161
Cambodian border, 146, 159
Cambridge, Duke of, 2
Camilla Creek, 180
Camilla Creek House, 176, 178, 179-180,
    184
Camp, Corporal, 183
Canberra, 130, 142, 151, 153
Canberra, Defence Department in, 128
Canungra, Jungle Training Centre, 129
Cape Town, 88
Carne, Lieutenant-Colonel James (Fred),
    43, 45, 47, 49, 51, 55, 71, 85; actions at
    Imjin battle, 61-62, 65-68; in captivity,
    69-70; carves Celtic Cross, 70; death,
    71; invested with VC, 70; reasons for
    award of VC, 55-56; task at Imjin batt-
    le, 61; VC in regimental museum, 72
Carne, Mrs. Jean, 71-72
Casey, Lord, 129
Cassels, Major-General James, 75, 78, 82,
    85
Castle Hill, 38, 39; battle for, 41, 43-48, 51, 62
Castle Site, 43, 44, 48-51
Cawnpore, 5
Celtic Cross, 70-71
Ceylon, HMS, 25
Chambers, Lieutenant-Colonel, 54
Chap Toi mountain, 120
Chavasse, Captain Noel, 6
Chelsea Pensioners, 2

Chelsea Royal Hospital, 88
China, 19, 20
China Fleet Club, 74-75
Chinese, 26; attack KOSB on 'United' and
    Hill 317, 78-84; holds Hills 355 and 317,
    74, 76-77; at Imjin battle, 56, 59, 64, 68,
    75
Chinook helicopters, 177
Choksong, 43, 44, 50
Chosin reservoir, 20
Church Crookham, 109
Civil Irregular Defence Group (CIDG),
    118, 121, 123, 125, 126
Claret operations, 91, 98, 108
Clement, Captain, 134, 135, 141
Clement, Sergeant Jack, 161
Coad, Brigadier Aubry, 25, 32
Coe, 2nd Lieutenant Mark, 182, 186
Collet, Sergeant-Major Tom, 32
Commonwealth Reception Centre, 70
Commonwealth troops in Brunei, 90; cas-
    ualties of in Brunei, 91; troops in Korea,
    128
Commonwealth War Graves Cemetery,
    Korea, 37
Congressional Medal of Honor, see
    Decorations & Medals
Cook, Corporal, 47
Cooper, Padre David, 177, 189, 203
Coronation Point, 179, 181
Corps
    1st Corps, 57, 65, 75
    Royal Army Medical Corps
    (RAMC), 6
    Royal Engineers, Corps of (RE), 6
    Cottam, Sergeant Frank, 48
Craig, Lieutenant Hedley, 63
Cranham, 71
Crete, 6
Crimean War, 2, 4
Crosland, Major, 179
Cuneo, Terence, 190
Curtis, Lieutenant Philip, 40, 41, 73, 85;
    background, 40-41; character, 51;
    death, 51; defends Castle Hill, 45-46;
    joins Glosters, 41; mounts counter-
    attack, 48-51; posthumous VC for, 52;
    VC sold, 53
Curtis, Mrs. Florence, 52
Curtis, Phillipa Susan, 40, 41, 52
Custar, Captain James, 134

Daffodil, HMS, 5
Daily Express, 52
Daily Telegraph, 53, 73

Dak To, 161
Da Nang, 126, 137
Darjeeling, 95
Darwin, 177, 178, 180-183, 189, 202
Davies, Padre Sam, 42, 69-72
Davis, Captain John, 172
Dean, Major-General William, 20
Decorations & Medals
    Air Medal (US), 130
    Armed Forces Honour Medal (S. Vietnam), 130
    Army Meritorious Unit Commendation (US), 115
    Bravery Medal (Aust), 115
    British Empire Medal (UK), 55
    Bronze Star (US), 151
    Commendation for Brave Conduct (Aust), 115
    Congressional Medal of Honor (US), 5, 6
    Cross of Gallantry with Palm (S. Vietnam), 128, 130
    Cross of Gallantry with Palm Unit Citation (S. Vietnam), 115
    Cross of Valor (Aust), 115
    Distinguished Conduct Medal (UK), 9, 39, 51, 55, 84, 85, 108, 128, 143, 146, 155
    Distinguished Service Cross (US), 37, 159
    Distinguished Service Order (UK), 4, 9, 55, 70, 74, 84
    George Cross (UK), 8, 39
    Indian General Service Medal, 25
    Legion of Honour (Fr), 4, 6
    Member of the British Empire (UK), 55, 176
    Member of the Victorian Order (UK), 109
    Mentioned in Despatches (UK), 4, 25, 39, 55, 82, 108
    Military Cross (UK), 9, 48, 55, 85
    Military Medal (UK), 9, 39, 55, 89
    National Order of the Republic of Vietnam (S. Vietnam), 128, 130
    Officer of the British Empire (UK), 176, 190
    Purple Heart (US), 130
    Silver Star (US), 130, 135, 158
    Star of Courage (Aust), 115
    US Presidential Unit Citation, 54
    Victoria Cross (UK), see Victoria Cross
    Vietnamese Wound Medal (S. Vietnam), 130

Delhi, 15
Dellwo, Sergeant Gerard, 161, 164, 166
Dent, Captain Chris, 187
Devonport, 40
Dharkarma Rai, Sergeant, 102
Dhofar, 156
Ding, Commander, 69
Ding Do, Private, 124, 126
Divisions
    1st ARVN, 138
    1st Cavalry, 26
    187th Chinese, 46, 61, 65
    188th Chinese, 61, 65
    189th Chinese, 61, 65
    1st Commonwealth, 75
    1st in Crimea, 2
    51st Highland, 75
    1st Republic of Korea, 43, 57
    3rd US Infantry, 57
    24th US Infantry, 20, 27, 32
Donnington, Ordnance Depot at, 4
Douglas Settlement, 194
Duke of York's School, 2
Duncan, Sergeant 'Dolly', 83
Duntroon Military College, 129, 153, 168
Durban, 88
Dutch, 90

Eagles, Drummer, 47, 63, 68
Eames, Sergeant, wins MM, 38; murdered on Hill 235, 39
Edinburgh, 87
Edinburgh, HRH Duke of, 15
Edington, 2nd Lieutenant John, 30-33
Elizabeth II, HM Queen, 3, 115, 128; approves VC to Rambahadur Limbu, 108; approves Wheatley's VC, 128; invests Colonel Carne, 70; invests Lance-Corporal Rambahadur Limbu, 108-109; invests Private Speakman, 11-16, 74; invests WO Payne, 169; invests WO Simpson 151; presents Lieutenant Curtis' VC, 52; presents Mrs. Jones with husband's VC, 190; presents Mrs. McKay with husband's VC, 203
Elizabeth, HM The Queen Mother, 3, 12
English China Clays, 53
Estancia House, 194, 198
Estancia, Mount, 195
Eton College, 176, 190
Europe, 3
Excellent, HMS, 2
Exeter, 71

Falkland Islands, 9, 91, 171-174, 190; East Falkland 172, 194; war in, 174, 176, 177, 194, 202; West Falkland, 172
Falkland Sound, 172
Falmouth, 71
Farrar-Hockley, Captain Anthony (later General Sir), 8, 47, 49, 67, 71
Farrar-Hockley, Major Dair, 181, 184-186, 188-189
Faulkner, Colour-Sergeant, 199
Fazekas, Captain Felix, 118; actions in Tra Bong valley, 119, 120-126, 128
Fitzgibbon, Andrew, 5
Flanders, 3
Flodden, battle of, 202
Forbes, Lieutenant, 160, 163
Fort Bragg, USA, 129, 142, 155, 169
Fox, Lieutenant Douglas, 99, 106
Frederick William, Prince, 2
Free World Headquarters, 113, 167
Frimley, 37
Fry, Lieutenant-Colonel John, 53
Fuller, Sergeant, 202, 203

Gallagher, Sergeant-Major, 51
Gallipoli, 91
Galla Wala, 96
Genghis Khan, 19
George Cross, see Decorations & Medals
George VI, HM King, 11, 13, 74; last investiture by, 37
Germans 4
Germany, 74, 87
Giachino, Lieutenant-Commander, 171
Gill, Warrant Officer, 147, 148
Gillies, Major Jim, 29, 32, 35
Glenton, Robin, 86
Gloster Crossing, 44, 46, 47, 61, 62, 64-65
Gloster Hill, battle on, 56, 61, 63, 64, 66-68, 70
Gloucester, 70, 71
Gloucester Cathedral, 70
Goose Green, 177, 178, 180-182, 186, 189, 202
Gordon-Ingram, Major Alastair, 29, 31, 32, 34, 35
Government House, 171
Governor, of Falklands, 171
Greece, 91
Green, Captain, 146, 149, 150
Grieve, Sergeant-Major John, 3
Griffin, Mrs. Susan (nee Curtis), 53
Grist, Major, 65
Gunong Tepoi, 98, 100, 102, 106; description of, 100-101

Gurkha, Queen's Orderly Officers, 16, 109
Gurkha Reserve Unit, 90, 110
Gurkha Signals, 110
Gurkhas, in Brunei, 89; campaigns of, 91; characteristics of, 94; in Vietnam, 128

Hac Bao Company, 138, 140
Halpin, Corporal, 49, 50
Hamilton, General Sir Ian, 6
Hamhung, 20
Hancocks, Messrs, 4
Hantan River, 59
Harding, Major Dennis, 63, 69, 71
Hardman, Corporal, 182, 187
Harriers, See Aircraft
Harriet, Mount, 196
Harrison, Major Philip, 77, 80, 82, 84
Harvey, Captain Mike, 69
Hastings, Sergeant, 188
Hay, Major-General, 151, 167
Haynes, Mrs. Beatrice, 41, 52
Haynes, Miss Joan, 40
Hayward, Mr. John, 53
Healey, Denis, 91
Heaver, Padre Derek, 203
Hecla, HMS, 5
Hickey, Captain, 39, 69
Hill 235, see Gloster Hill
Hill 282, 24; A & SH's battle for, 28-35
Hill 317 (Maryang-San), battle for, 75; 1 KOSB's defences of, 78-80
Hill 355 (Kowang-San), battle for, 75
Hill 388, 24; dominates Hill 282, 28, 30
Hill Selection, procedures of, 96
Himalayas, 94
Hinchinbrook, 169
Hobbs, Regimental Sergeant-Major, 71
Hoffman, Chaplain, 127
Holmberg, Sergeant, 147, 150, 151
Holt, Harold, 129
Holt's Wharf, 25
Hong Kong, A&SH in, 25; Speakman in, 74, 86
House of Commons, 91
Hudson, Lieutenant Bruce, 45, 46; death of, 51
Hue, 135-138
Hunter, Private, 47
Huth, Major, 67
Hyde Park, 1, 3

Imjin River, battles at, 8, 39, 43, 44, 46, 54, 56-62, 144
Imperial War Museum, 203

Imphal, battle of, 91
Inchon, 20
Indian Mutiny, 5
Indonesia, 90, 91, 99
Indonesian Army, 98-100, 106
Indrahang Limbu, Company Sergeant-Major, 103
Inkerman, battle of, 2
Iris II, HMS, 5
Iron Cross, 4
Israelis, 176
Italy, 91

Jackson, Brigadier, 127, 128
Jalapahar, 96
James, Lieutenant, 160, 163-165, 166
Japan, 19, 20, 41, 70, 144, 152
Japanese, 143
Johnson, Major-General, 110
Jolly, Lieutenant-General Sir Alan, 108
Jones, Lieutenant-Colonel 'H', 175, 181; actions at Darwin/Goose Green, 182-187; awarded posthumous VC, 174, 175, 190; burial, 189-190; character, 176-177, 189; killed, 187-188; other decorations, 176, 190; problems facing, 178, 180-181; sons of, 190-191
Jones, Mrs. Sara, 177, 190; attends investiture, 190
Jones, Commander Timothy, 190
Julius Caesar, 175

Kaesong, 70
Kalimantan, 90
Kamak-San, 58, 59, 61, 63
Keeble, Major Chris, 118, 189
Kelly, Warrant Officer, 147, 149, 150, 153
Kennedy, J.F. Center, 129, 155
Kent, Mount, 198
Kenya, 12, 78, 177
Kharbakahadur Limbu, Rifleman, 98, 105
Kim Il Sung, 20, 22
Kingswear, 190
Konoqwal, Corporal Filip, 5
Kontum, 158
Korea, 3, 9, 11, 19, 41, 45, 85, 144, 145; winter in, 22
Korean War, 8, 20-22, 75, 85, 128, 143, 144, 156, 176; A&SH in, 23-36; casualties in, 20; Chinese enter, 26; North Korea, 22; North Koreans, attacks on A&SH, 24, 31, 32; driven back to Yalu, 26; 38th Parallel, 19, 75; prisoners in, 22; South Korea in, 20, 22, 23; South

Koreans, at Imjin battle, 59-60
Koruh, 100-103, 106
Kowang-San, 75
Kowloon, 25, 74
Krishnabahadur Rai, Corporal 106
Kuching, 98
Kyushu, 19

Laos, 157, 159
Latham, Warrant Officer Kevin, 158-161, 163
Lea, Major-General, 98
Leakey, Sergeant Nigel, 4
Legion of Honour, see Decorations & Medals
Little Big Horn, battle of, 54
Lloyd, Lieutenant-Colonel, 148-151
London, 108, 128
Londonderry, 192
London Gazette, 11
London Stock Exchange, 108
Longdon, Mount, 5, 193, 194, 196, 198, 200, 204
Loos, battle of, 91
Lord Chamberlain, 14-16
Lucas, Charles, 5
Lutyens, Sir Edwin, 15

Mackay, 156, 169
Macmillan, Lieutenant-General Sir Gordon, 36
Mairs, Lance-Corporal, 50
Majuba Hill, battle of, 6
Malaya, 87, 91, 95, 98, 117, 143, 145
Malayan Emergency, 90, 131, 143, 156
Malayan Scouts, 86
Malaysia, Federation of, 90, 141
Manchus, 19
Mao, Chairman, 59
Marchwood Military Port, 202
Margaret, HRH Princess, 12, 203
Marines, US, 20
Martin-Leake, Surgeon-Captain Arthur, 6
Masters, Corporal, 51
Maunsell, Captain 'Kit', 97, 108; actions at Gunong Tepoi, 97, 99-106; plans for attack on Gunong Tepoi, 101
Maycock, 2nd Lieutenant John, 39, 44, 48; death of, 48
MacArthur, General, 20
McCraken, Captain, 200
MacDonald, Lieutenant-Colonel John, 77, 78; made brigade commander, 78
McKay Memorial Cottages, 203

McKay, Mrs. Marica, 203; attends investiture, 203; gives husband's medals to Parachute Regt, 203
McKay, Sergeant Ian, 5, 9; actions at Mount Longdon, 195, 198-201; background of, 193; on 'Bloody Sunday', 192; character, 193-194; children, 203; death, 201; father, 193; funeral, 202-203; mother, 204; posthumously awarded VC, 193, 195
McKellar, 2nd Lieutenant Peter, 30
McKinnon, Sergeant, 202
McMillan-Scott, Lieutenant, 80-81
Mekong Delta, 132, 151
Melbourne, 114
Melia, Corporal, 184
Menadue, John, 153
Mentioned in Despatches, see Decorations & Medals
Mercer, Private Sam, wounded on Hill 235, 38, 39; on Castle Hill, 40, 49, 50, 52
Military Cross, see Decorations & Medals
Military Medal, see Decorations & Medals
Milne, Corporal, 200
Ministry of Defence (MOD) 4, 176
Mitchell, Major Paul, 65
Mongols, 19
Montagnard tribesmen, 114, 118, 132, 147, 149, 150, 151, 157, 158, 160, 161-167, 206
Montez, Sergeant 'Monty', 160-167, 169
Moody Brook, 171
Moore, Major-General Jeremy, RM, 189
Muir, Colonel, attends investiture, 37; death of, 37
Muir, Major Kenneth, 73, 85; actions on Hill 282, 24, 33-36; as 2IC A&SH, 26; award of VC, 37; background, 24-25, 36; buried, 37; death, 35; medals at Stirling Castle, 37; takes command on Hill 282, 33
Murdoch, Sergeant-Major, 81, 82, 83, 84; receives DCM, 84
Murray, Sergeant-Major, 34
Murrell River, 196, 198
Mustangs, see Aircraft
Myers, Lieutenant-Colonel, 108

Nainabahadur Rai, Rifleman, 89
Naktong River, 24, 27
Nam Hoa, 132
Napalm, characteristics of, 23; attack on A&SH, 34
Nash, John, 13
Neame, Major, 182, 184

Neilson, Lieutenant-Colonel Leslie, 25, 28, 29, 32, 34-36
Nepal, 91, 93, 94, 108, 109
New Guinea, 143
New York, 142
New Zealand, 6, 84
Nha Trang, 146, 149
Norman, Major RM, 171
Norman, Sergeant, 184-185, 187-188
Normandy landings, 173
North Africa, 3, 39
Northern Ireland, 25, 176, 177, 191, 193
North Korea, see Korea
North Koreans, see Korean War
North Vietnam, see Vietnam
North West Frontier, 25, 27
Nott, John, 189
Nui Hon Doat mountain, 120
Nunn, Lieutenant Richard RM, 188

Okinawa, 137
Olympic Games, 22
Oman, 156
Operation Commando, 74, 76-78
Operation Minden, 75
Osborne, HMS, 2
O'Sullivan, Sergeant John, 30
Outer Hebrides, 173

Pakistan, 95
Palestine, 12
Paoksok-tong, 80
Papworth, Corporal, 50, 51
Parallel, the 38th, see Korean War
Pashpati, 95
Payne, Warrant Officer Keith, 9, 115, 152, 206; actions on 24 May, 1969, 162-167; award of VC, 164, 167-168; character, 156-157, 168-170; commands 212th company, 158, 160; illness, 157; other decorations, 158-159; retirement, 169; service in Oman, 156-157
Pejiru, 99
Peng Te-Huai, 59, 69
Penman, Captain John, 31, 34
Pennethorne, Sir James, 14
Perth, 145
Pettinger, Sergeant, 199
Phu Thu, 133
Pi-Chong-Ni, 69
Pike, Lieutenant-Colonel Hew, 196, 203
Pindaree War, 91
Pitkeathly, Corporal, 30
Pleiku, 157, 161

Plymouth, 40
Popular Forces (S. Vietnamese), 132, 133
Port San Carlos, 189, 194
Portsea, Officer Cadet School, 132, 142
Port William, 172
Preece, Lieutenant-Colonel, 128
Pucaras, see Aircraft
Puransing Limbu, Lieutenant (QGO), 103
Pusan, 26

Quang Dien, 136
Quang, 2nd Lieutenant, 118-119; actions in
    Tra Bong Valley, 120-121, 124-126
Queen's Gurkha Officers, 97, 109
Queensland, 113
Queensland Sun, 170

Raby, Commander Henry James, 3
Radcliff, Captain, 24
Radfan, 87
RAF, 40
Rambahadur Limbu, Lance Corporal,
    action on Gunong Tepoi, 104-105, 107;
    award of VC announced, 108; Bhakte,
    son of, 109-110; boyhood, 93-95; career,
    97, 109; Chandraprakash, son of, 110;
    character, 102, 106, 110; deserts, 95;
    nicknamed 'VC Sahib', 109, 110, rejoins
    Army, 96-97; VC citation, 92; visits
    Britain, 108; wife dies, 107
Ranjit Rai, Lieutenant (QGO), 98, 103-104
RASC, 40
Raynor, Lieutenant William, 5
Reading University, 191
Regiments
    7th Argentinian, 195; 49th Berkshire
    2; Black Watch, 12, 16, 73, 74, 75;
    Cameron Highlanders, 2; 7th Cav-
    alry, 54; Coldstream Guards, 2;
    Devon and Dorset, 176, 190, 191;
    2nd Dragoons, 3; 6th Dragoons, 2;
    Duke of Cornwall's Light Infantry,
    40; 1 Field Regiment RAA, 131,
    132; Fusiliers, 2; Gloucestershire,
    74, see also Battalions; 24th Regi-
    ment of NVA, 159; 27th Regiment
    of NVA, 159; Grenadier Guards, 2;
    67th Hampshire, 5; 8th Hussars, C
    Sgn of at Imjin battle, 57, 64; 11th
    Hussars, 2; King's African Rifles,
    4, 55; Leicestershire, band of, 25;
    1st Life Guards, 2; 2nd Life Guards,
    2; 64th North Staffordshire, 5;
    Parachute Regiment, 174, 176, 193,

202; 5th Regimental Combat Team,
    27; Rifle Brigade, 2, 6; Royal Aus-
    tralian, 113, 117; South Wales Bor-
    derers, 54; Sudan Defence force, 25;
    West Yorkshire, 40
Regional Forces (S. Vietnamese), 132, 133,
    136, 138
Repatriation Commission, 155
Repatriation Review Tribunal, 155
Returned Servicemen's Club, Paddington,
    153
Rhee, President Syngman, 20
Rice, Major Tony, 184
Ridgway, General Matthew, 43, 50
Risau, 99, 100, 106
Roneo, 40
Rookwood, cemetery, 129
Rorke's Drift, battle of, 54
Rossville Flats, 192
Rossville Street, 192
Rotherham Grammar School, 193, 203
Rothwell, Captain, 149-150
Royal Army Medical Corps, see Corps
Royal Artillery Units
    8 Commando Battery, 179; 70 Field
    Battery, 45, 64; 45 Field Regiment,
    44, 57; at Imjin battle, 59, 64; Horse
    Artillery, 2; Royal Regiment of
    Artillery, 6; C Troop, 170; Indepen-
    dent Mortar Battery, 46, 57
Royal Engineers, see Corps
Royal Marines, 2, 171-174; senior chaplain
    of, 189; Special Boat Squadron of, 194
Royal Navy, 172, 173
Russo-Japanese War, 19

Sabah, 90
Saigon, 22, 113, 127, 144, 151, 167
Salvadores, Major Carlos, 196
San Antonio, 169
San Carlos, 181
Sandhurst, 193, 194
Sarawak, 98, 100
Sabarots, Lieutenant-Commander, 171
Sari Bair, 91
Saudi Arabia, 9
School of Infantry, 176, 190
Scottish United Services Museum, 88
Searle, Major-General, 57
Seoul, 22, 26, 57-59, 65
Serikin, 99
Sershen, Staff-Sergeant Theodore, 119,
    121, 123, 125, 126, 129
Sharp, Sergeant James, 127
Sikkim, 95-97

Simpson, Mrs. Shoko, 144, 145, 152-154; pension problems of, 151 155
Simpson, Regimental Sergeant-Major, 189
Simpson, Warrant Officer Ray, 158, 168, 206; action on 6 May, 1969, 147-148; action on 11 May, 1969, 148-150; awarded VC, 143, 144, 146, 148, 151-152; background and early career, 143, 144, 145; character, 146, 155; death, 153; final discharge, 152; funeral, 153; later career 152; other decorations, 143, 151; wounded in leg, 145
Sindae, 47
Singapore, 22, 86, 89, 91, 98, 107, 113
Sir Bedivere, 190, 202
Sir Walter Scott, 88
Skorzeny, Otto, 146
Slim, Captain John, 36
Snitch, Private Rachel, 87
Solma-Ri, 55
Songju, 23, 27, 31, 32, 36
Sophia University, 153
Sotheby's, 53
South Africa, 6, 24, 88
Southampton, 88
South Devon, 190
South Vietnam, see Vietnam
Speakman, Private William, 9, 109, 144; allegations of drunkenness refuted, 73; appearance and background, 73-74; awarded VC, 84, 85; in battle on 'United', 78, 80-84; changes name, 88; court conviction, 87; effect of publicity on, 85-86; investiture, 11-16; joins B company KOSB, 77; later career, 86-88; marriage, 87; medals, 74; myths surrounding, 73; receives VC ribbon, 85; sells medals, 87
Special Air Service (Aust), company of, 145, 155
Staff College, Camberley, 176
Stanley, 171-173, 179, 194-196
Steward, Warrant Officer Jock, 160
St Ives, 87
Strong, Captain, 172
Sukarno, President, 89, 90
Sun, Comrade, 69
Sunday Express, 86
Suoi Tra Voi, 121
Sussex Mountain, 179
Swanton, Warrant Officer 'Butch', 116, 127; actions in Tra Bong Valley, 119, 121-126; arrives at Tra Bong, 117; funeral of, 127
Sweeny, Corporal, 30
Sydney, 117, 121, 127, 142, 143

Sydney Sun, 127
Sydney Rugby Football Union, 129
Syria, 91
Ta Ko, 145,
Tadman, Major Dennis, assumes command of 1 KOSB, 78
Taku Fort, 5
Taylor, Brigadier George, 75; sacked by Cassels, 78
Teal Inlet, 195
Team, The, see Australian Army Training Team, Vietnam
Temple, Lieutenant Guy, 48, 61
Tepoi, see Gunong Tepoi
Terendak Camp, 131, 141
Tet offensive, 114
Texas, 169
Thatcher, Mrs. 190
Thermopylae, battle of, 54
Thomas, George Sergeant 1st Class, 134, 135, 142
Thompson, Brigadier Julian, 177
Thompson, Lieutenant-Colonel Colin, 177
Thomson, 2nd Lieutenant, 80
Thau Thien, 132, 133
Times, The, 1, 2
Tokyo, 145
Tolley, Warrant Officer Barry, 159, 160-164
Torquay, 88
Tra Bong, 117-119, 125-126
Tra Co/Tra Dong river, 118
Tuggey, Sergeant Norman, 41, 47, 49-51
Tumbledown, Mount, 196
Two Sisters, 196

Ulster Crossing, 62
Unicorn, HMS, 25
Union Castle, 88
United Nations, 12, 20, 22, 41, 56-59, 65, 75
United States, in Vietnam 113-114; President of, 142
UN Security Council, 20
Upham, 2nd Lieutenant Charles, 6
US Special Forces, 114, 126, 127, 151; 'A' Team of, 118; association of, 169
USSR, 20

Van Fleet, General, 56
Vernet, Mount, 195
Viaticum, 42-43
Victoria Cross, the, 4, 11, 39, 55, 73, 85, 92, 107, 108, 114-115, 128, 143, 151, 155, 159, 176, 195, 203, 205; Bar to, 6; Commonwealth award, 4; foreign

awards of, 5; investiture procedure for, 11-16; in Korea, 22; Royal Warrant establishing, 1, 5, 128; sale of Lieutenant Curtis' VC, 53; unusual awards of, 5-6; witnesses for, 4; see also Badcoe, Carne, Curtis, Jones, McKay, Muir, Payne, Rambahadur Limbu, Simpson, Speakman, Wheatley
Victoria Cross & George Cross Association, 3, 88
Victoria, Queen, 1-4, 9
Viet Cong, 114, 131, 133, 145, 154, 157, 158, 159; action on 6 May 1969, 146-147; action on 11 May 1969, 148-150; at An Thuan, 138-141; at Phu Thu 134-135; at Quang Dien, 135-137; in Tra Bong valley, 118-126
Vietnam, 9, 10, 23
Vietnam, Republic of, 116, 117, 127, 144, 155, 156, 157, 159, 176; awards by, 115, 127
Vietnam War, Australian involvement in, 113-115
Vinh Tuy, 121, 125
Vo Trong Chan, Private, 123
Vung Tau, 129

Waegwan, 36
Walker, Major-General, 98
Wallis, 2nd Lieutenant Guy, 182
Walsh, Warrant Officer, 146-147, 149-150
Walters, George, 2
Wanchai, 74
Ward, Major Guy, 45, 62
Ward, private, 51
Warren, Councillor and Mrs. 12
Warrenpoint, 177
Waters, 2nd Lieutenant Terry, 8, 40, 42,

48, 51; death of, 39; in defence of Castle Hill, 45
Watt, Private, 35
Weeks, Warrant Officer, 200-201
Wessex helicopters, 177
Western Desert, 91
Wheatley, Mrs. Edna, 117, 127-129
Wheatley, Warrant Officer 'Dasher', 116, 127, 141, 151, 206; actions in Tra Bong valley, 119, 121-126; arrives at Tra Bong, 117; awarded posthumous VC, 116, 127-128; background, 117; funeral, 127; George, son of, receives father's VC, 129; other decorations, 127-128
Widgery, Lord Chief Justice, 192
Wilson, Captain, 39
Wilson, Corporal, 83
Wilson, Harold, 129
Wilson, Major David, 28, 34
Wireless Ridge, 196, 198
Wolseley, General Sir Garnet, 24
Wong, Chinese interpreter, 69
Wood, Captain David, 184, 187
Wood, Corporal, 83
Worsley-Tonks, Captain, 184
Wylie, Colonel, 109
Wyton, 87

Yalu River, 20, 26
Yang-Teh-Chi, General, 61
Yeoman of the Guard, 15
Yokohama War Cemetery, 153
Young, Lieutenant-Colonel, 64

Zeebrugge, 5
Zimbabwe, 176